Prudes, Perverts, and Tyrants

Prudes, Perverts, and Tyrants

PLATO'S *GORGIAS* AND
THE POLITICS OF SHAME

Christina H. Tarnopolsky

PRINCETON UNIVERSITY PRESS

PRINCETON AND OXFORD

Copyright © 2010 by Princeton University Press
Published by Princeton University Press, 41 William Street, Princeton, New Jersey 08540
In the United Kingdom: Princeton University Press, 6 Oxford Street, Woodstock, Oxfordshire
OX20 1TW

Library of Congress Cataloging-in-Publication Data

Tarnopolsky, Christina H., 1964–
Prudes, perverts, and tyrants : Plato's Gorgias and the politics of shame /
Christina H. Tarnopolsky.
p.   cm.
Includes bibliographical references (p.) and index.
ISBN 978-0-691-12856-6 (hardcover : alk. paper)
1. Plato. Gorgias. 2. Shame—Political aspects. 3. Democracy—
Philosophy. I. Title.
B371.T37 2010
170—dc22   2009028126

British Library Cataloging-in-Publication Data is available

This book has been composed in Minion Pro

Printed on acid-free paper. ∞

press.princeton.edu

Printed in the United States of America

1   3   5   7   9   10   8   6   4   2

For My Family

———————————————

CONTENTS

PART TWO: *Plato's* Gorgias *and the*
Contemporary Politics of Shame   141

CHAPTER FIVE
Prudes, Perverts, and Tyrants: Plato and the Contemporary
Politics of Shame and Civility   143

CHAPTER SIX
What's So Negative about the "Negative" Emotions?   172

TABLES

ACKNOWLEDGMENTS

A FIRST BOOK all about shame should never happen to anyone, but because this one happened to me, I must thank the following people and institutions. It is to them that I owe most of the joyful and intellectually stimulating moments of this project.

First, I wish to thank Richard Schultz, Jacob Levy, and McGill University for providing me with course relief during the fall semester of 2008 in order to complete this manuscript. For providing a wonderfully fertile intellectual setting that greatly facilitated the completion of this manuscript, I thank all of my political theory colleagues at McGill University: Arash Abizadeh, Jacob Levy, Catherine Lu, Victor Muñiz-Fraticelli, William Roberts, and Hasana Sharp. I thank the following undergraduate and graduate students who helped with the final research for this book: Liam Churchill, Leslie de Meulles, Virginia DiGaetano, Eli Friedland, Sohini Guha, Douglas Hanes, Warren Huard, D. Clifton Mark, Nina Valiquette Moreau, and Xiangzhen Wang. I am grateful for the financial support provided during my first years at McGill by a Standard Research Grant from the Social Sciences and Humanities Research Council of Canada.

I wish to thank my junior and senior colleagues, students and associates at Harvard University for all of the wonderful insights and helpful advice that they offered me during my years in the Department of Government and the Committee on Degrees in Social Studies. If I were to write down all of this advice, this section would be as long as Plutarch's *Lives*. I also wish to thank all of the students in my graduate seminars at Harvard and McGill for helping me to discover new insights about shame in the *Gorgias*.

I thank my following undergraduate professors and tutorial leaders who first turned me away from law school and toward the study of political philosophy: Clifford Orwin, Thomas Pangle, Michael Alexander, Rebecca Comay, Julian Patrick, Geoffrey Payzant, and David Leibowitz. Although none of them was directly involved in this project, they profoundly influenced the way I study texts. I thank Clifford Orwin for telling me that I should avoid exclamation marks at the end of my sentences unless I aspire to write comic strips.

The dissertation upon which this book is based was completed at the University of Chicago under the masterful guidance of Nathan Tarcov, Charles Larmore, Patchen Markell, Danielle Allen, and Gary Herrigel. Their extensive and insightful feedback on many countless drafts of my dissertation helped transform my inchoate thoughts on Plato and shame into a coherent philosophical project. I could always count on their comments and criticisms to discern the deepest philosophical issues I was dealing with, and to show me where I needed to think more deeply. I am also grateful for the financial support provided during and after graduate school by the University of Chicago, the John M. Olin Fellowship program, the Mellon Foundation's Final-Year Dissertation program, and the Bradley Foundation Post-Doctoral Fellowship program.

A number of people have generously read various versions or portions of this book or shared conversations with me about ideas that influenced this book: Arash Abizadeh, Danielle Allen, Leah Bradshaw, Fonna Forman-Barzilai, Joseph Carens, Mary Dietz, J. Peter Euben, Michaele Ferguson, Leonard Ferry, Hawley Fogg-Davis, Jill Frank, Bryan Garsten, Lisa Guenther, Peter Gordon, Cheryl Hall, Gretchen Helmke, Andrew Hertzoff, Bonnie Honig, Robert Howse, Horst Hutter, Barbara Koziak, Sharon Krause, Rebecca Kingston, Jacob Levy, Jill Locke, Nancy Luxon, Catherine Lu, Harvey Mansfield, Patchen Markell, Sara Monoson, Glyn Morgan, Darra Mulderry, Jennifer Nedelsky, Davide Panagia, Lorraine Pangle, Andrew Rehfeld, William Roberts, Reuel Rogers, Nancy Rosenblum, Stephen Salkever, Arlene Saxonhouse, Hasana Sharp, Marlene Sokolon, Aleksandra Wagner, Lisa Wedeen, Stephen White, Shelley Wilcox, Iris Marion Young, Karen Zivi, and John Zumbrunnen. I owe Jill Frank, Catherine Lu, Sharon Krause, Gretchen Helmke and Hasana Sharp special thanks for encouraging me to continue with this project whenever I felt that my future was better suited to a life of violin making.

I have presented earlier versions or portions of my chapters to audiences at Concordia University, Northwestern University, Yale University, University of California at Berkeley, University of California at San Diego, University of Chicago, University of Toronto, as well as at meetings of the American Political Science Association, Canadian Political Science Association, and Midwest Political Science Association. All of these audiences provided extremely helpful feedback on my work.

Jill Frank, Melissa Lane, Nina Valiquette Moreau, one anonymous reviewer at Princeton University Press and one at Harvard University Press have read different versions of this manuscript in its entirety and offered extremely helpful advice and criticism. Eric MacGilvray, Will Kymlicka, and Ian Shapiro also read an earlier version of the manuscript and generously awarded it the Leo Strauss Award in 2004.

An earlier version of chapter 5 was published as "Prudes, Perverts and Tyrants: Plato and the Contemporary of Shame" in *Political Theory* 32, no. 4 (August 2004). An earlier version of chapter 3 was published as "Plato on Shame and Frank Speech in Democratic Athens" in *Bringing the Passions Back In: The Emotions in Political Philosophy*. Parts of chapter 2 appeared in a different form in "Platonic Reflections on the Aesthetic Dimensions of Deliberative Democracy" in *Political Theory* 35, no. 3 (June 2007). Parts of chapter 6 appeared in a different form in "The Pedagogies of Shame: What's So Negative about the Negative Emotions?" in *Cabinet: A Quarterly of Art and Culture*, Issue 31 (Fall 2008). Thanks to Sage Publications, the University of British Columbia Press, and *Cabinet* for permission to reprint this material.

At Princeton University Press, my terrific editor Ian Malcolm's wisdom, sense of humor, patience, and encouragement sustained me throughout the entire publication process. I would like to thank Robert Dobbin for copyediting, David Luljak for help with the index , and I owe special thanks to Sara Lerner for the exceptional job she did as production editor.

All errors, misinterpretations, random non sequiturs and irrelevant observations are completely my responsibility. I can only hope that these are not the only unique contribution to Platonic scholarship to be found in these pages. I wish to thank my cat, Isaac, for being shameless and exemplifying the role of petty tyrant in our many daily non-interactions. I wish to thank the people who played the role of tyrant in my personal life because their behavior allowed me to experience the joys and horrors of interacting with this type of person just as I was formulating my thoughts about the Platonic tyrant. I wish to thank Rousseau's endnotes to his *Second Discourse* for showing me that sometimes you can put important thoughts in your notes.

Finally, I wish to thank my close friends Tracey, Dianne, Gaby, Debbie, and Robin, and my family, Helen and Bill Dimitroff, Walter and Joanne Tarnopolsky, Mark and Jackie, Sasha and John, Michelle and Andrea, Greg, Stephanie, Alanna, Milla, Josephine, Anna, Elizabeth, Dick, Anne, Rachel, and Bob. Without their love, support, encouragement, joyful company, and insightful conversations about everything under the earth, on this earth, and in the heavens, I would never have been able to produce anything at all.

Prudes, Perverts, and Tyrants

INTRODUCTION

CONTEMPORARY ATTITUDES TOWARD SHAME

Shame is a peculiar phenomenon. It has the potential to fracture our social ties in the very instance that it reveals them. It helps to establish the permeable and ever-unstable psychic boundary between the 'self' and the 'other,' both individual and collective, but it often does this in response to the painful awareness that this boundary has been unsettled or disrupted in some way.[1] Shame thus has a complex and ambiguous character. While it can function to help us negotiate our interactions with others in a decent and respectful manner, it can also cause us to turn away from such engagements, or to lash out against what gets uncovered in these interactions. Finally, as Greek tragedies and modern psychological case studies attest, it can even cause a person to commit suicide.[2]

In contemporary democratic societies shame is often construed as one of the negative emotions that we need to avoid in our deliberations, institutions, and practices, and it is not hard to see why shame comes to light as a negative emotion when we consider some of the pernicious ways in which it has been used in all of these diverse settings. Gays and lesbians, women, the disabled, and members of different races have all been shamed and stigmatized, both explicitly and implicitly, by certain laws, policies, or norms of deliberation that have sought to either punish them or exclude them altogether from the public realm because of their allegedly shameful characteristics or behaviors. The institution of marriage has been just one of the many ways in which gays and lesbians and members of different races have been excluded from the kinds of recognition that underpin self-esteem, and from the financial and social resources that allow one to participate as a full member of society. The horrific prison abuses at the Abu Ghraib prison, perpetrated against Iraqi prisoners during 2003 and 2004 in the course of the Iraq War, surely illustrate some of the worst manifestations of the emotions of both shame and humiliation in the realm of international relations. Finally, the different colored stars and triangles

---

[1] Throughout this book, I shall be talking about shame as a phenomenon that operates between both individual and collective 'selves' and 'others.' As will become clear over the course of this book, the 'other' before whom the 'self' feels ashamed can be external, internal, actual, imaginary, fantastical, realistic, singular, collective, specific or general. All subsequent references to 'self' and 'other' are not in single quotes. Cf. Kingston (2008, 113) who argues that one of the fundamental principles that Plato and Aristotle share is the view that all passions can be understood as individual and as collective phenomena.

[2] Basing her argument on a number of contemporary psychological and psychoanalytic accounts of shame, Toni Massaro (1999, 89) argues that in extreme cases, shame can lead to a "profound and complete loss of self that inspires a desire to die."

placed on Jews, Gypsies, gays, and lesbians served (and continue to serve) as horrific symbols of one of the most extreme ways in which a regime can devote itself to a systematic shaming and stigmatization of certain groups as a justification for eliminating them altogether. Anyone who has contemplated the horrific atrocities that have been committed against various individuals, groups, and entire races throughout world history cannot help but think that shame is one of the most negative, i.e., hierarchical, primitive, inhuman, demeaning emotions that mankind has in its repertoire. Indeed it is tempting to think that as we progress toward more democratic practices in our own polities, and more humanitarian interventions in foreign countries, shame will be the emotion that we will try to eradicate more and more from the human condition.

But before moving from these situations to an outright condemnation of shame, isn't it first necessary to ask whether shame, in all of its manifestations, leads to these sorts of pernicious outcomes? Moreover, isn't it also important to ask whether there aren't certain manifestations of shame without which we could not perform our deliberations as citizens or political leaders; contemplate our future actions with others in the domestic and international realm with humanity, dignity and respect; or protect ourselves and others citizens from certain types of damage and harm? Don't we wish that people like Hitler or Eichmann had felt ashamed of their treatment of Jews, Gypsies, and gays? Don't we admire, respect, and dignify people like Martin Luther King, Jr. who shame the American public for its mistaken equation of democratic equality with segregation and "separate but equal facilities" for blacks and whites? Don't we (as I surely did) scan the horrific pictures of prison abuses at Abu Ghraib prison trying to find just one person actually turning their head in shame rather than giving us the thumbs up and proudly smiling at the camera? Isn't it necessary for nongovernmental organizations like Human Rights Watch to explicitly shame regimes that carry out torture that is not sanctioned by the Geneva Conventions, or to shame regimes that stigmatize and punish unwed mothers in developing countries who have AIDS? Isn't it shameful when a political leader ignores the dire needs of one of his own cities in the aftermath of a hurricane because there just aren't enough rich white people living there, or when a political leader tries to sell a Senate seat to the highest bidder because that's what everyone else in Illinois does? Finally, don't we want our media to shame these leaders and politicians when they do engage in these sorts of actions, especially if they do them in the very undemocratic hope that they will never be divulged to the public?

THE THEORETICAL DEBATES SURROUNDING SHAME

These ambiguities that swirl around shame in our ethical and political lives also get reproduced in much of the contemporary theoretical literature that focuses specifically on this emotion. Political theorists who condemn shame do so because they see it as something that threatens certain necessary conditions for democratic participation and deliberation. Shame can threaten the mutual respect necessary for democratic deliberation by diminishing a person in the eyes of his audience or even in his own eyes, thus causing the person to withdraw from the discussion, and it can do this in a way that may be much more effective than a show of force. Utilizing Gabrielle Taylor's psychological work on shame, John Rawls describes it as "the feeling that someone has when he experiences an injury to his self-respect or suffers a blow to his self-esteem."[3] As self-respect is for Rawls a "primary good" and necessary condition for active participation in moral and political life,[4] shame is dangerous precisely because it can instill apathy and cynicism in the person, either by making everything seem worthless or by weakening the will to strive for things one values.[5] Similarly, building upon the psychological theories of Donald Winnicott, Martha Nussbaum has argued that shame (or more precisely a primitive form of shame that continues to linger in all of us to some degree)[6] ought to be banished from our legal systems because it contains dangerous aspirations to omnipotence that endanger rather than foster the "institutional and developmental conditions [necessary] for the sustenance of a liberal respect for human equality."[7] Finally, Jill Locke has recently argued that feminists and democrats should be skeptical of shame because the "negative global self-assessment" it involves and the weariness it induces actually forecloses rather than opens up the kinds of counterpublics and alternative spaces "where freedom can dwell," especially for "shame-ridden and shame-prone" subjects.[8]

In a somewhat similar vein (though from a different angle), queer theorist Michael Warner has argued that a politics of shame is pernicious to democratic deliberation because it isolates certain groups from the public by asserting a norm of what is acceptable and then silencing or concealing any "deviant" voices. In Warner's work, the "politics of shame" denotes the practice of diverting or avoiding the feeling of sexual shame by pinning it on someone else. Shame is the central mechanism by which the false moralism of the majority restricts the sexual autonomy of certain individuals by making their experi-

---

[3] Rawls (1971), 442.

[4] Rawls (1971), 62.

[5] Rawls (1971), 440.

[6] Nussbaum (2004), 15. For a full discussion of Nussbaum's book, see chapter 6.

[7] Nussbaum (2004), 16. Cf. Massaro (1997 and 1999), who utilizes a number of different psychological and sociological theories of shame to show why shame should not be introduced into the contemporary legal system in the form of shaming penalties. As will become clear in this book, I also do not support shaming penalties as a part of any legal system, but I do want to argue that another type of shaming is important for democratic politics.

[8] Locke (2007), 153–55, 159. She borrows the term "where freedom can dwell" from Hannah Arendt's book *On Revolution*.

ences and pleasures seem disgusting and therefore unworthy of acknowledgment. Equally problematic for Warner is the fact that instead of striving to circulate accurate knowledge about, and challenge the predominant view of their practices, these "perverts" strive to become "normal" by presenting themselves in accordance with the image of the "normal" citizen.[9]

On the opposite side of this debate, theorists of civility, such as Jean Elshtain, have argued that shame can provide the necessary conditions for democratic deliberation by excluding and thereby protecting the private lives of citizens from the gaze of the public. For Elshtain, individuals who parade their sexuality or intimate lives in the public breach the "boundary of shame" because they transpose the bodily functions, feelings, and interpersonal relationships that are meant for a private audience into the public sphere. Instead, for her, the public sphere should only be concerned with the activities of "arguing for a position, winning approval, or inviting dissent as a citizen."[10]

Similarly, Christopher Lasch has argued that America is actually suffering from a culture of narcissism and shamelessness in which the mass media regularly parade the "most outlandish perversions, the most degraded appetites," and moralists and psychoanalysts are in the business of getting people to accept and celebrate rather than judge and try to overcome these perversions.[11] As he puts it, "We do children a terrible disservice . . . by showering them with undeserved approval . . . Self-respect cannot be conferred; it has to be earned. Current therapeutic and pedagogical practice, all 'empathy' and 'understanding,' hopes to manufacture self-respect without risk."[12] Without the sting of shame, individuals never learn the individual initiative that is forged by overcoming obstacles and failures, nor do they develop respect for impersonal standards of competence that underpin any true form of education.[13]

Alternately, communitarian theorists of civility such as Amitai Etzioni argue that shame is necessary not so much to protect the individual from dangerous intrusions by the state or to educate him to self-reliance, but rather to express and reinforce the shared moral values that countries such as America are in danger of losing.[14] Etzioni and others have even gone so far as to favor the reintroduction of shaming penalties, e.g., forcing child abusers or drunk drivers to wear signs or bumper stickers publicizing their crimes.[15] According to

[9] Warner (1999). For a full discussion of Warner's book, see chapter 5. For similar accounts of the normalizing effects of shame see Goffman (1963), 128–35; and Nussbaum (2004), 173–74, 217–19.

[10] Elshtain (1995), 55. Cf. Saxonhouse (2006, 204) who argues that a rejection of shame may lead to a loss of the civility that is necessary for the coherence of a political community.

[11] Lasch (1995), 198; See also Lasch (1979); Twitchell (1997); and Gurstein (1996).

[12] Lasch (1995), 206.

[13] Lasch (1995), 206.

[14] Etzioni (2001).

[15] Etzioni (2001), chapter 2, 37–47; and Kahan (1996). For criticisms of shaming penalties, see Massaro (1997); Karp (1998); and Nussbaum (2004), chapter 5.

Etzioni such penalties are actually democratic because they express society's collective disapproval of certain acts, and they can be far more just than imprisonment because incarceration, unlike public penalties, often subjects prisoners to harsh conditions, offers few possibilities for parole, and fosters recidivism far more than rehabilitation.[16] Shaming penalties, on the other hand, express society's disapproval of the behavior while simultaneously giving the individual the possibility of showing his remorse and of reconciling with and reintegrating back into society.[17]

Although this kind of defense of shame may seem to lend itself to a conservative political agenda, William Miller and Dan Kahan have recently argued that emotions like shame and disgust can play a progressive role by marking out those moral matters for which there can be no compromise in a liberal democratic society, e.g., crimes such as "rape, child abuse, torture, genocide, predatory murder and maiming."[18] By expressing our collective abhorrence of these crimes and forms of cruelty, shame and disgust become virtues that track these vices and are necessary for the proper functioning of a liberal-democratic society.[19] Alternatively, John Braithwaite, who is an opponent of the kinds of shaming penalties favored by both Etzioni and Kahan, has argued that shame can play a positive role in the criminal justice system through "reintegrative shaming conferences."[20] Such conferences involve bringing together two "communities of care": the victims of the crime and their families or supporters, and the offenders together with their families and supporters. Because violent offenders have often erected a shield to protect themselves from feeling sympathy for or shame toward their victims, the victims' statements will instead affect the mothers or friends of the offender, and their reactions will in turn cause the offender to feel ashamed of his actions because of his respect and care for this latter group.[21] As Braithwaite puts it, "It is the shame of letting down those we love and trust that has the greatest power over us," and it is this kind of shame that is more likely to get criminal offenders to take the hard road of behavioral modification.[22] Finally, Braithwaite's work on shame has recently been utilized in the theories and practices of restorative justice, and of truth and reconciliation commissions after war, mass atrocities, and genocide.[23]

---

[16] Etzioni (2001), 42, 46.

[17] Etzioni (2001), 44.

[18] Miller (1997), 36. See also Kahan (1996) and (1999).

[19] Miller (1997), 202; and Kahan (1999), 64. (Miller and Kahan both draw upon Judith Shklar's work *Ordinary Vices* for this view of liberalism as the avoidance of cruelty.)

[20] Braithwaite (2000), 119–21.

[21] Braithwaite (2000), 120.

[22] Braithwaite (2000), 120.

[23] For excellent treatments of shame in these contexts, see Drumbl (2002) and Lu (2008).

Plato's Relevance to the Contemporary Politics of Shame

As this brief overview of the politics of shame illustrates, there is a great deal of disagreement about the place of this emotion in contemporary democratic politics. Some of the opposition to shame comes from the fact that it *is* a discomforting and unpleasant emotion to experience, and from the ample empirical evidence that shame *can* be used to stigmatize and isolate people causing them to withdraw from the political realm.[24] This latter empirical evidence cannot be denied and, as I will show in chapters 1 and 2, it is sometimes on display in Plato's *Gorgias*, just as it was sometimes on display in ancient Greek politics more generally. However, as Plato's dialogues and human life make abundantly clear, guilt, empathy, compassion, pity, love, anger, fear, remorse, or even calm calculation can be and have been just as crippling, disruptive, and pernicious to individuals, groups, or polities in the history of mankind.

Indeed, one of the most important corrections that both Plato and Aristotle can make to contemporary theories about the role of emotions in politics is to illustrate the fact that no emotion is a virtue in moral and political life, but rather that all emotions have the possibility of becoming an integral part of our democratic virtues or vices. For Plato, a desire to be without shame does connote a certain viciousness of character and a tyrannical personality; however, the presence of shame in no way guarantees that we possess virtue, even if it can often underpin our false pretensions to it. Shame, like the equality that Tocqueville examined in *Democracy in America*, can lead us either toward new and subtler forms of tyranny and despotism in our psyches and our polities, or toward new and subtler forms of liberty, democracy, and reciprocity. This book on shame is meant to show the many ways that, and reasons why, shame led in both of these directions for the Greeks in the fifth and fourth centuries BC, and for ourselves in our own recent history, so that we can devise the democratic institutions and practices that will tip the scale toward liberty, democracy, and reciprocity.

Second, as my overview also illustrated, some of the disagreements arise from certain ambiguities about what is meant by shame, and from the particu-

---

[24] Both Massaro (1997) and Nussbaum (2004) marshal significant and substantial evidence from the psychoanalytic and sociological literature on shame to show that hiding can be one of the reactions to shame. I think they are right to think that hiding is the dominant reaction to a certain type of shame or shaming by others. However, this is because they are primarily thinking of shame and shaming in terms of the kinds of stigmatizing penalties involved in shaming penalties, such as making people wear signs or bumper stickers that publicize their crimes or, even more problematically in the case of pedophiles, their particular mental illnesses. This is the dominant form in which shame has been conceptualized in the legal literature and actualized in the legal system, but it is not the only and certainly not the salutary form of shaming that I shall be supporting in this book.

lar manifestation of the emotion that is actually being praised or condemned. Many contemporary theories of shame and civility focus on only one aspect of shame, thus making their appreciation of shame's political and psychological work necessarily partial. Is Elshtain's "boundary of shame" an emotion, a virtue, an institutional arrangement, a set of practices within liberal democracies, or a character trait like civility, and how are these things related to one another? Is her "boundary of shame" or "veil of civility" actually necessary to ensure that the feelings of shame Rawls denounces are excluded from the public sphere? In other words, might they not both agree that respecting others as equals requires a politics of shame (understood as the civility made possible by our sense of shame) that avoids the pernicious practice of stigmatizing and humiliating others? This, of course, would be something very different from the politics of shame that Warner criticizes, and it may well amount to what he himself speaks of in other parts of his work as the possibility of finding a common human dignity in shame.[25] Related to this possibility, however, is the question of whether one can acquire a sense of shame or attain a dignity in shame without *ever* experiencing the painful feelings of inadequacy and the blows to one's self-esteem that characterize the primary occurrence of shame.[26] As Martha Nussbaum points out, "We do not think that the solution to all problems of shame lies in the effacement of the uncomfortable feelings,"[27] and we may even think that self-respect requires feeling shame "in various circumstances of reversal or failure."[28]

These ambiguities all point to the necessity of examining the complex manifestations and diverse forms of shame as a preliminary step to answering the question of whether or not shame has a place in democratic politics. The fact that ordinary language allows us to denote these various manifestations of shame with the same word suggests that there are complex and dynamic connections between these feelings, practices, and character traits that need to be theorized. This kind of analysis is required before one can argue either that shame is a necessary support for democratic interactions and deliberations or that it necessarily undermines these things by weakening the resolve, respect, and self-esteem that underpin human communicative interactions. The solution to our problems of shame then requires us to articulate the connection between the psychological and the political phenomena of shame. What does it mean to speak of the "politics of shame" or the "politics of emotion" more generally? Alternatively, how are political and social actions

[25] Warner (1999), 36.

[26] As Massaro (1999, 87) puts it, "One who truly felt *no* shame . . . would be a radically unsocialized, deeply disturbed individual who lacked a most basic inhibition—so basic that it is likely that very few (if any) utterly shameless individuals exist."

[27] Nussbaum (1980), 400.

[28] Nussbaum (1980), 404.

incorporated into the psyche in the form of shame? Can we have a democratic politics that preserves the kind of shame that is constitutive of respect and civility while avoiding the shame that stigmatizes and isolates certain groups from the public sphere?

In this book I explore these complexities that characterize shame in its dynamic capacity to move us simultaneously outward to sociality and political life and inward to the ongoing creation of a unique self. I do so through the lens of Plato's dialogue the *Gorgias,* not only because the emotion of shame was central to Greek political life and thought, but more importantly because it continues to be central to our own political life, even if this is often in the form of vehement denial.[29] Plato's analysis offers critical leverage on our contemporary democratic theories and practices because it offers one of the most profound meditations on how imperialistic democracies degenerate into tyrannies in part through their very disavowal of shame, and their desire to see shame as a simplistic and outdated emotion, and shamelessness as a form of freedom and courageousness.[30]

This desire to be without shame in order to be free is no less true of many of the world's current democratic polities, and of the kinds of psychosocial phenomena that led to the situation within which these polities now find themselves.[31] Contrary to what the leaders, media, and pundits now tell us, we do not have only the Depression of the 1930s to look to for a model of the kind of moderate and self-limiting democracies we might now all want to become. Plato's Athens was coping with similar problems and had just come out of an imperialistic war, a tyrannical democracy, the regime of the Thirty

---

[29] The same is also true of shame's constant companions like honor and esteem. As Brennan and Pettit (2004, 8) put it, "The assumption . . . that ordinary folk have no interest in honour and esteem and that it belongs only to the aristocracy is a grievous error."

[30] At *Republic* 8.560d–e Plato describes the tyrannical individual as a person who renames shame "simplicity" and shamelessness "courage." (All references to and translations of the *Republic* are from the translation by Allan Bloom, *The Republic of Plato,* Second edition (New York: Basic Books, 1968), unless otherwise noted.) This encapsulates what Plato brings out in great detail in his depiction of the potential Athenian statesman, Callicles, in the latter half of the *Gorgias.* As I will show in this book, the *Gorgias* contains Plato's most careful and sustained treatment of the relationship between shame, democracy, and tyranny.

[31] I borrow the term "psychosocial" from Danielle Allen (2000b). As Allen (2000b, 333 n.3) puts it, "The word 'psychosocial' [describes] the ways in which an individual's participation in social practices and ideas interacts with the *individual psyche* (or meets the needs of the individual psyche) and serves to foster *social cohesion.* The word indicates how social cohesion at once supports individual cognitive and psychological mechanisms and needs their support." Like Ober (1989, 11), Allen (2000b, xi) and Frank (2005, 3–5), I think that the Greek notions of the Athenian constitution (Ober), or authority and desert (Allen), as well as the Aristotelian notions of action and practice (Frank) lie at the intersection between structures and individual agents, between institutions and beliefs. The same is also true of Plato's notion of shame. It is a phenomenon made possible by the interaction of certain types of institutions and certain types of individual psychic states and beliefs.

Tyrants, and a period of unparalleled prosperity built partially upon greed, injustice, and the desire to banish shame from their collective psyche and polity.[32] Plato's writings are all deeply marked by these experiences of the late fifth century BC, and by his experience of the poorer but more moderate and democratic Athens that existed within the very different world order of the fourth century BC.[33]

If our own current problems arose in part from the *lack* of self-regulation and self-limitation within each of our polities' economic and political institutions and practices, I hope to show that such self-regulation and self-limitation are at the heart of a very important kind of democratic shame. As we rebuild the physical infrastructures or territorial boundaries of our polities to redress our current economic and political woes, it is my hope that we will also try to rebuild the psychosocial infrastructures and boundaries that predispose us to see our worldwide "depression" as an intractable crisis, rather than as an opportunity for change in a new and more democratic direction.[34] Shame can be one of the last safeguards of our democratic constitutions and by this I mean both our psychic and our political constitutions. Shame can be (and always has been) an important guide at such difficult crossroads, even if it is a guide that always threatens to lead us astray or down paths we have traveled before. More specifically, I argue that Plato's analysis of shame in the *Gorgias* supplies a deeper understanding of the necessary but dangerous role of this emotion in human life and democratic politics than either the proponents or the opponents of the contemporary politics of shame and civility. I do this by articulating the three different kinds of shame and shaming practices that can characterize human communicative interactions and democratic deliberations. In what follows, I refer to these different models of a politics of shame as 'flattering,' 'Socratic respectful,' and 'Platonic respectful' shame.[35]

This turn to Plato will of course strike some readers as odd, so before discussing Plato's specific insights on shame and democracy, I shall outline my reasons for making precisely this move. First, as certain Platonic scholars have argued, Plato's middle dialogues contain some of the most profound consider-

---

[32] The "Thirty Tyrants" refers to the pro-Spartan oligarchy that was set up after the surrender of Athens at the end of the Peloponnesian War in 404 BC. See Balot (2001, chapter 7) and Frank (2007) for excellent accounts of how Plato's *Republic* responds to the greed (*pleonexia*) and injustice (*adikia*) that plagued Athens during the period of the Peloponnesian War and the oligarchic revolutions of the late fifth century BC.

[33] Ober (1989) offers an excellent account of how the ideology that was forged and re-forged by mass and elite citizens in democratic Athens during the fourth century BC (partially in response to the excesses of the previous century) served as a crucial support for this more moderate and less tyrannical democracy.

[34] The notion of a worldwide "depression" is an excellent example of the kinds of psychosocial phenomena that I will be speaking about in this book. It suggests both the psychological state and the political-economic institutions that reciprocally create and sustain our current situation.

[35] All subsequent references to these terms are not in single quotes.

ations on human psychology, the role of emotions in politics, and the dynamic relationship between the psyche and the polity.[36] The famous analogy between the soul and the city in the *Republic* is the most obvious example of these Platonic concerns.[37] Trying to understand exactly what the analogy between the thumotic, erotic, and rational parts of the soul and the corresponding classes in the city means is one of the most difficult challenges to any reader of this dialogue. Similarly, all of the other dialogues of this period—the *Gorgias*, the *Symposium*, and the *Phaedrus*—contain profound reflections on the relationship between the psyche and the polity. More specifically, the *Gorgias* contains one of the first and most sustained reflections on the complex relationships that can exist between shame in the psyche and the shaming practices of democratic politics.

The second reason for turning to Plato consists of the need for thinking outside of certain early modern conceptual paradigms. Contemporary theorists of the emotions have stopped speaking about them as *either* raw feelings *or* unique forms of cognition because they have begun to realize that such binaries fail to capture the complex phenomena of the emotions. Such strict binaries have been inherited from early modern thinkers like René Descartes who conceived of passion and reason as completely distinct faculties,[38] or from the psychologist and philosopher William James who famously wrote, "*Our feeling of [bodily changes] as they occur IS the emotion* [James' italics]."[39] Instead, the current notion of a "politics of emotion" stresses the need to theorize the connections between feelings, thoughts, behaviors, and practices in ways that evade the static and binary categories of inner/outer, reason/emotion, mind/body, and public/private.[40] These strict dichotomies that characterize the early modern turn in political philosophy are simply not present in the Platonic corpus, even though these dualisms have characterized our interpretations and distortions of Platonism. The very asocial and unencumbered selves that we now need to think beyond are remnants of a way of thinking that is foreign to the Greeks, and here I think that elements of their very strangeness

---

[36] See Kaufer (1978); Irwin (1977), 191–216; Irwin (1979), 191, 195, 218, 221; Klosko (1983); Vlastos (1991), 45–81; Cooper (1999), chapters 2 and 4; and Lear ([1998], 1999). For a full discussion of the ordering of Plato's dialogues and the particular characteristics of his middle dialogues, see chapter 1.

[37] One of the best treatments of this theme in the *Republic* is Lear ([1998], 1999). For an excellent account of the dynamic and reciprocal relationship between characters and institutions in the works of Aristotle, see Frank (2005).

[38] For an account of Descartes' problematic dualisms, see Kingston (2008).

[39] I borrow this citation from Solomon ([1998], 2008), 189.

[40] For examples of this new approach and some of the debates within it, see Lutz and Abu-Lughod (1990); Damasio (1994); French and Wettstein (1998); Reddy (1997); Blackburn (1998); Elster (1999); Redding (1999); Koziak (2000); Nussbaum (2001); Marcus (2002); Solomon (2003) and ([1998], 2008); Walzer (2003); Hall (2003) and (2005); Konstan (2006); Clarke, Hoggett and Thompson (2006); Gross (2006); Sokolon (2006); Krause (2002) and (2008); and Kingston (2008).

can help us get away from these problematic early modern modes of thinking about the self and the emotions.[41]

Finally, I believe that Plato can help us think more deeply about the differences between a shame that is grounded in respect for others, and a shame that stigmatizes others and that depends upon a rigid and irreversible hierarchical structure between the shamer and the shamed. A number of theorists of shame have pointed to the fact that Attic Greek, unlike English, has two words for shame: *aidōs* and *aischunē*.[42] It is tempting to think that the two Greek words give us the necessary distinctions between a bad kind of hierarchical shame that is linked only to dishonor and disgrace (*aischunē*) and a good kind of shame linked only to awe, reverence, modesty, and respect (*aidōs*).[43] When I first began work on this book, I myself felt (and hoped) that this might well be the case. Unfortunately, by the time of Plato and Aristotle, many of these distinctions had begun to blur.[44] *Aischunē* had come to be used as a synonym for *aidōs* in many contexts, and the verbal form of both words (*aischunomai* and *aideomai*) when used with an accusative referring to another person or persons could be used either in the sense of "I feel ashamed before," or "I respect."[45] (As I will show in chapter 2, this bipolar or two-directional aspect of Greek shame (*aidōs/aischunē*) is essential for understanding the intersubjective character of this phenomenon.) Plato himself often uses forms of *aidōs* and *aischunē* interchangeably,[46] or uses the same word (*aischunē*) when articulating very different manifestations of shame.[47]

Although both *aidōs* and *aischunē* shared the possible connotation of respect for an other in Plato's time, there were still subtle distinctions between the two terms which are important for understanding the relationship between Plato's *Gorgias* and our own contemporary notions of shame. The more archaic and poetic word, *aidōs*, was originally used primarily in martial and

---

[41] Cf. Kingston (2008, 113) who argues that Plato and Aristotle can redress the modern tendency to see an emotion as either a wholly internalized phenomenon or a solely individual one.

[42] See for example Riezler (1943), 457; Cairns (1993), 415; Williams (1993), 194 n.9; Scheff (1997), 209; Konstan (2006), 93; Nieuwenburg (2004), 466 n.12; and Saxonhouse (2006), 61 n.9. All Attic Greek terms are transliterated.

[43] This is the argument of Riezler (1943) and Scheff (1997). Konstan (2006, 91–110) also thinks there is an important distinction between the two terms, but for him this arises more out of the fact that *aischunē* can have a prospective and a retrospective character, whereas *aidōs* can have only a prospective character. In other words, the object of *aischunē* can be a past, present, or future blow to one's self-esteem, but the object of *aidōs* can only be a future blow to one's self-esteem.

[44] See Cairns (1993), 415 and 455; Williams (1993), 194 n.9 and Nieuwenberg (2004), 466 n.12.

[45] Cairns (1993), 415 and 455.

[46] See for example *Euth.* 12b; *Rep.* 8.560c–9.571d. Konstan (2003, 95–100) argues persuasively that Aristotle differentiates between *aidōs* and *aischunē* because he only uses *aidōs* in a prospective or restrictive sense while he uses *aischunē* in both a prospective/restrictive sense and a retrospective or remorseful sense. I have not found this distinction to be true of Plato's use of the terms.

[47] In the chapters that follow I argue that this is precisely what happens throughout the *Gorgias*.

religious settings and had positive connotations of awe, respect, and reverence for the gods, or respect and modesty before one's superiors, guests, or strangers, especially in Homer.[48] With the development of Athenian democracy in the fifth and fourth centuries, the word *aischunē*, which first occurred solely with the meaning of disgrace,[49] gradually began to take on some of the more positive connotations of respect that had been characteristic of the archaic term *aidōs*. Now, however, this respect was directed more toward other men and their man-made codes than toward the gods. Indeed, one of the few subtle but important distinctions between *aidōs* and *aischunē* that persisted in Plato's time was the fact that there was no active verb form of *aidōs*, but there was an active verb form of *aischunē*, which (in the first person singular) was *aischunō*.[50] In other words, while it was possible to *aischunō* (shame or dishonor) another person, it was impossible to *aideō* another person. This of course makes sense if *aidōs* was originally that particular emotion brought about by the irreversible hierarchical relationship between man and the gods, and this actually makes *aischunē* closer to our contemporary notion of shame, in the sense that it can refer both to the felt experience of shame and to the action of shaming that we direct toward others.

This also explains why the only word used throughout the *Gorgias* to describe the kinds of shame and acts of shaming that were experienced and performed by democratic Athenians and by Socrates is *aischunē*. When Plato uses the word *aischunē* in the *Gorgias* the connotations of dishonor and disgrace are still foremost, but he also uses it to describe the motivation that prompts Socrates to relentlessly question and shame his fellow citizens into perplexity and uncertainty out of an attitude of respect. As Socrates tells Callicles, he (Socrates) would be ashamed (*aischunoimēn*) if he could not render his particular brand of help to himself or to others (*Gorg.* 522d).[51] There is thus within the dialogue an attempt to articulate two related but different kinds of shame (*aischunē*) that can be felt before or wielded against one's peers and fellow citizens, and that can lead either in the direction of conformity and flattery or critical reflection and respect.

[48] Latimer (1926), 2–4, 35–37; Cairns (1993), 49–146; Riedinger (1980). (Cairns (1993, 135), however, argues that *aidōs* is never used exclusively in a religious sense in Homer. He (1993, 138–39) also argues that even in certain Homeric passages *aidōs* and *aischunē* were used synonymously to refer to instances of disgrace or dishonor before other men.)

[49] Konstan (2003, 294 n.11) argues that the noun *aischunē* "first occurs in the sixth-century poet Theognis [verse 1272], in the sense of being a 'disgrace,' and becomes common toward the middle of the fifth century BC." While the more archaic and poetic term *aidōs* is only cognate with *aischos* (disgrace) and *aischron* (ugly or dishonorable), *aischunē* is clearly derivative from them.

[50] Liddell and Scott (1996), 43.

[51] All references to and translations of the *Gorgias* are from the translation by James Nichols, Jr., *Plato: Gorgias* (Ithaca: Cornell University Press, 1998). All citations refer to the Stephanus pages and sections of his translation.

The other subtle distinction between the two emotions that persisted in classical Athens was the association of *aidōs* with the virtue of modesty and the metaphor of a covering mantle, and the association of *aischunē* with the virtue of courage.[52] In the deft hands of Plato, this subtle distinction is used both in the *Apology* and especially in the *Gorgias* to remind his fellow citizens that the only truly courageous person in a democratic polity is the person (i.e., Socrates) who feels a certain shame (*aischunē*) before the very activity of philosophizing, and who thus refuses to flatter his democratic audience.[53] Indeed, as I will argue at great length in chapters 3 and 4, Plato's *Gorgias* offers both his contemporary Athenians as well as his future readers a vivid image of the kind of courage needed in order to reciprocally shame one's fellow citizens out of their complacency, false moralism, and problematic conflation of shamelessness with courage and freedom.

The fact that a philosopher like Plato can help political theorists think more deeply about an emotion like shame in the aforementioned ways is, of course, a relatively uncontroversial claim. However, my book goes further and challenges the traditional and canonical view of Plato as a virulent anti-democrat by examining the ways in which his dialogues actually utilize and develop certain Athenian democratic ideals within and alongside his critique of Periclean imperialistic Athens.[54] By repositioning Plato in this way, I am better able to utilize his insights into the complex role of shame in Athenian democratic politics in order to address the issues I outlined earlier in the contemporary politics of shame and civility.

In doing so, I also challenge the prevalent view, most famously espoused by Gregory Vlastos, of a democratic Socrates and an anti-democratic or authoritarian Plato.[55] By this I do not mean that I think of Plato as an avid supporter of fifth- and fourth-century Athenian democracy, nor do I think that the democracy was justified in putting Socrates to death for what they took to be inherently anti-democratic activities.[56] I think that whether these thinkers were

---

[52] Konstan (2003), 95 and 296 n.17. Konstan here cites Thucydides' *History of the Peloponnesian War* 1.84.3 for this distinction. For an excellent argument against conflating shame with modesty in a very different literary and historical context, see Wagner (2008).

[53] For an excellent account of this form of Socratic courage in the *Apology* and the *Gorgias*, see Balot (2008).

[54] This approach to Plato was first developed by Euben (1997); Saxonhouse (1996) and (1998); Wallach (1997) and (2001); and Monoson (2000). Other thinkers who offer nuanced and sympathetic readings of Plato's attitude toward democracy include Wardy (1996); Balot (2001); and Frank (2007) and (2008).

[55] Vlastos (1983c) and (1991). Thinkers who have argued for Plato's anti-democratic attitudes include Vickers (1988), 88–89; Vlastos (1991); Roberts (1994); Ober (1998); and Nehamas (1998). Thinkers who have argued for Plato's authoritarian attitudes include Popper (1945); Havelock (1957); Taylor (1997); Dombrowski (1997); and Shorris (2004).

[56] For the argument that the Athenian democracy was justified in prosecuting Socrates for anti-democratic activities and sentiments, especially concerning the practice of free speech, see Stone (1988).

enemies or friends of Athenian democracy is a very complicated question and the solution is not contained in the notion of a democratic Socrates and an authoritarian Plato.[57] In certain instances, both Plato and Socrates were opposed to specific practices and policies of democratic Athens, e.g., they both objected to the kind of mass decision making characteristic of the Athenian democratic assembly and law courts.[58] However it is important to see that, in some cases, their opposition was to the particular form that democracy took in Athens during the fifth and fourth centuries BC. This was a form of democracy that was far more direct and participatory than our contemporary democracies: it lacked most features of our modern-day bureaucracy, civil service, or representative institutions; a number of key political offices were filled by lot; and citizens could debate, offer amendments to, and vote on things as diverse as war policies, taxation, public works, and diplomatic negotiations.[59] In contrast, at the beginning of the twenty-first century, many of us take for granted the authority of an entrenched elite,[60] a civil service, and a bureaucratic state structure, and the fact that the average citizen's participation in government is limited mainly to voting.

It should hopefully be obvious that, for me, this is a descriptive, not a prescriptive characterization of our contemporary democracies. I also do not mean to overlook alternative forms of contemporary democratic participation such as social movements or aesthetic practices. I only want to emphasize the fact that modern-day citizens do not (and cannot) participate in the direct governance of a democratic polity to the same degree that the Athenian male citizen did. Second, I also want to suggest that before decrying the elitism of Socrates and/or Plato it is necessary to ask ourselves whether we would want the most important political offices of our own democracies to be chosen by lot.

These significant differences between their situation and our own does not mean that what Socrates and Plato have to say about democratic concepts such as liberty, equality, and majority rule have nothing to offer us as we continue

---

[57] For theorists who examine the relationship between Socrates and Athenian democracy, see Monoson (2000), 11 n.23. For a list of theorists who examine the relationship between Plato and Athenian democracy, see Monoson (2000), 12 n.24.

[58] I owe this point to Danielle Allen. See also Monoson (2000), 11 n.22. See Frank (2005, 6) for the argument that Aristotle also felt that truth was rarely a matter of mass majority rule. (Here she quotes *Meta.* 1009b2.)

[59] See Finley (1985), 20, 25–26; (1991), 75–76; Hansen (1991), 3; Samons (2004), 28–31; and Rhodes (2006), 56–62. Cf. Ober (1989, 151) who argues, "[the fact] that there was a relatively direct and causal relationship between the opinion of the majority, and state policy and legal decisions is a fundamental difference between Athenian democracy and modern governmental systems."

[60] Ober (1996), 5. For the argument that Athenian leaders, including Pericles, did not form anything like an entrenched and self-perpetuating elite see Finley, (1985), 24–25; Ober (1989), 16–17, 21.

to grapple with these same concepts ourselves. It is also important not to make the mistake of thinking that because they do sometimes make assertions that are anti-majoritarian, anti-liberty, or anti-equality, they are therefore anti-democratic thinkers. Their criticisms of these concepts were often directed at the most radically democratic articulations of these ideals, or at the perverted forms of liberty, equality, and majoritarianism that they thought were being practiced by the imperialistic and tyrannical democracy that Athens had become at the end of the fifth century BC. A deeper understanding of what they actually mean by equality, liberty, and majoritarianism can still have relevance for our own thinking on these topics,[61] and as I show in this book their concerns about the corrupt forms of these democratic ideals actually do have very direct relevance for our own current political situation.

Thus, in chapter 3, "Plato on Shame in Democratic Athens," I argue that a more indirect approach is necessary before applying Platonic insights to our contemporary problems. The first part of this approach involves reconstructing aspects of the Athenian democratic "normative imagery" and then juxtaposing these to Plato's own account of philosophical practice.[62] This is necessary because, as both A.H.M. Jones and Josiah Ober have pointed out, although we have a number of classical texts that are critical of democracy, we lack any surviving statements of the theory upon which Athenian democracy was premised.[63] When this is done a new reading of Plato becomes possible. More specifically, it becomes clear that although Plato relentlessly attacks flattering rhetoric and the democratic leaders Pericles and Themistocles throughout the *Gorgias,* he does so because they *fail* to live up to certain ideals that are in fact shared by Platonic philosophizing and certain strands of Athenian democratic ideology. It also becomes clear that philosophy requires the same openness to being shamed by an other that is exemplified in the democratic ideal of *parrhēsia* (free/frank speaking) and in the Socratic elenchus.

The second part of this new approach involves distinguishing between the representations of democracy and democratic leaders in Plato's dialogues and the actual historical institutions and theories of democracy that were prevalent in Athens at the time. As Peter Euben has argued, the "democratic leaders," Pericles and Themistocles, and the "democratic citizen," Callicles, (all of whom are relentlessly criticized by Socrates), actually fail to live up to certain ideals

---

[61] For a similar articulation of the relevance of Aristotle's thought for democratic theory today see Frank (2005), introduction.

[62] Monoson (2000), 12–15. Monoson borrows the term "normative imagery" from Loraux (1986). For other theorists who pursue this strategy in relation to Plato's dialogues, see Euben (1994) and (1997), chapters 8 and 9; Saxonhouse (1996), (1998) and (2006); Wallach (20001); and Balot (2001), chapter 7. For accounts of Athenian democratic ideology see Finley (1985); Farrar (1988); Euben, Wallach, and Ober (1994); Ober (1989), (1996), and (1998); Ober and Hedrick (1996); Monoson (2000); and chapter 3 below.

[63] Jones ([1957], 1979), 41; and Ober (1998), 147.

explicitly espoused by Athenian democratic discourse.[64] More specifically, I argue that Socrates' attacks in the *Gorgias* are directed at the supporters or leaders of Athenian democracy who dream of being tyrants, while falsely professing to be concerned with the common good. Socrates' shaming refutations of these interlocutors are thus meant to recall his fellow citizens back to the true practice of democracy. Because shame involves the recognition that we don't actually live up to the ideals we have of ourselves, it can also play a role in showing us that we don't live up to the corrupting image of the tyrant. Taken together, these two strategies allow me to treat Plato not as a total enemy of democratic Athens, but rather as an "immanent" critic of a corrupt Athenian democracy.[65]

In chapter 4, "Socratic vs. Platonic Shame," I go further and suggest that the *Gorgias* illustrates Plato's own criticisms of and corrections to his teacher's elenchic and ironic encounters with others from a standpoint that is in some ways *more* sympathetic to the perspective of Socrates' Athenian democratic audience.[66] These criticisms and corrections depend upon Plato's own deepening understanding of the role of shame in communicative interactions. Here I argue that Plato's use of myth at the end of the *Gorgias* both illustrates the shaming mechanism of the Socratic elenchus and exemplifies a comportment toward the audience that represents a different kind of respectful shame than the one exhibited by Socrates' own elenchic activities. The myth at the end of the *Gorgias* combines the pleasures of sight and sound, so integral to Gorgias' epideictic rhetoric, with the more painful and negative aspects of the Socratic elenchus to elicit a more positive reaction to the experience of being ashamed. This rearticulation of Plato's position *vis-à-vis* democratic Athens thus allows me to utilize his insights into shame as a way of deepening our own understanding of the role of this emotion in contemporary democratic politics.

PLATO'S *GORGIAS* AND THE POLITICS OF SHAME

One of the reasons it has been so difficult for scholars to see Plato as having any sympathies for Athenian democratic ideology arises out of the many mistaken interpretations of the very dialogue that I focus on in this book. Accordingly, in the first chapter I argue that the problematic distinctions between rhetoric

---

[64] Euben (1994), 208–14. See also Wallach (2001, 10) who points out that Plato's criticisms of political injustice and domination have often been mistaken for a criticism of democracy.

[65] Cf. Monoson (2000); and Wallach (2001). The term "immanent" criticism comes from Walzer (1987).

[66] Cf. Wallach (2001) who suggests that "Socrates is as much a problem as a hero in Plato's philosophical project" (9) and that Plato's project involved trying to resolve the tensions between the critical discourse (*logos*) of Socratic virtue and Athenian democratic practice (*ergon*) (7). Klosko (1983, 585) also argues that the "rejection of Socratic political tactics is a major element

and philosophy, emotion and reason, persuasion and argumentation, which Plato's *Gorgias* is credited with inaugurating, overlook the distinctions he actually makes between Gorgianic rhetoric, flattering rhetoric, the Socratic elenchus, and the true and noble brand of rhetoric that he forges out of an alliance between Gorgianic rhetoric and the Socratic elenchus. In this chapter I show how the dialogue itself performs a mediation between those elements of Gorgias' display (*epideixis*) rhetoric and Socrates' shaming elenchus, which Plato thinks are *both* necessary if shame (*aischunē*) is to have a salutary role in democratic deliberations. Although Plato critiques elements of both Gorgianic rhetoric and Socratic philosophy in the *Gorgias*, his method of critique (or what he calls the method of collection and division in the *Phaedrus*)[67] subsumes and preserves rather than wholly negates the salutary elements of these modes of comportment toward others. In doing so, I also challenge the neo-Kantian prejudice that sees respect as a product of practical rationality in isolation from the psychological and affective sources of this phenomenon, and I challenge Straussian interpretations of the dialogue that see it as a Platonic-Gorgianic alliance that is meant solely to protect Socratic and Platonic philosophy from politics. Far from banishing rhetoric and emotion from his own notion of a more philosophical democratic politics, Plato's *Gorgias* shows us exactly why a rhetoric of respectful shame is integral to the kinds of reciprocal and intersubjective relations that make self–other interactions in a democratic polity both critical and potentially transformative.

In the second chapter, "Shaming Gorgias, Polus, and Callicles," I offer a detailed analysis of the refutations of Socrates' three interlocutors in the *Gorgias* in order to show how the phenomenon of shame (*aischunē*) is itself constitutive of the structure of intersubjectivity that is necessary for this kind of potentially transformative ethical and political deliberation. Previous accounts of the role of shame in the *Gorgias* treat it as revealing either the ethical truth contained within the psyche of the individual, or the ethical truth contained within certain societal opinions and practices. Instead, I argue that shame points simultaneously inwards to what the individual desires and believes, and outward to the world of other individuals and groups, as well as to the laws and practices within which he moves and lives. This bipolar or two-directional character of shame is reflected in the fact that it involves the cognitive-affective gaze of an other that reveals a certain inadequacy in the self.

Second, I argue that understanding how a shame refutation works requires taking into account the two moments of any shame situation: the moment of recognition and the moment of reaction. Only by distinguishing between these two moments is it then possible to understand why it is that we can speak of

---

of the political teaching of the *Gorgias*," but he thinks that Plato's rejection of Socrates led him in an authoritarian direction (594). My position is obviously quite different from Klosko's.

[67] *Phdr.* 266b; cf. *Phdr.* 263a–266a.

individuals as either being ashamed of the truth or being too ashamed to speak the truth. In this chapter I illustrate these two moments through a detailed analysis of all three of Socrates' elenchic encounters with his interlocutors. Previous interpretations of the role of shame in the *Gorgias*, as well as of our own contemporary theories of shame in democratic politics, end up being partial precisely because they overlook these *two* moments that can both play a part in the kinds of evasions, transformations, and contestations made possible by any shame situation.

The moment of recognition within the primary occurrence of shame consists of the painful but potentially beneficial recognition of the gaze of an other that reveals a certain inadequacy in the self. It is painful because it involves some kind of diminution of the self in relation to an other. However, what is positive about this experience is that it disrupts or unsettles one's "blind" or unthinking identification with an image or ideal, which can actually be a good thing if who we are cannot be fully captured by an overly unitary or fantastical standard. For this very reason perplexity or a salutary kind of disunity and disorientation often characterizes the moment of recognition within the experience of shame, and this very perplexity opens up but does not guarantee the possibility of a radical transformation or contestation of the self or other involved in the shaming situation. What can also be positive and potentially beneficial about this experience is that it can reveal a common truth between the self and the other, e.g., the very vulnerabilities we share as human beings living in an uncertain and to some degree uncontrollable world. Finally, I argue that what endangers the salutary potential in any shame situation are the kinds of reaction that the self makes to what is revealed in the shaming situation, and the mode of comportment by the other doing the shaming (and these two things are often, though not necessarily, related to one another).

The third and fourth chapters, "Plato on Shame in Democratic Athens" and "Socratic vs. Platonic Shame," are thus devoted to articulating these two other elements of a shame situation. More specifically, in chapter 3 I focus on the kinds of reactions to the moment of recognition that led the Athenians to develop a sense of flattering shame that actually foreclosed rather than opened up spaces for contesting the problematic norms of democratic citizenship that were prevalent (if only implicitly) during Athens' imperialistic period. In chapter 4 I then turn to analyze the ways in which Socrates' own unique brand of respectful shaming may have inadvertently contributed to the less than salutary reactions on the part of his interlocutors and his polity more generally. I show how Plato's own revision to Socrates' brand of respectful shame exemplifies the kind of comportment toward a democratic audience that can prompt more salutary reactions to the experience of being shamed out of one's conformity or complacent moralism. Thus I argue that Plato's use of myth reflects certain criticisms of Socrates' engagements with others that are grounded in Plato's own deepening understanding of the mechanisms of shame, and of the kinds of comportment toward an other that are necessary to elicit a more positive reaction to the experience of being shown that we are not who we thought we were.

In the case of flattering shame (exemplified by the kind of rhetoric that both Polus and Callicles valorize and practice), one fixates on the pain that is inherent to the recognition that one has fallen below the standards of an imaginary or actual other. It is the painfulness of this recognition that becomes the "shameful" situation that one tries to avoid in the future. In flattering shame, one hopes to avoid the unpleasant experience of having one's identifications punctured by one's audience. What one considers "shameful" is the fact that one is seen by others not to be what one thought one was, and alternately, what one considers "good" is to be recognized by oneself or others as simply what one already takes oneself to be. The speaker's sense of shame thus attunes him to the view of the other or audience, but in such a way that this other can never again reveal any inadequacies or criticisms of his self. Nor is he (the speaker) oriented to revealing any inadequacies in his audience. Instead, both parties to the debate are oriented to maintaining the mythic unity of the objectified public image of the "virtuous" citizen. A false consensus then forms wherein "debate" becomes a kind of reciprocal exchange of pleasures or pleasantries, such that neither party ever has to endure the pain of having their identity or ideals criticized by the other. Those actions or aspects of the self that do not fit this mythic unity are then displaced onto other individuals or groups in the shaming practices of derision and stigmatization. The person whose sense of shame has fixated on the pleasures of mutual recognition and who is oriented to restoring the lost unity that is always sundered by feelings of shame may then try to escape the "shame" of failing to live up to the norm by displacing it onto others. This kind of flattering shame becomes especially problematic when the public image of the truly "virtuous" citizen in an imperialistic polity like democratic Athens actually embodies dangerous and tyrannical aspirations to omnipotence and to freedom *from* all restraints on these problematic desires for omnipotence.

In contrast to this, Socrates' own sense of shame offers a model of respect that is grounded in preserving our very openness to judgment by the other that is present in the primary occurrence of shame. This kind of respectful shame is oriented toward dissecting the mythical unity of these images of the "virtuous" citizen in the ongoing project of mutual reflection and criticism (as exemplified by the Socratic elenchus.) The morality grounded in this kind of respectful shame consists, not in assimilating to a standard or norm, but rather in remaining open to the ongoing possibility that who you are cannot be captured by any particular norm or self-image you currently possess. As Dana Villa puts it, "[Socrates'] essential task is to get his fellow Athenians to entertain the possibility that the demands of morality may, in fact, run counter to the established norms of the society and its conception of virtuous citizenship,"[68] and as he suggests, this activity provides a model of a kind of critical democratic citizenship that ought to complement the more participatory models of citizenship put forth by contemporary republican theorists.[69] Just as the Socratic shaming elenchus performs a kind of disruption of unity and identity, so a healthy democracy requires citizens who reciprocally perform and endure the pain of being rightfully shamed out of their conformity. In the *Gorgias*, Socrates performs this critical democratic citizenship role by trying to get his foreign and Athenian interlocutors to see that they are not in fact the tyrants they secretly or not so secretly profess to admire because they do actually admire certain other activities or ways of life that are inconsistent with tyranny.

Finally, Plato's own revision to this Socratic politics of shame reflects his additional consideration that although a certain amount of pain and struggle is integral to the discovery of ethical and political truths, a certain amount of pleasure and consensus is also integral to any act of intersubjective recognition and deliberation. I argue that Plato's model of respectful shame ultimately tries to find a place for the struggle and pain of Socrates' elenchic encounters and for the kinds of pleasures and benefits that can come from acknowledging the commonalities between one's self and one's fellow citizens, even while showing them why and how you disagree with them. Accordingly, I argue that the myth at the end of the dialogue represents a poetic-philosophic and friendly amendment to both Socrates' shaming elenchus and Gorgias' pleasant and spectacular rhetoric. In fact, it exemplifies a respectful shaming of both Socrates and Gorgias because it reveals the insufficiencies as well as the salutary aspects of their own modes of comportment toward others as this is displayed in the initial parts of the dialogue.

In chapter 5, I argue that once these insights into the various manifestations of shame are developed it becomes clear that there are often more striking similarities than differences between the contemporary proponents and opponents of shame and civility. Here I show how the proponents and opponents of shame tend to criticize or alternately to engage in the pernicious politics of flattering shame, while overlooking or misstating the possibilities of both Socratic and Platonic respectful shame that can bind individuals or groups together through the very recognition of their difference or distance from prevalent norms of citizenship. I also argue that Plato's treatment of shame actually extends upon the positive treatments of shame offered by Bernard Williams, Andrew Morrison, and John Braithwaite by showing how shame can open up possibilities of not just transforming the self in accordance with the other doing the shaming, but also of contesting and resisting the very self and other that are revealed in any shame situation. Finally, I show how Plato's incorpora-

---

[68] Villa (2001), 3.
[69] Villa (2001), 299.

tion and transcendence of his teacher's method of shaming others allows us to find a place for consensus and disagreement, deliberation and agonism within a democratic politics of shame.

In chapter 6, I extend my analysis of Plato and shame beyond the particular debates concerning shame and civility to show how the notion of respectful shame that I derive from Plato is actually consistent with some of the most recent findings in the neuroscientific study of the emotions and their significance in human deliberations. I also argue that Plato's understanding of respectful shame requires that we relinquish the oversimplistic division between "positive" and "negative" emotions and instead focus on the positive and negative manifestation of each and every emotion in human life and, more particularly, in democratic deliberations and practices. Related to this, I argue that in order to understand the place of emotions in human ethical and political life it is necessary to overcome the problematic distinctions (propagated by many psychoanalysts and political theorists in the past century) between shame as a primitive and amoral emotion and guilt as a mature and moral emotion.

Prudes, Perverts, and Tyrants

Finally, I should say a little about my title, even though the figures, especially that of the tyrant, shall rear their heads in various places throughout this book. I daresay they have also reared their heads recently in our own democratic polities. This should not be too surprising for as I hope to show in this book, they are figures that have a lot to do with those aspects and types of shame that we continue to share with the Greeks.

As I will argue in chapter 5, the prude and the pervert are the two figures or personality types that we moderns tend to think of most when we think about shame and civility. Two things are important about this fact. The first is that these figures center around questions of sexuality where our fundamental vulnerability to the subtle or not so subtle intrusions of others is most manifest, but they also inevitably intersect with political questions surrounding valorized or problematic forms of intersubjectivity. Hence, it is no coincidence that these figures have tended to rear their heads in discussions of gay marriage or AIDS activism. The original perceptions of AIDS as a "gay plague" as well as certain contemporary criticisms of gay marriage both assume that a particular sphere or form of intersubjectivity must be protected from the intrusions of certain "perverts" who threaten the kinds of activities that are to be fostered in these circles of care and concern. They also implicitly convey concerns about just why the activities of these alleged "perverts" should disqualify them from access to the kinds of rights and resources necessary to participate fully as democratic citizens.

If our own modern-day "perverts" tend to be "cross-dressers" or "sadomasochists" who breach the boundary of shame and civility by openly parading their perversions in the public sphere,[70] the Greeks had their own variation on the "pervert" in the form of the catamite. The catamite was the passive partner in a male-to-male sexual relationship who, by virtue of his passive sexuality, was denied citizenship rights because he was deemed incapable of taking on the role of the active citizen, future soldier, and defender of Athens.[71] He was also seen as a figure of shamelessness because he failed to put up the kinds of restraints or boundaries necessary to participate fully as a rational and active citizen, and instead passively gave in to his shameful and excessive sexual desires.[72] Socrates' suggestion in the *Gorgias* that such a person might actually be consistent with Callicles' own valorization of indiscriminate hedonism as the best way of life for human beings invites a harsh rebuke from Callicles, simply because it poses such an affront to the accepted norms of Athenian democratic citizenship (494e). Callicles interprets Socrates' comment as a shameless and perverse intrusion into the conversation, even though he (Callicles) had initially professed to be free of the kind of shame that ties one to conventional norms (482e–483e).

Second, as I hope to show in this book, the "prude" and "pervert" are figures that are actually constructed out of the more fundamental desire for very rigid boundaries between the self and the other. If shame is the emotion that helps us negotiate the boundaries between the self and the other, flattering shame involves the problematic desire that we fix this boundary once and for all by coming to see ourselves as the omnipotent and invulnerable beings or the perfectly "virtuous" citizens that we so desire to be. The "prude" is the person who wants shame to police these rigid boundaries to prevent the intrusion of shameless "perverts" into the collective self or polity. In the *Gorgias*, Callicles tells Socrates that it is fine to philosophize when one is a youth but that this childish activity should be given up when one reaches adulthood or else one becomes ridiculous and worthy of a beating because one becomes inexperienced in the customs and character of one's own polity (484c–e). It is Callicles' prudish desire that one could learn to become a virtuous citizen by simply attuning oneself to the prevalent norms of "virtuous" citizenship in imperialistic Athens, and this leads in turn to his desire to literally beat up anyone like Socrates who challenges these norms. Callicles' prudishness represents the fan

---

[70] These examples of "perverts" are drawn from Jean Elshtain's (1995, 54–55) description of the problematic politics of displacement and publicity in contemporary democratic polities. My own sense is that such displays of defiance against our modern-day Victorian prudishness are actually sorely lacking in most democratic polities.

[71] I discuss the importance of the catamite in the *Gorgias* in chapters 1 and 2.

[72] See Bradshaw (2005) and Monson (2000) for accounts of the ways in which excessive desire was also linked with female desire and female desire was in turn linked to tyranny.

tastical desire for strict and impermeable boundaries between the self and the other, and it also exemplifies the kind of flattering shame that led the Athenians to see Socrates as an "enemy" to their polity worthy of being sentenced not just to a beating, but to death. Socrates' refusal to flatter the imperialistic Athenians' problematic self-image of omnipotence and freedom from all restraints thus resulted in his own stigmatization as an enemy of the polis.

Ironically enough, Callicles' initial profession to be free of the kind of shame that attunes one to the conventional norms of one's polity (482e–483e), as well as his later contradictory desire to be completely attuned to these conventional Athenian norms (484c–e), actually show that the "prude" and "pervert" are simply the contradictory desires to police rigid boundaries (the prude) or to abolish all boundaries (the pervert) which are inevitably produced out of the refusal to perform the more difficult negotiation between truly open boundaries that are always vulnerable and permeable by an other in the ongoing and reciprocal relationships of respectful shame. Respectful shame performs the dissolution of these rigid boundaries between the self and the other because it keeps open the possibility that both the self and the other might actually be transformed or contested in and through the very actions of shaming and being shamed that are characteristic of a more democratic and less tyrannical form of political intersubjectivity. In contrast to this, Callicles, the character who tells Socrates that one must flatter one's regime if one wants to preserve oneself in a polity like Athens (521a), merely mimics the contradictory desires of his own imperialistic and tyrannical polity that broke the standing rules and conventions of warfare in its affairs with other Greek cities during the Peloponnesian War, even while it inculcated a rigid norm of active, male, and martial citizenship within the polity to support this imperialistic war.[73] For this very reason, Socrates' criticisms of the tyrannical democrat, Callicles, in the *Gorgias* can offer us important lessons for dealing with the tyrannical impulses that continue to plague our own democratic polities as we face new and novel challenges in the world we share with others.

Until very recently, it might have been tempting for us to think that the tyrant is not someone we need to think much about because we have institutional checks and balances, a division of power, higher laws, and bills of rights that play many of the restraining roles that the ancients thought had to be checked by a rigorous education to virtue. Even if shame did play an important role in restraining the tyrannical and overweening desires of certain individuals for honor, esteem, money, or power, it is no longer necessary (according to such a view), because we have regulations and institutions in place that have

---

[73] As Frank (2007, 445) puts it, the Peloponnesian War "broke the standing rules of warfare that had been in effect since the eighth century BCE, causing major changes in the practice of war," "destabilizing hitherto settled rules of engagement and categories of identity" and "giving free rein to *pleonexia* [overreaching] in all its registers, psychic, domestic, and imperial."

corrected many of the oversights of the direct and impetuous democracies of the ancients.[74]

As the first decade of the twenty-first century comes to a close, it is very unlikely that many people still believe that this is the case. Nonetheless, the first place that many people are looking to for answers to the troubling deregulation of our economies or the recent incursions on our political and civil rights is to more regulation or better protections of these rights. These are certainly going to be an important part of the solution to our current economic and political woes,[75] but it is also important to finally recognize that no external constraints, regulations, and checks on the tyrannical exercise of power can ever fully prevent future abuses of the power that we will always have to give to certain leaders or experts in our societies. They also cannot prevent the future tyrannical abuses that we as democratic citizens might well bring about because of our own desires for more money, bigger homes, more power, and more pleasure in our personal lives. There will always come a point when only the respectful shame of a political leader will prevent him from taking the tyrannical step of proroguing parliament to prevent a non-confidence vote by his democratic opponents, or turning away from the horrific abuses that are going on in various prisons set up around the world to fight terror, or forbidding newscasts of fallen soldiers who have died in the very war which was started to combat fantastical weapons of mass destruction. There will also always come a point when the desire to respectfully shame such leaders will be what gets democratic citizens onto the streets or the blogs to fight against these abuses of power because there is no current election they can vote in, or no new proposition that can overturn the one that has just denied them basic civil rights, or no media or news source that actually wants to play their antiwar message. Recognizing the tyrannical impulses in ourselves and our democratic leaders, a recognition that I will show in chapter 3 was actually elicited by Socrates' acts of respectful shaming, will always be a necessary part of self-limiting and responsible democratic citizenship, especially in the always-present absence of completely sufficient external regulations and laws.

Here Plato's characterization of the tyrant is helpful for diagnosing these tyrannical tendencies in our own psyches and polities. The figure of the "tyrant" is for Plato a personality type and a regime type developed by him in order to explain certain kinds of pathological psychosocial or psychopolitical

---

[74] As Euben, Wallach, and Ober (1994, 10) point out, "Debates over reform of the British Parliament and the French Revolution found conservatives criticizing the politics of their own day in terms of the excesses of democratic Athens and . . . *The Federalist Papers* did likewise to justify their redefinition of republicanism and the need for a distant federal government."

[75] In other words, respectful shame is not a replacement for better laws and bills of rights and I do not want to deny that these will always be necessary to curb the tyrannical impulses of certain people who prove incapable of engaging in "shameful self-assessment" (Locke, 2007), 156.

phenomena that he observed in the polities of his time, and especially within his own imperialistic, democratic Athens. As Nathan Tarcov argues, the ancients characterized the tyrannical regime in a number of different but interrelated ways: it involved any type of rule without legality, limitation, legitimacy, or consent.[76] However, Plato focused primarily on the tyrant as a soul-type that lingered to some degree in all of us.[77] One of the perplexing ideas that this book on Platonic notions of shame will illustrate is that there are no *completely* shameless people in this world. Rather the tyrant is the person who *desires* to be shameless, renames his shame simplicity, and tries to banish it from his soul, just as he tries to banish, stigmatize, or (in extreme cases) exterminate any person or other who threatens to make him feel shame.[78] Such a person develops a sense of flattering shame which links him to the fantastical other of the omnipotent individual who is completely free of all restraints on his immoderate desires.[79] As Plato illustrates in both the *Gorgias* and Book 8 of the *Republic*, this desire to be omnipotent and free of all restraint grows out of that which democracy itself defines as a good: freedom. In the case of the tyrannical democrat, dramatized in the *Gorgias* by the character of Callicles, this leads the person to the indiscriminate pursuit of any and all types of pleasure and the desire to be free of all restraints including those imposed by the laws and customs (*nomoi*) of his own democratic polity and by the shaming criticisms of his fellow citizens.[80] For Plato, the failure to moderate these desires leads in the end to its opposite: unfreedom or tyranny, because the people (who share these tyrannical desires for omnipotence) succumb to the flattery of demagogues who tell them that they can have these limitless desires satisfied, and who ostracize or kill any people who try to criticize them for these immoderate and lawless desires.[81] The democratic citizen whose flattering sense of shame attunes him to the desires and pleasures of a wholly omnipotent other inevitably tries to avoid the painful but potentially beneficial recognitions so central to the occurrent experience of shame by stigmatizing and even killing

[76] Tarcov (2005), 132. Cf. Tormey (2005) and Kalyvas (2007).

[77] Beiner (2005); Blitz (2005); and Tarcov (2005).

[78] As Plato points out at *Rep*. 8.567b, the tyrant gradually does away with any friend or enemy who speaks frankly (*parrhēsia*) to him and rebukes him for his actions. At *Rep*. 9.571c, Plato argues "that in such a state [the tyrannical individual] dares to do everything as though it were released from, and rid of, all shame and prudence."

[79] Quoting Euripides' *Trojan Women*, Plato criticizes the poets in book 8 of the *Republic* for extolling "tyranny as a condition 'equal to that of a god' "(*Rep*. 8.568b). It is this tyrannical desire to be a completely self-sufficient and omnipotent person or polity that Plato criticizes in both the *Gorgias* and the *Republic*.

[80] At *Gorg*. 484a, Callicles tells Socrates that the tyrannical individual tramples underfoot "our writings, spells, charms, and the laws that are all against nature." Callicles is also the interlocutor who ends up being least capable of submitting to Socrates' shaming elenchus and continually begs to be let out of the discussion (497b, 505c–d).

[81] Tarcov (2005), 127–28.

the person who tries to shame him out of his problematic conflation of freedom with shamelessness.

It is this kind of tyrannical action that Plato accuses the Athenian democracy
of committing against Socrates in response to his respectful shaming practices.
But more importantly, it is this kind of tyrannical action that Plato wants
readers of his dialogues to check within themselves so that they do not attempt
to eliminate the other in a tyrannical and anti-democratic attempt to become
fully autonomous.[82] The elimination of this other in our psyche is intricately
related to the anti-democratic elimination of any and all forms of opposition,
which any moderate democracy must preserve as a check on the tyrannical
impulses of the majority, especially when this majority does equate democratic
freedom with a complete lack of restraint or regulation of its desires for money,
glory, and power. Moreover, for Plato this kind of tyrannical impulse to trample on the laws and customs (*nomoi*) of one's polity arises precisely when a
democratic polity is faced with new challenges and circumstances that always
seem to exceed the standing rules and laws set in place for dealing with the
world it shares with others. However, as Plato also shows in the *Gorgias*, the
philosophic individual who does feel a certain shame (*aischunē*) before the
very activity of philosophizing is precisely the individual who rebukes his polity and plays the role of the other by respectfully shaming his polity and refusing to let the tyrannical self or polity escape from the salutary restraint of
shaming criticism.

[82] See Allen (2000b, 91–93) for an excellent account of why the move on the part of Creon and
Antigone in Sophocles' *Antigone* to become fully autonomous or self-legislating is characteristic
of the tyrant and his desire to be the source of laws from which he himself is exempt, and why it
is contrary to the kind of self-limiting authority that was central to the classical Athenian notion
of democratic laws (*nomoi*) and the democratic constitution (*politeia*).

PART ONE

Plato's *Gorgias* and the Athenian Politics of Shame

Chapter One

SHAME AND RHETORIC IN PLATO'S *GORGIAS*

PLATO's *GORGIAS* has long been recognized as the most political of all of his dialogues prior to the *Republic* because it contains an explicit discussion of a number of Athenian democratic practices and leaders, and because each of the characters in the dialogue highlights the importance of rhetoric, either by professing to teach it or by wishing to learn it so as to advance his career.[1] In the dialogue Socrates speaks with one of the most renowned practitioners and teachers of rhetoric in the late fifth century BC, Gorgias of Sicily, then with Gorgias' Sicilian student Polus, and finally with the potential Athenian statesman Callicles.[2] Socrates' faithful companion and supporter of the Athenian democracy, Chaerophon, completes the cast of five characters.[3] He briefly enters the dialogue to begin questioning Gorgias about rhetoric (*Gorg.* 447d–448c), but his characteristic ineptitude prompts Socrates to take over as the principal interlocutor for the rest of the dialogue. It is also important to note that the dialogue takes place in front of the audience who had initially come to hear Gorgias' display (*epideixis*) speech.[4] This audience intervenes in the dialogue with a roar of approval (*thorubos*) in order to get Gorgias to continue speaking with Socrates about rhetoric (458c), thus mimicking the kind of uproars that would have been heard in the mass deliberations characteristic of Athenian assembly debates and trials.[5] In a certain sense, then, the dialogue

[1] Dodds (1959), 31–34; Klosko (1983), 579; Wallach (2001), 145 (although Wallach also includes the *Protagoras* in this category). Many scholars have noted the similarities between the dramatic structure and interlocutors of the *Gorgias* and *Republic* 1, as well as the themes of the two dialogues. See for example Dodds (1959); Irwin (1979); Klosko (1983), 579; Klosko (1984), 130; Friedlander (1964), 244–45; Kahn (1996); Wallach (2001); and Stauffer (2006).

[2] For accounts of Gorgias' life and works see Dodds (1959), 6–10; Wardy (1996), chapters 1 and 2; and Wallach (2001), 181–84. For Polus, see Dodds (1959), 11–12; and Wallach (2001), 184–85. For Callicles, see Dodds (1959), 12–15; Wallach (2001), 185; and n.13 below.

[3] Chaerophon is the person who asked the Delphic Oracle whether any man was wiser than Socrates (*Apol.* 21a). Cf. Wallach (2001), 185.

[4] Dodds (1959, 188) notes that the presence of this audience is attested to at *Gorg.* 455c6, 458c, 473e5, 487b4, and 490b2. Lewis (1996, 196) argues that Socrates' efforts at persuasion are directed only toward these men and not toward Gorgias, Polus, and Callicles. This is too strong; while I believe that Socrates is trying to persuade members of this audience, this does not preclude the fact that he is also trying to persuade his immediate interlocutors (and that Plato is trying to persuade his contemporary and future readers of the dialogue).

[5] As Nichols (1998, 40 n.33) notes with respect to this passage, *thorubos* "can be the noise of approval, as here, or of disapproval, like the noise made against certain things that Socrates said at his trial (*Apol.* 17d, 20e, 21a, 27b, and 30c)." Ober (1996, 115) notes that "Athenian public

actually enacts the experience of being under the eyes of one's fellow citizens, which is so important to the phenomenon of shame, both for the Greeks and for ourselves.[6] Finally, at other times in the dialogue Socrates introduces the views of the imaginary audience of democratic Athens (452a–d, 461b–c, 474c, 482d–e, 494e) to get each of his interlocutors to consider how their remarks would be viewed by this imaginary yet still forceful and collective other.

The topics touched upon in the dialogue range from the character and function of rhetoric in democratic assemblies and law courts (Gorgias section); to the differences between democratic and tyrannical rule (Polus and Callicles sections); to lengthy discussions of the democratic virtues of justice (*dikaiosunē*) (Polus section) and moderation (*sōphrosunē*) (Callicles section). More specifically, the dialogue moves from Gorgias' initial profession of the power and moral neutrality of his rhetoric to Socrates' criticism of one type of rhetoric as a form of flattery (*kolakeia*). Polus and Callicles then successively enter the discussion both explicitly espousing the life of the tyrant (*turannos*) as the best life to live. In each shaming refutation (*elenchos*) Socrates attempts to wean them from this problematic love of tyranny by showing them that their own views about the best life for human beings actually fail to conform to their image of the tyrant, and instead fit better with a number of Athenian democratic ideals and practices. During the course of the discussion, Socrates makes a number of specific remarks about, and criticisms of, the Athenian democratic practices of delivering speeches before a mass audience (455a), calling witnesses to one's character (471e–472a), voting and electing officials by lot (473e), payment for service on juries and the council (515e), and ostracism (516d). Finally, he gives a lengthy critique of the careers of the famed Athenian political figures Pericles, Themistocles, Cimon, and Miltiades (515d–519b), many of whom were responsible for expanding the Athenian democracy and building the Athenian empire that eventually led to Athens' war with Sparta (the Peloponnesian War).[7]

The importance of all of these political themes is further supported by the dramatic date of the dialogue. Although this date is difficult to fix conclusively,

---

speeches were addressed to enthusiastic amateurs, not to judges or professional lawyers." I think the fact that the dialogue is held in front of an audience or crowd emphasizes its public and political character.

[6] Cf. Aristotle, *Rhet.* 1383b3, and 1384a17–18. Cf. Konstan (2006), 103; Sokolon (2006), 112. Konstan (2006, 103) adds the important proviso that, for Aristotle, exposure before others is not fundamental or necessary to feel shame but rather is "an aggravating factor." The same is also true for Plato, and indeed the *Gorgias* as a whole illustrates how both actual and imaginary others can figure in producing shame.

[7] Nichols, (1998), 100 n.125. As Stauffer (2006, 152) points out, Socrates specifically trains his sights on Pericles, who was the greatest leader of imperial Athens. For accounts of the rise and fall of the Athenian Empire see Meiggs (1972); de Ste. Croix (1972); Fornara and Samons (1991); Raaflaub (1994); and Samons (1998, 2004).

certain indications or allusions in the dialogue suggest a range of dates between 429 and 404 BC.[8] The recent death of Pericles (in 429 BC) is mentioned at 503c; Gorgias' first attested visit to Athens was 427 BC; Socrates makes a prediction about Alcibiades at 519a–b which would be most appropriate for 415 BC; Archelaus (a Macedonian tyrant who came to power in 413 BC) is said to have come to power "just yesterday or the day before" at 470d; Euripides' play *Antiope* (which was probably produced around 408 BC and which contained a well-known comparison between the active and the contemplative life), is mentioned at 485e and 506b; and, finally, Socrates' behavior at the trial of the generals at Arginusae (in 405 BC) is mentioned as happening "last year" at 473e.

During the time period in which Plato sets the dialogue Athens experienced a dangerous vacuum in political leadership. Pericles had recently died from the plague that had devastated Athens in 429 BC and Athens was still engaged in a lengthy and costly war with Sparta. Wealthy elites like Cleon and Alcibiades, exposed to the education offered by both Gorgias and Socrates, competed to become leaders of Athens by utilizing different rhetorical strategies in various assembly debates that followed Pericles' death.[9] Cleon based his career on maintaining the support of the masses, and was mocked in Aristophanes' *Knights* for being a lover of Demos.[10] In contrast to this, Alcibiades openly flaunted his wealth and ancestry and was successful at both winning over the votes of many Athenians and also of plotting and successfully launching an oligarchic coup in 411 BC.[11] In the *Gorgias*, Plato masterfully weaves together both of these aristocratic tendencies in his fictional character Callicles.[12] Callicles contains within himself the contradictory elitist impulses of both Cleon and Alcibiades, at one point telling Socrates that one must trample on the laws of the many (484a), and yet at other points telling Socrates that one must learn the ways and customs of the many and even flatter them to preserve oneself in a democracy like Athens (484d, 521a).[13]

All of these historical allusions point to the central themes of the dialogue: what kinds of rhetoric (*rhētorikē*), teachers of rhetoric, and political *rhētores*

---

[8] For a full discussion of the dramatic date, see Dodds (1959), 17–18 and Irwin (1979), 109–10.

[9] See Ober (1989), 92–93; Wallach (2001), 180–81; and Gish (2006), 55.

[10] Ober (1989), 93. Cf. Zumbrunnen (2004). Socrates will characterize Callicles in just this way at 481d.

[11] Ober (1989), 93–94.

[12] Dodds (1959, 12), Nichols (1998, 25), and Wallach (2001, 185) all note that Callicles is one of the few characters in the Platonic corpus about whom no records survive. This has been taken by some scholars to attest to his fictional character, although Dodds (1959, 13) argues that, as a young man just embarking on a political career (515a), he may have died too early to be remembered by anyone but Plato. His name means beautiful fame or fame for beauty.

[13] *Contra* Dodds (1959, 13–14) and Kastely (1991, 101–2), who characterize him as showing only aristocratic disdain for the people. Stauffer (2006, 147) and de Romilly (1992, 160) correctly note his ambivalent contempt and love of the people (*dēmos*).

(speakers) does a democracy in Athens' situation require?[14] What life is the best for human beings: action or contemplation; and what kind of political life is best for the great individual: tyranny or democratic rule? What kind of democracy should Athens aspire to: the imperial one that led to the Peloponnesian War or the more moderate one of the recent past?[15]

Moreover, these issues facing Plato and his fellow Athenians should not be seen as obscure or obsolete problems obsessing a bunch of weird men in togas. The rhetoricians in democratic Athens played many of the same roles now played by our "spin doctors," campaign managers, institutions of higher education, informed and educated citizens, and even political leaders. So if it is true that today "politicians are taunted by their opponents and exhorted by political commentators to cut out the rhetoric and tell us what they would really do to deal with our problems," the same was no less true of democratic Athens.[16] The orator who displayed too much skill or specialized knowledge left himself open to the charge of elitism or of trying to deceive his audience.[17] In order to avoid this charge a number of orators developed the "my opponent is a skilled speaker but I am just like you" strategy and put it to use 2400 years before both George W. Bush and John McCain used it in their debates against Senator Kerry and Senator Obama in the 2004 and 2008 presidential debates.[18] Finally, if the Athenians felt a dangerous vacuum in their leadership, a need to rethink their imperialistic and economic policies and the ways in which citizens and leaders collectively decided upon the fate of their city, it is safe to say that most modern democratic polities are now finding themselves in a very similar situation.

In response to such problems, Plato's *Gorgias* examines the different types of rhetoric and the different ways in which many emotions, but especially the

---

[14] The term *rhētōr* literally means "speaker" but it had both a broad and a more specific sense. Broadly, it referred to any citizen who put forward proposals for laws and decrees in the assembly or for public actions in the courts. More specifically, it could designate citizens (generally the wealthy) who regularly did this and who thus took on something of a leadership role. See Ober (1989), 109–10; Yunis, (1996), 9–10; and Nichols (1998), 28 n.12.

[15] For a discussion of the critique of imperialism launched in the *Gorgias,* see Dodds (1959), 32–34 and Saxonhouse (1983), 165–67.

[16] Nichols (1998), 2. See Nichols (1998), 1–24 for an excellent essay explaining why a fresh look at Plato's *Gorgias* can help us think about rhetoric in our own times. The most persistent comment made by the (still) undecided voters after the Presidential debates between Barack Obama and John McCain was that both candidates were "merely spouting rhetoric" and not really telling them what they would do to solve the economic crisis facing the nation.

[17] Ober (1989), 173. Ober (1989) outlines the complex ways in which the elite speakers and the mass audience of Athenians interactively constructed a number of rhetorical techniques and tropes that could overcome the tensions generated by the economic or educational inequalities that existed between them.

[18] For the trope "my opponent is a skilled speaker," see Ober (1989), 174–77. Socrates actually uses this strategy at the beginning of the *Apology.*

emotion of shame (*aischunē*), can facilitate or endanger the kinds of collective deliberations necessary to cope with these sorts of problems. There are, however, two prominent interpretations of the political character of the *Gorgias* that pose a significant threat to my own project of utilizing it to understand the pernicious and salutary roles of shame in contemporary democratic theory and practice. First, because it contains Plato's most direct criticisms of democratic Athens (472a–c, 515e–519d), the *Gorgias* has been interpreted as Plato's own "Apology" in which he sets out his reasons for forgoing a career in Athenian democratic politics in favor of opening his Academy.[19] Second, it is often considered to be *the* dialogue that inaugurates the problematic binaries between rhetoric and philosophy, emotion and reason, and persuasion and argumentation, which have plagued Western philosophy and political theory ever since the fateful encounter between Socrates and the two rhetoricians Gorgias and Polus that opens the dialogue.[20] In fact, the history of rhetoric has even been characterized as a response to Plato's attack upon it in the *Gorgias*.[21] In chapter 3, I will show precisely why Plato's criticisms of democratic Athens do not make his teaching in the *Gorgias* inherently anti-democratic or irrelevant for contemporary democratic theory and practice; however, in this chapter I want to deal with the second interpretation: Plato's alleged attack on all forms of emotion, rhetoric, and persuasion.

Such an interpretation obviously poses a significant threat to my own project of utilizing Plato's teaching about the nature of shame (*aischunē*) to help us think about the *salutary and pernicious* roles it can play in contemporary democratic politics. Even more importantly, I think elements of this position continue to linger in certain contemporary theories about the emotions generally, and shame in particular. (I address this problem extensively in chapter 6.) Instead of targeting all emotions as irrational, it has been very tempting to target shame and other emotions, like disgust, jealousy, or humiliation, as either inherently irrational, unreasonable, or anti-democratic.[22] According to such an interpretation, shame is pernicious for politics because it is an emotion that the rhetorician cleverly uses to stigmatize, silence, or exclude certain parties from the debate, or to get other parties to make insincere assertions that mask their real thoughts or preferences. By producing either silence or insincerity, the rhetorician's use of shame actually forecloses any kind of real deliberation.

---

[19] For theorists who treat the *Gorgias* as Plato's "Apology" and wholesale rejection of Athenian democratic politics, see chapter 3, n.1 below.

[20] Theorists who treat the *Gorgias* as displaying Plato's hostility toward rhetoric include Kennedy (1964), 14–15; Friedlander (1969), 247–55; Kerferd (1981), 4; Klosko (1984), 137; Vickers (1988), 88–90; de Romilly (1992), 71; Garver, (1994), 30; Yunis (1996), 117–71; Gross (2006), 138; and Olmsted (2006).

[21] Lee (1962), 3–7.

[22] For an interesting treatment of the ways in which even humiliation discloses aspects of our intersubjectivity and can be a possible site of resistance, see Guenther (2008).

While it is certainly true that this is part of what Plato wants to show us about a certain form of shame and a certain kind of rhetoric in the *Gorgias*, this is by no means the whole teaching on shame or rhetoric in this dialogue. In this chapter, I will show that these misinterpretations, or, more accurately, partial interpretations of shame and rhetoric arise out of an inadequate understanding of the full drama of the dialogue and a misunderstanding of the centrality of shame to *all* of the different forms of rhetoric that are examined or exemplified in the dialogue, including the rhetoric of both Socrates and Plato.[23] In fact, only when the dramatic context is understood in all of its complexity can the centrality of shame (*aischunē*) to the other two themes of the dialogue—the character of rhetoric (*rhētorikē*) and the best way of life for human beings (*eudaimonia*)—be fully appreciated.[24] Far from banishing all rhetoric from the best type of polis or confining philosophers to the Academy, Plato is concerned to distinguish his noble (*kalon*) and true (*alēthes*) brand of rhetoric from the rhetoric involved in flattery (*kolakeia*) and from the painful (*lupēron/aniaron*) but beneficial (*ōphelimon*) rhetoric practiced by Socrates.[25] This also means that what is tested/put to shame/refuted/examined (*elenchein*) by Plato (as the writer of this dialogue) is not just each interlocutor that Socrates meets, but also Socrates himself and his elenchic practices.[26]

---

[23] Theorists who are attentive to the dramatic structure of the *Gorgias* and who think this structure is important for understanding Plato's full teaching in the *Gorgias* include Klosko (1983), 585; Saxonhouse (1983); Lewis (1986); Benardete (1991); Nichols (1998); Kastely (1991); Wardy (1996); Weiss (2003); and Stauffer (2006). Numerous commentators of the *Gorgias* have noticed the central role played by shame (*aischunē*) in all three of the refutations (*elenchea*): Dodds (1959), 30, 221, 263; Kahn (1983); Lewis (1986), 108; McKim (1988); and Gish (2006), 62–69. As Dodds (1959, 30) astutely points out, it is precisely because the dialogue deals with the best way of life for human beings and not just a formal doctrine that shame (*aischunē*) is so important. I address McKim and Kahn's extensive treatments of shame in chapter 2. Finally, Kaufer (1979); Lewis (1986); Benardete (1991); Nichols (1998); Kastely (1991); Weiss (2003); and Stauffer (2006) all recognize that Socrates is using a type of rhetoric in the *Gorgias* and that Plato himself may be arguing for some kind of alliance between Socratic rhetoric and Gorgianic rhetoric. I address the similarities and differences between my position and theirs later in this chapter.

[24] Dodds (1959, 1–2) notes that in the medieval manuscripts and in the catalogue quoted by Diogenes Laertius, the *Gorgias* bears the subtitle, *ē peri rhētorikēs* ("or on rhetoric"). He also notes, though, that rhetoric's relationship to the best way of life for human beings is implicit throughout the Gorgias section and explicit throughout the Polus and Callicles sections.

[25] The rhetoric of flattery is first described at 462b–466a and then later at 480b, 500e–501d, 517a–d, 521a–b, 521e–522a. The painful but beneficial rhetoric is first described at 480c–481b, and then later at 502b. The noble rhetoric is described at 503a–b. The true rhetoric is described at 517a.

[26] The first important treatment of the problematic character of the Socratic elenchus dramatized in the *Gorgias* is Gregory Vlastos, "The Socratic Elenchus," in *Oxford Studies in Ancient Philosophy* I (1983): 27–58. [Henceforth referred to as Vlastos (1983a)]. This article is reprinted (with very minor revisions) as "The Socratic Elenchus: Method is All" in *Socratic Studies*, ed. Myles Burnyeat (Cambridge: Cambridge University Press, 1994), 1–33. [Henceforth referred to as Vlastos (1994a)]. Throughout this book I have cited the original text because the other commenta-

This interpretation, however, depends upon my own controversial beliefs about the *Gorgias*, which I mentioned in the Introduction, but which I now want to defend fully. The first (and least controversial) claim is that the *Gorgias* is a transitional dialogue between the early "Socratic" dialogues that depict the historical Socrates, and the dialogues of Plato's middle period where "Socrates" is now also a mouthpiece for certain Platonic doctrines. The second is that these transitional and middle dialogues contain Plato's own deepening understanding of the *psychological* motivations of both Socrates and his various foreign and Athenian interlocutors. These two claims actually lay the groundwork for my most controversial claim: that Plato's reflections in the *Gorgias* do not lead him to reject Athenian democracy and rhetorical practices in favor of an undemocratic, expert form of knowledge, but rather to perform an immanent critique of both the Socratic elenchus and the flattering rhetoric that he feared was involved in imperialistic Athenian democratic politics.[27]

Situating Plato's *Gorgias* within the Platonic Corpus

Turning then to the first claim. There is broad general agreement among Platonic scholars that Plato's dialogues can be divided into three periods: early, middle, and late, based on stylometric tests that include such things as the formulae of response and the use of particles.[28] More controversially, however, certain commentators have argued that there are significant doctrinal distinctions between the dialogues that correspond very closely to this stylometric evidence.[29] More importantly for my own argument, specific doctrinal and stylistic criteria (which I will outline below) suggest a further distinction within the early group between those that are wholly "Socratic" and those that are transitional between these early dialogues and Plato's middle period, resulting in the following classification:

---

tors whom I discuss all refer to Vlastos' original, and because the revisions do not affect Vlastos' argument regarding the problem of the Socratic elenchus. I include the page references for both articles in the footnotes and I have included the text of the revised edition in square brackets where it includes any substantial differences from the original. Other theorists who note Plato's problematizing of the elenchus in the *Gorgias* include Irwin (1977), 130–31; Irwin (1979), 4–5; Kahn (1983), 75; McKim (1988), 35–36; Klosko (1983), 585; and Weiss (2003), 204.

[27] Although Plato does have Socrates say for the first time in the *Gorgias* that only he and a few other Athenians practice the true political art (*alēthēs politikē technē*), this does not amount to an expert form of knowledge because Plato expands the notion of *technē* to include knowledge of one's own ignorance, which is only discovered in the dialectical relationship with an other in both the *Gorgias* and the *Republic*.

[28] For a general overview of the most important stylometric analyses, see Brandwood (1992). See also Dodds (1959), 18–19, and Vlastos (1991), 46 n.2.

[29] See Dodds (1959), 20–24; Rowe (1976), 40; Irwin (1977), 291–293, n. 33; Irwin (1979), 4–8; Vlastos (1991), 45–80; and Penner (1992), 121–169.

Group 1a: Socratic/Elenchic Dialogues: *Apology, Charmides, Crito, Euthyphro, Hippias Minor, Ion, Laches, Protagoras, Republic* I.

Group 1b: Transitional Dialogues: *Gorgias, Euthydemus, Hippias Major, Lysis, Menexenus, Meno.*

Group 2: Plato's Middle Dialogues: *Cratylus, Phaedo, Symposium, Republic* II–X, *Phaedrus, Parmenides, Theaetetus.*

Group 3: Plato's Late Dialogues: *Timaeus, Critias, Sophist, Politicus, Philebus, Laws.*[30]

Stylistically there are a number of things about the *Gorgias* that suggest it is a transitional dialogue between Plato's early and middle dialogues. First, it shares important characteristics of both the early and the middle dialogues. Thus, like the early dialogues it is a direct dialogue rather than an indirect narration (as is the case with the *Republic* and *Symposium*), but like the middle dialogues Socrates espouses a significant amount of positive doctrine, both in his own voice and by relating the stories of others.[31] In part because of this more dogmatic Socrates, the *Gorgias* is one of the lengthiest of Plato's dialogues, shorter only than the *Republic*, the *Timaeus*, and the *Laws*.[32] Second, the significant amount of elenchic exchange between Socrates and his interlocutors suggests a connection to the earlier dialogues where Socrates is shown to engage in the incessant questioning that made him so famous and notorious in Athens. However, the fact that the dialogue ends with a myth points to stylistic similarities with Plato's middle dialogues like the *Republic, Phaedo,* and *Phaedrus.*[33]

Doctrinally, the fact that the *Gorgias* myth contains views or speculations about a future life links it closely to the myths of judgment in the *Republic* and *Phaedo.*[34] The significant references to Pythagorean doctrine (including

---

[30] My classification follows Vlastos' own (1991, 46–47), except for my placement of the *Gorgias.* Here I follow Dodds (1959); Irwin (1979); Klosko (1983); Brandwood (1992); and Penner (1992) in thinking that the myth and Pythagorean doctrines in the *Gorgias* all confirm that it is transitional to Plato's middle period. Although Vlastos (1991, 46–47, nn.4 and 8) excludes it from his list of transitional dialogues: *Euthydemus, Hippias Major, Lysis, Menexenus, Meno;* he does admit that it is probably the last of the early dialogues.

[31] Dodds (1959, 6) notes the difference in style between the direct dramatic form of Plato's early dialogues and the indirect dramatic form of his middle dialogues. Dodds (1959, 16–17), Rowe (1976, 40), Irwin (1979, 6) and Klosko (1983, 580) note the fact that the *Gorgias* contains significantly more positive doctrine than Plato's early dialogues. Irwin (1979, 6) stresses the fact that the transition from dialogue to pure exposition is much more marked in the *Gorgias* than it is in those earlier dialogues, like the *Crito, Apology,* and *Protagoras* that do contain positive doctrine.

[32] Dodds (1959), 20.

[33] Dodds (1959, 17); Penner (1992, 124–25); and Irwin (1979, 7) all note the significance of the myth at the end of the *Gorgias* for placing it close to or within Plato's middle period.

[34] See Dodds (1959), 20; Annas (1982a), 122; Klosko (1983), 580; and Vlastos (1991), 55–56. I treat the *Gorgias* myth extensively in chapter 4.

the doctrine of rebirth mentioned at 493b–c) suggest a close link with both the *Phaedo* and *Meno*, and distinguish the *Gorgias* from the early dialogues.[35] Finally, the doctrine of virtue as a kind of grace or order (*kosmos*) of the soul (*psuchē*) (506e–507a, 508a) suggests the influence of the rhetorician Gorgias and the Pythagorean Archytas. Since Plato would probably have met Archytas on his first visit to Sicily around 389–387 BC, this places *Gorgias* closer to the time period when he wrote his middle dialogues.[36]

Furthermore, these doctrinal elements are not found in the early dialogues and Plato often has Socrates introduce his teaching about these new doctrines in a way that denies his own authority for these teachings. Thus he has Socrates introduce his teaching on desire/love (*erōs*) in the *Symposium* as something he learned from a Mantinean woman, Diotima (*Symp.* 201d); on spiritedness (*thumos*) in the *Republic* as a story he has heard that he trusts (*Rep.* 439e); on the transmigration of the soul in the *Meno* as something he has heard from priests and priestesses (*Meno* 81a); on the myth of the jars in the *Gorgias* as something told to him by one of the wise and explained to him by a myth-telling Sicilian or Italian (*Gorg.* 493a); and on virtue as a kind of grace or order (*kosmos*) of the soul in the *Gorgias* as a story told by the wise (*hoi sophoi*) (507e).[37] This disavowal of authority suggests that Plato is explicitly signaling to the reader that these are new doctrines that were not held by the historical Socrates.[38]

More importantly, the notion of virtue as a kind of *kosmos* requires at least some kind of division in the soul that challenges the "virtue is knowledge" doctrine Socrates holds in all of the early dialogues.[39] This, of course, would be necessary if the desires, appetites, and emotions are now recognized as having their own place or unique role in the soul.[40] Indeed, most of Plato's

---

[35] Dodds (1959), 20. See also Klosko (1983), 581 n.8; and Penner (1992), 124–25.

[36] For the importance of the theme of *kosmos* in Gorgias' *Encomium of Helen* see Wardy (1996), 29–30 and Gish (2006), 53–54. For the importance of the theme of *kosmos* in Pythagorean doctrine see Dodds (1959), 337–38. For this and other evidence that supports placing the dialogue after Plato's Sicilian visit, see Dodds (1959), 26 and Penner (1992), 124.

[37] Dodds (1959, 338) argues that "the wise" in the *Gorgias* passage are probably meant to refer to the Pythagoreans. Cooper (1999, 63) argues that Plato uses this device in the myths of the jars at 493a–494a to show that the teaching on the soul that the myths imply are Pythagorean and Platonic, but not Socratic.

[38] Dodds (1959, 297) points out that Plato uses the same kind of formulation at *Republic* 583b (referring to the illusory character of physical pleasures) in order to indicate clearly that these views are not Socratic.

[39] Irwin (1979), 7; Klosko (1983), 581. See Klosko (1983), and Cooper (1999), chapter 2 for more detailed accounts of the ways in which the Polus and Callicles sections anticipate the tripartite soul doctrine of the *Republic*.

[40] Irwin (1979), 221; Cooper (1999), 65; and Kaufer (1978), 68. Plato sometimes treats these as separate parts of the soul and sometimes as simply separate capacities. One of the virtues of the *Gorgias* is that it doesn't treat shame (*aischunē*) as a separate part of the soul from reason

middle dialogues contain profound meditations on these elements or capacities of the soul, i.e., desire/love (*erōs*), appetite (*epithumia*), spiritedness (*thumos*), and shame (*aidōs/aischunē*), and the ways in which they can either promote or undermine the virtues required by citizens. More specifically, the *Phaedrus* and *Symposium* focus on *erōs*, the *Republic* focuses on *epithumia* and *thumos*, and the *Gorgias* on *aischunē*.

The *Gorgias* is, in fact, unique in the Platonic corpus because each of the three refutations Socrates engages in involves shame at a crucial step in the argument.[41] Plato actually has two of Socrates' three interlocutors pointedly complain that shame (*aischunē*) has been used as the crucial element in Socrates' refutation of the other interlocutors: Polus asserts that Gorgias "was ashamed (*ēischunthē*) not to agree further with [Socrates] that the rhetorical man also knows the just, noble and good things" and that he would teach his students this if they did not know it already (461b). Callicles then reiterates this charge with regard to Gorgias (482d), and adds that Socrates caught Polus himself being "ashamed (*aischuntheis*) to say what he thought" and so agreeing insincerely that doing injustice is more shameful than suffering injustice (482d–e). Finally, Socrates himself twice states that shame (*aischunē*) has been involved in his refutations of Gorgias and Polus (487b, 508b), and his lengthy encounter with Callicles involves repeated attempts to make Callicles feel ashamed of the consequences of his indiscriminate hedonism thesis (494c–499b). What is even more significant is that Socrates himself admits that he would be ashamed if he were unable to protect himself or his friends from committing an injustice against other human beings or gods (522d).

The Dual Character of the Socratic Elenchus

In fact, the connection between shame (*aischunē*) and refutation (noun = *elenchos*; verb = *elenchein*) is much easier to make in the Greek because the verb, *elenchein*, means to disgrace, put to shame, cross-examine, question, prove, refute, confute, and get the better of.[42] The Greek word blurs the distinction between the logical and psychological, the cognitive and affective dimensions of the experience.[43] Accordingly, as Gregory Vlastos puts it, the Socratic elenchus in the *Gorgias* has a dual objective:

(*logos*). This is important for my view that some form of shame (*aischunē*) is integral to knowledge of one's own ignorance in the *Gorgias*.

[41] See chapter 2 for a detailed analysis of the role of shame (*aischunē*) in each refutation.

[42] Liddell and Scott (1996), 531.

[43] Krause (2008, 2) points out that contemporary models of democratic deliberation (including Rawls' and Habermas') often suffer from a neo-Kantian reluctance "to tie the content and authority of moral and political norms to the psychological states of individuals." One of the advantages

to discover how every human being ought to live [the philosophic objective] and to test that single human being that is doing the answering—to find out if he is living as one ought to live [the therapeutic objective]. This is a two-in-one operation. Socrates does not provide for two types of elenchus—a philosophical one, searching for the truth about the good life, and a therapeutic one, searching out the answerer's own life in the hope of bringing him to the truth.[44]

Thus, throughout the *Gorgias* the compulsion the interlocutors feel when subjected to the Socratic elenchus is not just logical but also psychological.[45] They don't reject certain premises because these premises seem integral to the way of life that they follow or find attractive. As Charles Kahn puts it, "In an argument with a real interlocutor one cannot, but also need not, close all logically possible escape routes: if our opponent is not willing or able to take a given way out, 'the reply that somebody else might take it does not help his case against us. In this respect, all moral arguments are *ad hominem*.' "[46]

In fact, in the *Gorgias* Socrates does not *logically* refute Callicles' indiscriminate hedonism thesis that pursuing any and all pleasures is the best way of life for human beings:[47] the life of the catamite (*kinaidos*) (494e) and the life of cowards rejoicing at the retreat of their enemies (498e) are still left open as logically possible ways of life. It's just that even Callicles cannot stick with his thesis if these "shameful" ways of life are its logical conclusion: in Athens, the *kinaidos* was the passive partner in male-to-male sexual relationships whose very passivity suggested that he was taking on the role of a woman, and this in turn led to the suspicion "that he abjured his prescribed role as a future soldier and defender of the community."[48] Indeed, "the conception of a *kinaidos* was of a man socially deviant in his entire being, whose deviance was principally observable in behavior that flagrantly violated or contravened the dominant social definition of masculinity."[49] More importantly, in Athens a

---

of Plato's middle works is that they focus precisely on the intertwining of the logical and psychological aspects of ethical and political deliberation.

[44] Vlastos (1983a), 37; Vlastos, (1994a), 10.

[45] See Kahn (1983), 80; McKim (1988), 37; and Kraut (1983), 59–70. *Contra* Vlastos (1983a, 22) who seems to overlook this dual character at certain points in his article and even questions why Polus himself does not just jettison his premise *q* (that doing injustice is more shameful than suffering it) "with the feeling 'good riddance'."

[46] Kahn (1983), 80. Kahn is here quoting Richard Hare, *Freedom and Reason* (Oxford: Clarendon Press, 1963), 111.

[47] On the relationship between the doctrine of hedonism defended in the *Protagoras* and the one attacked in the *Gorgias*, see Irwin (1977), 122–25; and Klosko (1984), 131–32. For criticisms of Irwin's view, see Cooper (1999), 69–75.

[48] Dover (2002), 28. Cf. Kahn (1983), 106.

[49] Winkler (1990), 177. See chapter 2 for a discussion of the role that this image plays in the refutation of Callicles.

citizen could lose his political rights for this kind of behavior.[50] Both the coward and the *kinaidos* conflict with the masculine ideal of democratic citizenship that Callicles himself most admires and that he has absorbed from his Athenian upbringing. There are then logically possible ways of life that a human being can find simply unlivable and what Plato dramatizes in the *Gorgias* is that shame is one of the most important emotions for revealing these kinds of moral truths.

What Plato also illustrates is that Socrates is actually more adept at manipulating the weapon of shame than his interlocutors, Gorgias, Polus, and Callicles.[51] This is true whether he uses shame to reveal certain universal ethical truths about humanity (i.e., that some pleasures are better than others and some pleasures need to be restrained (499b–e),[52] or to reveal the conventional norms of the Athenian polity, or, even more problematically, when he uses these conventional norms to get his interlocutors to agree to premises they don't fully believe. There are various occasions where Socrates coerces his interlocutors into continuing with the conversation and accepting conclusions they don't fully understand only to "save face," avoid embarrassment, or gratify the other interlocutors (and the crowd gathered to watch this conversation), who are eagerly following Socrates' every move and like to see a good battle (*agōn*). In the *Gorgias*, as in some of the other early dialogues, it is Socrates who knows how to "work" the crowd so that they are cheering on his refutations while some of his interlocutors squirm with discomfort or anger, and, at times with little regard for the seemingly outrageous conclusions he is espousing.[53]

I believe that these problematic responses show that Plato is just as concerned to interrogate the psychological character of the Socratic elenchus as he is its logical character, and to understand the kinds of reactions both positive and negative that Socrates' interlocutors have to the painful shaming refutation that they undergo at the hands of Socrates.[54] Moreover, the same is also true of the other forms of communication that are illustrated in the *Gorgias*,

[50] Sokolon (2006), 113.

[51] Lewis (1986, 196) notes Socrates' prowess in a public forum in the *Gorgias*.

[52] It is important to note that when Plato thinks shame is revealing a universal ethical truth about human beings and not just a conventional norm, he has Socrates or one of the interlocutors (at 499b it is Callicles) assert that this is what all human beings really believe to be the case.

[53] The refutation of Polus illustrates the case where an interlocutor ends up agreeing to theses that he finds strange and does not fully understand: "To me, Socrates, [these conclusions] seem strange (*atopa*) indeed; but perhaps you make them agree with the things said before" (480e). The refutation of Callicles illustrates (repeatedly) how Socrates infuriates some of his opponents to the point where they finally refuse to care anymore about the argument (505c, 510a).

[54] Cf. Klosko (1983), 586, 594. To put it more accurately, whatever we moderns may think about the need to separate logical, normative/ethical, and psychological phenomena, the same was not true for Plato's investigation of shame (*aischunē*) in the *Gorgias*. Cf. Kaufer (1978, 64) for a slightly different treatment of this point. For an excellent treatment of the ontological, psychological, ethical, and intersubjective character of shame, see Guenther (2008).

i.e., Gorgias' display (*epideixis*) rhetoric and the rhetoric of flattery that both Polus and Callicles favor. What Plato does over the course of the dialogue is to diagnose the particular problems with each of these styles of comportment toward a democratic audience, even as he preserves certain elements from some of them in order to construct a new form of rhetoric that will instantiate a more salutary form of intersubjective relationship between democratic speakers and their audiences.

From Gorgianic Rhetoric to Platonic Rhetoric

In order to see this, it is important to follow the movement of the dialogue as it shifts away from the original distinctions made between rhetoric and philosophy in the opening discussion with Gorgias and Socrates, and toward the distinct types of rhetoric that are outlined in the latter parts of the dialogue. The dialogue opens with a contrast between Gorgianic rhetoric and Socratic dialectic that Gorgias and Socrates develop together (447a–461a). (See Table 1 below.) After Polus jumps into the discussion it moves to a characterization of one type of rhetoric as a form of flattery (462b–463e) and then to a fuller discussion of the differences between flattering rhetoric (a subset of the four different kinds of flattery [*kolakeia*])[55] and the political art of justice (a subset of the four different kinds of political art (*politikē technē*) (463e–466a). (See Table 2 below.) Even the description of rhetoric as a form of flattery (*kolakeia*) is not the last one that is supplied by Socrates in the dialogue because at 480b–481b he distinguishes between a rhetoric that is used to speak in defense of the injustice of oneself, one's friends, and one's fatherland, and one that is used to compel oneself and one's friends to submit well and courageously to justice "as if to a doctor for cutting and burning—pursuing what's good and fine, not taking account of what's painful . . ." (480c). (See Table 3 below.) In fact, for the remainder of the dialogue, the distinctions "Socrates" now makes are between different types of rhetoric and not between rhetoric and philosophy or dialectic. Even the distinction between flattering rhetoric and just rhetoric is subsequently displaced (in the Callicles section of the dialogue) by a distinction between flattering rhetoric and noble rhetoric. (See Table 4 below.) Then, finally, toward the end of the dialogue, distinctions are made which suggest that a true form of rhetoric can redress a specific problem shared by both flattering rhetoric and Socrates' true political art, i.e., their mutual inability to preserve the speaker who uses them. (See Table 5 below.)

---

[55] Dodds (1959, 225) notes that the Greek term *kolakeia* is conventionally translated as "flattery" but it applied to a wider range of actions and carried a more emphatic implication of moral baseness. In modern English, "flattery" can sometimes be used to connote only that an utterance aims at what is pleasant to the listener or receiver (and thus is not necessarily a base practice).

I now want to show how these different contrasts actually reveal the criticisms Plato makes of Gorgianic rhetoric, flattering rhetoric, and the Socratic shaming elenchus, and culminate in a true and noble form of rhetoric that preserves the best aspects of Gorgianic rhetoric and Socrates' shaming elenchus. Turning to the first set of distinctions:

TABLE 1
Gorgianic Rhetoric vs. Socratic Dialectic

Gorgianic rhetoric	Socratic dialectic
1. Involves a display (*epideixis*) and lengthy speech (*makrologia*) (*Gorg.* 447a–449c).	1. Involves dialogue or discussion with questions and answers and brief speech (*brachulogia*) (447a–449c).
2. Provides the greatest good and is the cause both of freedom (*eleutheria*) for human beings themselves and at the same time rule (*archē*) over others in each man's own city (452d7–9).	No specific contrast is made on this point.
3. Addresses itself to a multitude (*plēthos*) or mob (*ochlos*) in various public gatherings: the law court (*dikastērion*), the assembly (*ekklēsia*), the Council (*boulē*) (454e–459b).	3. Addresses itself to the individual (to whom Socrates' speech is directed) and bids the many (*hoi polloi*) farewell (474a–b).
4. Has the power/ability (*dunamis*) to get an unwilling patient to take a drug (*pharmakon*) or submit to a doctor for surgery or cautery, when the doctor is unable to do so (456b).	No specific contrast is made on this point.

The first thing that it is important to notice about Gorgianic rhetoric and Socratic dialectic is that there are potentially anti-democratic overtones to both of them. Athenian democracy was characterized by the fact that the speakers (*rhētores*), both in the law court and the assembly, always spoke before a mass audience.[56] Socrates' description of his dialectical/elenchic activity (Table 1, Item 3), while still intersubjective and dependent on the agreement with another individual, is not democratic by this Athenian standard. However, Gorgias' suggestion (Table 1, Item 3) that the mass audience he speaks to is the multitude (*plēthos*) or mob (*ochlos*) is also not necessarily democratic by Athenian standards; or, to be more exact, there is a great deal of ambiguity about

---

However, we do still use "flattery" to connote a pernicious or vicious practice, especially when the utterance is intended to deceive the receiver.

[56] See Ober (1989), 8; Yunis (1996), 5–6; and Nichols (1998), 33 n.22.

whether this formulation is democratic, aristocratic, or tyrannical. As Josiah Ober points out, the common ancient sources describe the Athenian citizen-masses as the mass (*to plēthos*) or the many (*hoi polloi*), whereas the mob (*ho ochlos*) was deliberately insulting.[57] Gorgias' formulation thus suggests an aristocratic or tyrannical disdain for the people, and Plato and Aristotle both thought that the tyrant could arise through demagoguery when a base people (hence a mob or *ochlos*) allowed themselves to be deceived by flattery.[58]

There is also a certain amount of ambiguity in the formulation Gorgias uses to describe his rhetoric in Table 1, Item 2: To say that his rhetoric produces "freedom for human beings themselves" and "rule over others in each man's own city" is actually closer to an aristocratic and even a tyrannical formulation of freedom (*eleutheria*) and political rule (*archē*), by classical Athenian standards.[59] As Aristotle makes clear in the *Politics*, the Athenian conception of democratic rule entailed both ruling and being ruled in turn, but Gorgias' description seems to leave out the all-important passive element of this formula.[60] However, the Greek itself is somewhat more ambiguous and some have translated Gorgias' formulation "*eleutherias autois tois anthrōpois*" to mean that the freedom is bestowed "to mankind at large"[61] or to "a man himself."[62] The ambiguity is, I think, important because it is never fully made clear in the dialogue whether Gorgias himself is being deliberately ambiguous or is confused about the exact character and power of his rhetoric. That the tyrannical formulation is indeed what Polus and Callicles understand Gorgias to be saying comes out in *their* explicit defense of the life of tyranny. It is precisely this licentious and tyrannical notion of freedom as a kind of freedom from ever being ruled or restrained by an other that actually lies at the heart of the flattering rhetoric that Plato subsequently criticizes in both the Polus and Callicles section of the dialogue.[63]

In contrast to the problematic and anti-democratic elements of both Gorgianic rhetoric and Socratic dialectic, the noble rhetoric that is introduced much

---

[57] Ober (1989), 11.

[58] Aristotle, *Politics*, 4.4.1292a21–24; 5.11.1314a2–3; and Plato, *Rep.* 8.566e.

[59] Irwin (1979, 116) notes the aristocratic and even Homeric character of this notion of freedom. Wallach (2001, 189) and Weiss (2003, 203) both note the despotic character of this rule, although Weiss thinks that this is Plato's own true notion of freedom.

[60] The formula *archein kai archesthai* can actually mean to rule and to be ruled (active and passive) or to rule and to begin (active and middle). See Beck (2003), 43–44. The fact that Socrates does emphasize the importance of passivity when he later describes his elenchic activity to Gorgias at 458a shows that his elenchus was, at least in this respect, quite close to the classical Athenian notion of democratic rule. As Allen (2000b, 91) points out, the democratic notion of law (*nomos*) specifically connoted the fact that the laws were acceptable to those who lived under them.

[61] Lamb (1925), 279.

[62] Irwin (1979), 19. For a more detailed account of the ambiguity, see Cooper (1999), 33.

[63] For the argument that tyrannical rule in classical Athens was linked to a notion of being autonomous (self-ruling) or the sole source of the law, see Allen (2000b, 91–93). For the argument

later at 502e is a form of rhetoric that is now said to explicitly aim at the common good and not simply the good of the individual delivering the speech (unlike Gorgianic rhetoric), and it is a form of rhetoric addressed to individuals, friends, associates, mass audiences, and even one's fatherland (unlike Socratic dialectic).[64] Given this fact, such a noble rhetoric is actually more democratic (and closer to the Athenian notion of democratic rhetoric) than either Gorgias' or Socrates' initial descriptions of their own activities.[65]

The other thing it is important to note about the initial contrasts between Gorgianic rhetoric and Socratic dialectic relates to Item 1 of Table 1. The contrast between Gorgias' lengthy speech (*makrologia*) and Socrates' brief speech (*brachulogia*) is actually something that Socrates himself *fails* to stick with in the later parts of the dialogue. Although there are certainly many examples of brief exchanges between Socrates and a specific interlocutor, there are also many instances where Socrates *rather than Gorgias* engages in both display (*epideixis*) and lengthy speech (*makrologia*).[66] Socrates accuses himself of *makrologia* at 465e and describes this as strange or out of place for himself (*atopon*), which suggests that Plato is signaling to the reader that "Socrates" is now becoming more Platonic. In fact, Socrates describes his famous comparison between the art (*technē*) of politics (*politikē*) and flattery as an *epideixis* at 464b. Indeed the lengthiness of his speechifying depends in large part on the recalcitrance of his specific interlocutor. So Callicles, who continually begs to be let out of the discussion, is actually subjected to very lengthy speeches by Socrates. When he refuses to go any further Socrates engages in a strange mono-dialogue and even ends the whole encounter with the first lengthy speech (*muthos*) in the Platonic corpus about the afterlife (523a–527e), which he tells Callicles that he (Socrates) considers to be a rational account (*logos*) (523a). There is a progression from a Socrates whose elenchus is primarily negative or adversarial, aimed at getting his interlocutors to see the inconsistencies in their views about justice, to a "Socrates" who is willing to give a lengthy account of his own views about such things as justice and moderation. There is also a progression from a Socrates who claims to speak only with one man alone (at 474a–b) to a "Socrates" who claims that his just rhetoric is aimed at one's friends, family, and even one's fatherland (480c–e).

I want to suggest that this "Socrates" is now the more Platonic Socrates who does think that *makrologia* (lengthy speech) and *epideixis* (display) can be useful in the conversion of one's fellow interlocutors to a new way of life. As

---

that tyrannical "freedom" actually designated the downfall of freedom for the tyrant's subjects, see Monoson (2000); Tarcov (2005, 127–28); and Kalyvas (2007, 416).

[64] This is also true of Plato's characterization of rhetoric in the *Phaedrus*.

[65] Although Wardy (1996, 62–63, 75–76) does a very good job of showing why both Gorgianic rhetoric and Socratic dialectic would be anti-democratic within the Athenian context, he makes the mistake of seeing rhetoric and philosophy as opposed throughout the dialogue.

[66] *Contra* Wallach (2001), 194 who argues that the *Gorgias* illustrates Plato's rejection of *makrologia*.

I will explain in more detail in chapter 4, Plato felt that there was something problematic about simply using the shaming elenchus to get people to see that they are not who they think they are without replacing this with a more positive view of the kind of person they might become if they were to transform themselves in accordance with the new insights gleaned in their encounter with Socrates. The exchanges between Callicles and Socrates vividly illustrate how negatively certain people react to feeling ashamed (especially when they are shamed in a specific way), while the myth reflects a new form of Platonic respectful shame that is meant to overcome the limitations of both Callicles and Socrates, as these come to light in the *Gorgias*.[67] In the latter sections of the dialogue, Plato highlights the failed acts of communication between Socrates and Callicles, to remind the reader of the adversarial character of Socrates' shaming elenchus, and to make it clear that the new myth-telling "Socrates" will now be espousing certain Platonic views that Plato in fact learned from Gorgias and the Pythagoreans.[68] Thus, the retuning or refinement of rhetoric which Plato makes in the *Gorgias* is meant to redress the limitations of what he diagnoses in the rhetoric of flattery and in the overly adversarial aspects of the Socratic shaming elenchus, and it involves combining elements of Gorgias' dazzling epideictic display rhetoric with the Socratic knowledge of one's own ignorance—but now in a new mythopoetic form of philosophy that is displayed in the myth at the end of the *Gorgias*.

Thus, what we see over the course of the dialogue is actually a progressive transformation from Socratic views to Platonic views that itself mirrors the work of conversion or transformation that Plato himself underwent as a person. Plato as a young man fell in love with Socrates just as his tyrannical counterpart, Alcibiades, had done. However, Plato, unlike Alcibiades, chose to pursue the life of philosophy that involves slowly understanding how you are both like *and unlike* the teachers you most admire. If Plato did not question and disagree with Socrates on certain things then he would have been a So-

---

[67] Both Rocco (1996) and Wardy (1996) note the coerciveness that comes along with Socrates' own use of *logos* (reason/account) in the *Gorgias*. However, I think this is due to the fact that elenchic refutation is always inextricably intertwined with shame, which has a psychological coerciveness that is not the same as the brute force of being beaten by someone (something Callicles says he wants to do to philosophers at 485c), but which can nonetheless be just as efficient in silencing one's opponents.

[68] Benardete (1991), Nichols (1998), Weiss (2003), and Stauffer (2006) all argue that Plato wants to form an alliance with Gorgias; however, my account differs from theirs because I do not want to equate Gorgianic rhetoric with the flattering rhetoric that Socrates' criticizes at 464b–466a. According to Weiss (2003), the rhetoric of justice in the *Gorgias* involves an alliance between Plato and Gorgias because it involves flattering people like Callicles in order to protect philosophy from the city. I think that Weiss (2003) (and Benardete [1991] and Stauffer [2006]) go too far in suggesting that it is *only* philosophy that needs to be protected from an irremediably sick city, when in fact Plato also wants to suggest that the city needs to be protected from an overly harsh or adversarial Socrates.

cratic disciple, not a Socratic philosopher.[69] That complete agreement with an other (or with oneself for that matter) lies at the heart of flattery comes to light in the Callicles section of the dialogue (521a–521b). Moreover, Plato met a number of other types of philosophers, rhetoricians, poets, and mystics over the course of his life, who all had a great influence on his way of life and his practice of philosophizing. What Plato dramatizes in his middle dialogues is a poetic-rhetorical-mystical-musical form of philosophizing that goes beyond, while incorporating elements from, the various Western and Eastern forms of philosophy, rhetoric, poetry, and religion to which he was exposed.

The fact that Plato begins to slowly incorporate some of Gorgias' views of rhetoric into his own characterization of "Socrates" comes to light in the second set of contrasts that are made between rhetoric and philosophy:

TABLE 2
Flattering Rhetoric vs. Socrates' Political Art of Justice

Flattering (kolakikon) rhetoric	Political art (politikē technē) of justice (dikaiosunē)
1. A knack based on previous experience (empeiria). It guesses at what produces pleasure (hēdonē) and grace/gratification (charis) without considering what is best (beltiston) (Gorg. 462e–463b, 464d).	1. An art (technē) based upon a rational account (logos) of the true nature (phusis) of the thing to which it administers and the things that it administers (465a–b).
2. Corresponds to cookery (opsopoiia), which aims at the pleasures of eating without regard to the good of the body (464e–465a).	2. Corresponds to medicine (iatrikē), which aims at what is best for the body (464e–465a).
	Note: The analogy with medicine (first used by Gorgias in his description of rhetoric in Table 1, Item 4) is transferred to the description of Socrates' art of justice.

[69] For Plato, philosophy is also a way of life and not just a set of doctrines that the individual simply applies to the world. That is why the only true Platonists are those people who strive *not* to be simply disciples of Plato. This does not mean that there is no set of beliefs that these people share with their mentors, rather it means that *living* a belief in, for example, justice or philosophy, is very different from memorizing, agreeing on, and applying every principle that one learns from one's mentor. Plato in fact incorporates elements of the Socratic elenchic method into the regulative principles of his own method of philosophizing, even as he goes beyond it with his notion of the method of collection and division. This latter method is performed via a constant orientation to both consensus (collection) and dissensus (division), which allows one to understand the world better than those tyrannical individuals or frameworks that foreclose this difficult in-between activity of philosophizing. Although Plato only specifically articulates the method of collection and division in the *Phaedrus* (and performs it on *erōs* in this dialogue), he actually performs it on shame (*aischunē*), rhetoric (*rhētorikē*), and justice (*dikaiosunē*) in the *Gorgias*. This shall become clear from my treatment of these themes in this book.

TABLE 2 *(cont'd)*
Flattering Rhetoric vs. Socrates' Political Art of Justice

Flattering (kolakikon) *rhetoric*	*Political art* (politikē technē) *of justice* (dikaiosunē)
3. Tools of persuasion: calls in "false witnesses" (*pseudomarturai*) of good repute to support the speeches (472a). Uses laughter, ridicule, or scare tactics (bogeymen) to refute (*elenchein*) one's opponent (473d–e).	3. Tools of persuasion: calls in one witness (*martus*) to support the speeches: the man to whom the speeches are directed (474a).

This set of contrasts is the one that most readers think of when they think of the strict distinction between rhetoric and philosophy in the *Gorgias*.[70] However, there are three things that I would like to point out about this contrast that challenge many of the misunderstandings that have been made of the dialogue as a whole. The first one is that immediately before making this contrast between flattering rhetoric and the political art of justice, Socrates explicitly says that this is how he is going to define a kind of rhetoric, but that he is not necessarily satirizing Gorgias' rhetoric "for from our recent argument, what in the world he considers it to be did not at all become manifest to us" (463a).[71] This proviso is important because it suggests that Plato is not going to throw out all aspects of Gorgianic rhetoric even if he does agree with Socrates that flattering rhetoric is always pernicious for ethics and politics. This is key for understanding the new kind of rhetoric and new type of shame that does eventually get displayed in the myth at the end of the *Gorgias*, and which I examine in great detail in chapter 4.

Second, as Irwin notes, Socrates criticizes flattering rhetoric for two reasons: "(1) It is shameful because it aims at the pleasant without the best. (2) It is not a craft because it offers no 'rational account,' (*logos*) (see 449de) and cannot give the 'cause' or 'explanation' (*aitia*: the cognate *aitios* is translated by

---

[70] This is also true of a number of commentators on the *Gorgias*. See for example, Yunis (1996); Wardy (1996); Wallach (2001); and Weiss (2003).

[71] Black (1958, 366) and Stauffer (2006, 44) both note this proviso, although I follow Black and not Stauffer in thinking that this is Plato's way of signaling to the reader that he is not equating Gorgianic rhetoric with flattery. Stauffer (2006, 44) argues that "the rhetoric that Socrates describes in such critical terms seems to be *exactly* the kind of rhetoric that Gorgias pursues." This conflation of Gorgianic rhetoric with flattering rhetoric leads both Weiss (2003) and Stauffer (2006) to think that even the noble rhetoric later introduced in the dialogue is Plato's way of protecting philosophy from the city by presenting a false or deceptive view of the moral character of Socratic justice that is more in line with the sick patient, Callicles, who believes deeply in justice and morality. It will become clear later in this book that I do not think that the noble rhetoric displayed in the myth of the *Gorgias* is a form of flattering rhetoric that presents a false picture of the philosophic life.

"responsible" at 452d) of its treatment; cf. 462c . . . [However,] Socrates never objects against rhetoric that it appeals to the emotions, hopes, fears and other non-rational aspects of its audience."[72] This makes sense if, as I argued earlier, what Plato is trying to understand in his middle dialogues is the complex interrelationships between *logos* and the *a-logon*, i.e., *pathos* (emotion/ passion) and *ēthos* (character/disposition/way of life).[73] In fact, in the discussion with Gorgias, Socrates had subtly suggested that what rhetoric might have knowledge of is the soul (453a).[74] In other words, what the new more Platonic "Socrates" is beginning to focus on is not just knowledge of the virtues but rather knowledge of how the virtues of justice, moderation, etc., are acquired (or fail to be acquired) through habituation and training of the various emotions or passions (*pathē*). A true rhetoric requires knowledge of the soul and of the kinds of pleasures and pains, desires, emotions, and reasons that are appealing to a particular person or mass audience, and I believe that if Plato excelled Socrates at anything, it was at his greater understanding of just what these *pathē* are and the complex roles they play in psychosocial relationships.[75] More specifically, the *Gorgias* examines the relationship between *logos* (narrowly understood as reason), *erōs* (desire/love), *ēthos* (character/ disposition/way of life) and *aischunē* (shame), and gives an account (*logos*) of the ways in which *aischunē* can lead to both vicious or virtuous forms of democratic politics.

One of the reasons this has been overlooked as a crucial element of Platonic philosophy, especially as this philosophy comes to light in the *Gorgias,* is the tendency to read *logos* in the narrow sense of "reason" rather than in the broader sense of "account" when Socrates uses this term to contrast the political art with flattering rhetoric.[76] (See Table 2, Item 1 above.) The focus of the contrast is not between a political art that relies on reason (*logos*) and a knack that relies on experience (*empeiria*),[77] but rather on the fact that the flattering rhetoric aims *only* at pleasure (*hēdonē*) or grace/gratification/gratitude (*charis*) *without* the best (*beltiston*),[78] and lacks an account (*logos*) of the thing it

---

[72] Irwin (1979), 135–36.

[73] As Abizadeh ([2002], 2008, 71) argues with respect to Aristotle: *pathos* and *ēthos* supplement abstract *logos* in the narrow sense. "Consequently, *logos* in the broad sense includes both *ēthos* and *pathos.*"

[74] Stauffer (2006), 27. Cf. Nichols (1998), 139.

[75] Cf. Klosko (1983) and Cooper (1999), chapter 2.

[76] Similarly, at the end of the dialogue, when Socrates describes the *muthos* he is about to tell Callicles as a *logos* (523a), he means *logos* in the broad sense which includes the connotations of both account and story.

[77] This is a distinction that also wrongly gets used to distinguish Platonic from Aristotelian science and knowledge. For an account of the importance of experience for correct judgment in Plato's *Republic*, see Frank (2007).

[78] As Ober (1989, 228–36) points out, the *charis* relationship was an important means of redistributing wealth from elite citizens to the masses through giving generous gifts and liturgies.

treats and the medicine it uses to treat the person. This distinction does not rule out the possibility that a true art of rhetoric could be focused on a kind of pleasure (*hēdonē*) or grace/gratification (*charis*) that is consonant with the good,[79] and this possibility is going to be exploited by Plato's later characterization of a noble rhetoric that can be either pleasant or unpleasant to the listeners (503a–b).

It is also important to note that this slightly more Platonic Socrates retains the example of medicine (Table 2, Item 2), which Gorgias had originally used to describe the power of his own rhetoric (Table 1, Item 4).[80] Indeed, it is the example of medicine and not mathematics that gets used for the remainder of the dialogue to comprehend all of the different forms of linguistic exchange or styles of comportment toward an other in the *Gorgias*.[81] The true rhetor is the one who understands the truth about the *pharmakon* he uses and about the patient to whom he administers the *pharmakon*.[82] (Here it is important to note that the Greek term *pharmakon* can mean a poison or a cure, and this ambiguity in its meaning is important for understanding the ambiguous character of the *pharmakon* of shame (*aischunē*) and the shaming elenchus that is administered by "Socrates" at various points throughout this dialogue.)

Now, anyone who has ever gone to a number of different doctors knows very well that even in the case of medicine, it is not just *what* the doctor says

---

However, bribery was naturally related to *charis*, and the verb *charizesthai* could be use in a negative sense to mean "to offer a bribe." Plato seems to be exploiting this possibility in his notion of flattering rhetoric.

[79] Stauffer (2006), 47.

[80] Benardete (1991), Nichols (1998), Weiss (2003), and Stauffer (2006) all note that an alliance between rhetoric and philosophy is suggested by the example of medicine that Gorgias first uses to describe his rhetoric. However, as shall become clear, I disagree with them about the character of this alliance. For them it is a Gorgias-Plato alliance that protects Socratic (and Platonic) philosophy from the city, because of the inherent limitations of politics. For me, it is a Gorgias-Plato alliance that works to harmonize Gorgianic rhetoric, Socratic philosophy, and democratic Athens by taming the harsher elements of all of these forms of comportment toward an other.

[81] *Contra* Vlastos (1983a), (1994a), and Wallach (2001, 193–94), who both argue that the *Gorgias* champions a geometrical method (such as the one outlined in the *Meno*) that does not rely on knowledge of "experience." Indeed, Vlastos (1983a, 52 and 1994a, 25) explicitly argues that in order to solve the logical problem of the Socratic elenchus, Plato must be making a "meta-elenctic" assumption to the effect that: "Anyone who ever has a false moral belief will always have at the same time true beliefs entailing the negation of that false belief. And he elaborates this in terms of what he calls "overt" and "covert" beliefs. His example (1983a, 51 and 1994a, 23) is as follows: "If I believe that a given figure is a Euclidean triangle, then I believe covertly the proposition which is so surprising when we first learn it in geometry, that the figure's interior angles sum to two right angles." Thus, Vlastos argues that in the *Gorgias* Plato thinks that moral truth is grasped using the same tools of logic by which mathematical truths are discovered.

[82] Cf. Wallach (2001, 184) for the use of *pharmakon* in the historical Gorgias' descriptions of his own rhetoric.

about our sickness, but also *how* he says it, and the bedside manner he displays toward us, that helps us make a decision, especially when there are two or three different opinions on offer. The same was surely true of Greek medicine and it explains why Gorgias, the dazzling and pleasant rhetorician, is able to brag that he had helped his brother and other doctors to get a sick patient to drink a drug (*pharmakon*) or submit himself to surgery or cautery (456b) when the doctors were unable to do so. The problem, of course, is that a doctor's bedside manner can lead us astray so that we (the patient) actually make a wrong decision. And Gorgias' subsequent utterance alludes to this problem: here he asserts that if a rhetorician and a doctor competed in the assembly or in any gathering to be chosen as doctor, the rhetorician and not the real doctor would win the contest (*agōn*) (456b–c).[83]

This latter use of rhetoric, however, is quite different from the way that the more Platonic "Socrates" uses medicine as an analogy for justice. When "Socrates" develops the analogy between medicine and the political art of justice, he reinstates the doctor's concern for his patient's health (i.e., the doctor aims at the best and not the pleasant), and he also tries to warn the patients of their own integral role in the goal of attaining health. He compares flattering rhetoric to cookery, which directs itself to the pleasures of the palate with no concern for the health of the body (464d–465a). As "Socrates" warns his interlocutors, the attainment of health requires some sort of knowledge on the part of the patient if he is not to be deceived into taking "remedies" (*pharmaka*) which taste pleasant but actually harm his body. Translating this medical analogy into the political realm, "Socrates' " critique of the citizens in imperialistic Athens is that they allowed themselves to be carried along by the pleasant and flattering rhetoric of political leaders whose promises to aggrandize the Athenian polity via an imperialistic war and an unjust extortion of funds from their own allies actually led to the downfall of Athens.[84]

This analogy with medicine also highlights the fact that both flattering rhetoric and the political art are addressed to a *particular audience* (See Table 2, Item 3). The critera for Socrates' claim to the universal character of the moral truths he discovers in the *Gorgias* thus do not rest upon the kinds of mathematical arguments that Plato will later try to elaborate in the *Meno*.[85] Instead, as Peter Euben puts it, the Socrates of the *Gorgias* puts forth a politically grounded notion of knowledge and wisdom. This type of knowledge

---

[83] Wallach (2001, 184) argues that the historical Gorgias did not himself seem terribly worried about this kind of adaptation of his rhetoric.

[84] As Strauss (2005, 237–38) points out, the Athenian Parthenon, which was characterized by Pericles as a monument to freedom, was actually paid for by excessive and forced tributes from her 250 allied cities, who later claimed that this was an act of barefaced tyranny, which had led to their collective enslavement rather than to freedom.

[85] *Contra* Vlastos (1983a), (1994a). See n.81 above.

relies crucially on the actual or anticipated "communications with others with whom I share a world and with whom I have to come to some agreement."[86] Even more importantly, the size of this other with whom one must reach an agreement in order to understand the best way of life actually increases over the course of the dialogue. Socrates' initial depiction of his dialectical activity describes it as an activity addressed to the individual alone that bids the many farewell (474a). However, he later describes himself as utilizing a type of just rhetoric that is addressed to collective audiences (480c–e). Here the contrast "Socrates" makes between flattering rhetoric and just rhetoric is not a contrast between the size of the audience, but rather the particular kind of comportment toward this audience that is taken by the rhetorician:

TABLE 3
Flattering Rhetoric vs. Socrates' Just Rhetoric

Flattering (kolakikon) *rhetoric*	*Socrates' just* (dikaion) *rhetoric*
1. Speaks in defense of one's own injustice and the injustice of one's parents, comrades, children, and fatherland (*Gorg.* 480b–c).	1. Is used to get oneself, one's parents, comrades, children, and fatherland to submit courageously as if to a doctor for cutting and burning—and pay the penalty (*dikē*) when they have done injustice (*adikia*) (480c–e).
	Note: Socrates now speaks with multitudes, even though his earlier description of dialectic and the political art was aimed only at the individual.
2. Corresponds to cookery (*opsopoiia*), which aims at the pleasures of eating without regard to the good of the body (464e–465a).	2. Corresponds to medicine (*iatrikē*), which aims at what is best for the body (464e–465a). (Hence the above analogy to cutting and burning.)

At this point in the dialogue, it is no longer the distinction between a mass audience as opposed to a single person that "Socrates" highlights when he contrasts his art of justice with flattering rhetoric (*contra* Table 2, Item 3 above). Instead, he argues that flattering rhetoric involves speaking in defense of one's injustice or the injustice of one's fatherland rather than rebuking and criticizing one's friends, comrades, and fatherland when they commit injustice. The new, more Platonic "Socrates" now suggests that there could be a democratic rhetoric addressed to mass audiences that would benefit the city through criticizing its unjust practices.

---

[86] Euben (1997), 211.

The other important distinction that is brought out in this contrast lies in the painfulness of Socrates' new democratic rhetoric of justice. Although "Socrates" is now presented as someone who is willing to speak to multitudes, his just rhetoric is still presented as involving a great deal of pain on the part of the patient who must submit to this rhetoric. The analogy with medicine introduced in the first contrast between flattering rhetoric and the Socratic art of justice (Table 2), is now used to highlight just how painful it is for a patient or polity to undergo the kind of *pharmakon* (poison/cure) that might be required for it to achieve a state of health. Here it is important to note that Greek medicine involved things like cutting, burning, bleeding, and various other painful cures, and not the kind of pleasant or at least pain-killing and serotonin-inducing medications our doctors can now prescribe. As becomes clear throughout the *Gorgias*, the particular *pharmakon* that Socrates applies to his interlocutors is shame (*aischunē*), which provokes the painful recognition on the part of the patient that he is not the person he thought he was. However, as also becomes clear in this dialogue, this recognition prompts a number of different responses on the part of the patient subjected to this *pharmakon.*

Indeed, as I shall outline in great detail in the next chapter, the success of the Socratic shaming elenchus depends in part on the particular reaction that the individual or audience has to the painfulness of being shamed by Socrates. The *Gorgias* explores the complex ways in which shame (*aischunē*) can lead to the discovery of a new ethical or political truth, or to perplexity and confusion, or, finally, even to the attempt to evade and hide from the truth that has been revealed in the shame situation. Thus, I believe that the *Gorgias* illustrates how the reaction to shame (*aischunē*) plays a crucial role in determining whether this *pharmakon* will turn out to be either a poison or a cure. Moreover, I believe that Plato not only wants to dramatize these different possible reactions to the painful recognition characteristic of shame (*aischunē*), but also to suggest ways in which the comportment of the doctor himself (i.e., Socrates) might have prompted the more negative reactions to shame precisely by over-looking the possibility of combining nonharmful pleasures with the more painful aspects of a just democratic rhetoric.

This becomes clear in the penultimate contrast between different types of rhetoric that Plato makes in the dialogue. In the latter sections of the dialogue, the Platonic "Socrates" makes a contrast between flattering rhetoric and a new noble form of rhetoric (see Table 4 below).

Here the contrast no longer focuses on the necessarily painful medicine that is administered by the democratic rhetorician, but rather on the fact that this rhetoric must say the best things for the polity "whether they will be more pleasant or more unpleasant to the hearers" (503a–b). With this subtle revision, Plato suggests that there might well be certain kinds of pleasures that are

TABLE 4
Flattering Rhetoric vs. Plato's Noble Rhetoric

Flattering (kolakikon) rhetoric	Noble (kalon) rhetoric
1. Involves flattery (*kolakeia*) and shameful (*aischron*) popular speaking that is done for the sake of one's private interest; it makes light of the common interest and seeks only to gratify (*charizesthai*) the citizens (*Gorg.* 502e–503b).	1. Makes preparations for the citizens' souls to be as good as possible and fights to say the best things, whether they will be more pleasant or more unpleasant to the hearers (502e–503b).
	Note: Noble rhetoric can be pleasant or painful and is aimed at a common good: the best life for both the speaker and listener.

not necessarily pernicious for a democratic audience to experience, even while they are being criticized or rebuked for certain other unjust practices or beliefs. Part of the overly adversarial character of Socrates' shaming elenchus, especially as this comes to light in Plato's early dialogues and in the initial elenchic sections of the *Gorgias*, arises out of the fact that Socrates rarely says anything at all that is either pleasant or complimentary about *any* Athenian democratic practices. Toward the end of the dialogue Plato even has his Socrates assert that he would not at all be surprised if this kind of elenchic activity were to bring about his own death, if he were ever brought before an Athenian law court (521d). This passage is not meant to show that there is an irreconcilable tension between philosophy and the city, but rather to suggest that Socrates' own mode of comportment toward his Athenian polity was insufficient to bring about a positive transformation in this patient and assuage the feelings of anger and confusion that were so often produced by his shaming elenchus.

Far from banishing rhetoric, Plato reinstates rhetoric's concern for the preservation of its practitioner in light of the fact that Socrates himself was unable to preserve himself from the condemnation of Athens. Thus, in the latter sections of the dialogue Plato argues that a true brand of rhetoric would actually preserve both the pilot (or rhetorician) himself, while also making sure that his ship (or democratic polity) safely negotiated the rough passage across a dangerous sea (see Table 5 below).

While Plato is at pains throughout the dialogue to show just how different Socrates' painful but just rhetoric of shaming one's democratic polity for its pleonectic (greedy and overreaching) desires is from a democratic rhetoric which merely flatters and indulges these desires, he does subtly suggest that there might be another form of rhetoric that would actually preserve the doctor who practices it. Although certain commentators have argued that this true and noble rhetoric is not really developed by Plato until he writes the *Phae-*

TABLE 5
Flattering Rhetoric vs. Socrates' Political Art vs. Plato's True Rhetoric

Flattering (kolakikon) rhetoric	Socrates' political art	True (alēthes) rhetoric
1. Is unable to preserve the rhetor himself and prevent him from being condemned by his democratic audience (*Gorg.* 517a).	2. Is unable to preserve the rhetor himself and prevent him from being condemned by his democratic audience (521d–522c). Socrates admits that if he were tried before a law court he would be killed (522b4).	2. Like the pilot's art, is able to save the person who uses it (511d–512d, 517a). *Note:* True rhetoric can ensure the preservation of the individual who uses it.

drus,[87] I believe that the *Gorgias* itself contains a dramatization of this rhetoric in two ways. First, over the course of the dialogue, we see a "Socrates" who is more willing to espouse positive (and more detailed) doctrines about justice and moderation. As I will show in subsequent chapters these are doctrines that were in fact shared between Socratic and Platonic philosophizing and certain moderate strands of Athenian democratic ideology: that it is better to suffer injustice than it is to do it (474b), that knowledge (*epistēmē*), goodwill (*eunoia*), and outspokenness (*parrhēsia*) are necessary if two parties are "to make a sufficient test of a soul's living correctly" (487a), and that certain base pleasures and desires need to be restrained (503c–d). Second, the pleasures of sights and sounds, for which Gorgias' epideictic rhetoric was famous, are actually displayed in the spectacular and memorable myth at the end of the *Gorgias*, and they are displayed before the very captive audience who had originally come to hear and witness Gorgias' display. In the myth itself, Plato's noble rhetoric utilizes the pleasures of sight and sound that would be familiar to an Athenian democratic audience who constantly went to various theatrical plays and spectacles in order to envision their own democratic polity as well as to learn how to be active spectators or critics of this polity.[88]

Both of these innovations by Plato reflect his own corrections to the problematic intersubjective relationship that he himself had witnessed between his own teacher, Socrates, and the Athenian democratic polity. As I will show in the next chapter, part of the reason for the more negative reactions to Socrates' shaming elenchus arose out of the fact that the "doctor," Socrates, was simply

[87] See Yunis (1996) and Nichols (1998).

[88] See Monoson (2000), chapter 8. For the close connection between Athenian political rhetoric and Athenian drama, see Ober and Strauss (1990).

too strange and unfamiliar (*atopon*) for his Athenian democratic audience to even judge whether his way of life might be something that they would want to incorporate into their own lives as Athenian democratic citizens. The problem with Socrates' characteristic strangeness arises out of the fact that in debates about justice or moderation the relationship between the manner, way of life, or character (*ēthos*) of the "doctor," and the cure (*pharmakon*) that he is prescribing, is even more integral to the act of judgment than it is when we are patients of real doctors. If we are concerned to figure out what the just or moderate course of action is, then it will matter in our deliberations whether the person offering this advice is himself just or moderate.[89] Similarly, if we are going to transform ourselves in accordance with the insights offered by a "doctor" in a shaming refutation, then it is important that this "doctor" give us some concrete and memorable view of the way of life which he is urging us to practice in order to become healthy.

In chapter 3, I will show how the Platonic "Socrates'" presentation of himself as the only truly courageous *parrhēsiastēs* (free or frank speaker) in the *Gorgias* builds upon significant elements of the image of critical citizenship valorized by the Athenians themselves. Second, as I will show in great detail in chapter 4, the myth at the end of the *Gorgias* illustrates the painful but beneficial character of Socrates' shaming elenchus in a number of traditional motifs that would have been familiar to an Athenian democratic audience, even while it also provides an image of the new way of life that might open up to a person who transformed himself in accordance with some of the insights that have been revealed over the course of the dialogue. In other words, the myth at the end of the dialogue assuages the perplexity and even anger that I will now show in chapter 2 were actually produced by Socrates' respectful shaming of interlocutors like Polus and Callicles. This is because it involves an attunement to the practices of justice that were prevalent and hence comprehensible to Socrates' interlocutors, even while it slowly introduces a new and memorable image of just and critical democratic citizenship into the Athenian democratic normative imagery.

[89] For an account of how this works in Aristotle's notion of political deliberation, see Yack (2006).

Chapter Two

SHAMING GORGIAS, POLUS, AND CALLICLES

IN THE LAST CHAPTER, I argued that far from banishing rhetoric from the *Gorgias*, Plato actually constructs a new and noble form of rhetoric that transcends while still preserving elements of Gorgias' epideictic rhetoric and the Socratic shaming elenchus or political art of justice. I now want to turn to an examination of each of the three shaming refutations in the *Gorgias* in order to begin to articulate the peculiar character of a shame situation as well as the potentials and dangers that underlie this whole phenomenon. In other words, I want to show exactly what Plato learned about shame by witnessing Socrates' shaming elenchus and by witnessing the reactions that Socrates' interlocutors had to this experience.

As I mentioned in the last chapter, many commentators of the *Gorgias* have noted the central role played by shame in each of the three refutations (*elenchea*) of the dialogue, but their accounts have all failed to bring out the full complexity of Plato's teaching.[1] The first problem is that they usually assume that shame works in the same way in all three refutations (*elenchea*). Thus, for example, Charles Kahn argues that the interlocutors assert out of shame what they really believe to be false, whereas Richard McKim argues that they assert out of shame what they really believe to be true.[2] However, an important part of their disagreement arises from the fact that they each focus on two different senses of shame in their treatments of the *Gorgias*. To be shamed into telling a lie and to be ashamed of the truth are two different things. In the first case, shame involves the imagined threat of having the inadequacies (in one's beliefs, actions, or character) revealed to an other, thus causing one to conceal these with more appropriate beliefs or actions.[3] In the second case, shame involves

---

[1] See chapter 1 n.23 for a list of commentators who have noted the central role shame plays in the *Gorgias*. In this chapter, I will be focusing primarily on the accounts of shame in the *Gorgias* offered by Charles Kahn and Richard McKim because their accounts provide the most detailed analysis of the way that shame allegedly works in each of the three different refutations. However, what I have to say about their accounts will also address the limitations of the other accounts of shame in the *Gorgias*.

[2] Kahn (1983), 75–121. (Although parts of this were reprinted in Kahn [1996], I use the original because this contains the most sustained treatment of shame and because other commentators on Kahn refer to this article.); McKim (1988), 34–48.

[3] Konstan (2006, 101–4) persuasively argues that the classical Greek notion of *aischunē* did not refer solely (or even predominantly) to situations in which the unavoidable defects in one's character or self are revealed by an other. Rather, a situation that provoked *aischunē* consisted of three

the experience of being unmasked by an other and discovering a truth about one's inadequacies, which causes one to feel the acute pain so central to the emotion of shame.[4]

Instead, I argue that the *Gorgias* contains illustrations of both of these possibilities, as well as a third possibility, that is, that the shamed individual is simply perplexed and uncertain about just what it is that he believes, precisely because Socrates' shaming elenchus has introduced a great deal of confusion or novelty into his existing belief structure.[5] However, the cognitive state of perplexity is very different from both sincerity and insincerity because the person is in the process of acquiring a wholly new other or exemplar for action about which he can subsequently be sincere or insincere. Indeed, part of what was so perplexing and *atopon* (out of place, extraordinary, strange, marvelous, paradoxical, foul, and distasteful)[6] about Socrates for his Athenian interlocutors was that he was attempting to introduce a wholly new way of life or exemplar for action within their existing normative framework.[7] I will argue in this chapter that in order to be clear about all of these distinct possibilities, it is necessary (1) to distinguish between the moment of recognition and the moment of reaction in any shame situation;[8] and (2) to understand the differ-

---

elements: "a particular act (throwing away one's shield in battle); the fault of character that is revealed by the act (cowardice); and the disgrace or loss of esteem before the community at large." In chapter 6, I argue that our modern notions of shame and guilt also do not divide easily into a distinction between character flaws (shame) and morally culpable actions (guilt), even though some psychoanalysts and political theorists mistakenly think this is the case.

[4] This distinction should not be confused with the distinction between prospective and retrospective shame utilized by Cairns (1993); Williams (1993); Nieuwenburg (2004); and Konstan (2006). Prospective and retrospective refer to whether the ill or evil that makes one feel shame is in the future (prospective) or in the present/past (retrospective). However, this distinction does not refer to whether the feeling of shame makes the person utter a sincere or insincere statement in response to the feeling of shame.

[5] Stauffer (2006) also argues that Polus and Callicles are more confused and ambivalent than sincere or insincere about the arguments that Socrates presents, but this, for him, is because of the fundamental confusion that all humans (except Plato and Socrates) have about justice, nobility, and virtue. Adkins (1960, 268) also points to this confusion in the case of Polus, but he asserts that this is due to the ambiguities in the ordinary Greek notion of the shameful/ugly (*aischron*) and noble/beautiful (*kalon*) during this time period. I address Adkins's point in chapter 3.

[6] Liddell and Scott (1996), 272.

[7] For a discussion of the politics of paradigm shifts in Plato's dialogues see Allen (2000a and 2000b, chapter 10), and chapter 4 below.

[8] This distinction between the *different moments in any shame situation* should not be conflated with the many distinctions that have been used to distinguish between *different kinds of shame*. In the latter category I include the retrospective and prospective distinction (Cairns [1993]; Williams [1993]; Nieuwenburg [2004]; Konstan [2006]); the concealing and transformative distinction (Williams [1993]; Abdel-Nour [2003]); the primitive and constructive distinction (Nussbaum [2004]); the stigmatizing and reintegrative distinction (Braithwaite [1989], [2000]) and my own flattering, Socratic respectful, and Platonic respectful distinction (chapters 3 through 6). It will become clear over the course of this book just how my own distinctions between flattering, So-

ent types of other, both individual and collective, that can be involved in pro-
voking the recognition or reaction (or both).[9]

Second, I argue that the *success or failure* of a shame refutation depends in
part upon the reactions of the individual. Although commentators such as
McKim and Kahn illuminate many of the ways in which recognition is a crucial
element of the phenomenon of shame, they tend to assume that the reactions
of the interlocutors to this phenomenon are always identical. Thus, while Kahn
thinks that none of Socrates' interlocutors in the *Gorgias* has a conversion
experience, McKim thinks that they all do.[10] Instead I argue that the *Gorgias*
reveals a number of positive and negative reactions to the feeling of shame.
These are shown both by the interlocutors' immediate reaction to Socrates,
and by the ways in which they re-enter the dialogue during the refutations of
other interlocutors. As I argue below, Callicles' reaction is predominantly one
of trying to hide from the very truths that he and Socrates have just discovered
(*Gorg.* 497b, 504c, 505c). Gorgias, on the other hand, re-enters the dialogue
at a number of crucial moments even after he has been shamed by Socrates
(497b, 506a–b), thus suggesting that he is ready to learn something new from
Socrates and to transform himself in reaction to what he is now learning. As
I argued in chapter 1, whether Socrates' shaming refutations (*elenchea*) benefit
the souls of his interlocutors depends, in part, upon the "patients' " reaction
to them. This, however, does not exempt the "doctor," Socrates, from his own
crucial role in determining the outcome of a shame situation. Indeed, as I shall
argue in more detail in chapter 4, Plato's project in the *Gorgias* is not just to

---

cratic and Platonic respectful shame differ from the other kinds of shame that people have identified. One problem with some of their distinctions is that they tend to be unclear about whether
they are distinguishing between the different kinds of recognitions or reactions that an individual
has when experiencing shame, or the different kinds of attitudes that shamers have to the one
being shamed, or whether their distinctions include some combination of all three of these things.
Finally, the distinction between the moment of recognition and the moment of reaction do not
quite map onto the distinction between the occurrent feeling of shame and the disposition or
sense of shame, although as I will show in chapter 3, how we react or are taught to react to shame
over time does play a role in our development of a sense of shame. I follow Nieuwenburg (2004)
and Konstan (2006) (*contra* Cairns [1993]), in thinking that the prospective and retrospective
distinction does not map onto the distinction between the dispositional (or sense of shame) and
the occurrent feeling of shame. As Nieuwenburg (2004, 466 n.16) puts it, "prospective shame" is
"ambiguous between (1) the prospect of shame and (2) shame at a prospective blow to one's
reputation." I partially agree with Konstan (2006, 295 n.15) that it is the "restrictive" or prospective sense of *aischunē* that is in play in the *Gorgias*, but, for me, this only applies to the refutations
of Gorgias and Polus. As I show in this chapter, the Callicles section dramatizes both the prospective and retrospective senses of shame (*aischunē*) equally.

[9] The shame situation can be very complex especially when the self being shamed or the other
doing the shaming is a collective entity. For an excellent account of the many different types of
recognitions and reactions that were prompted in the collective selves of Germany and Japan by
the shaming of the U.S. and its allies in the aftermath of World Wars I and II, see Lu (2008).

[10] Kahn (1983); McKim (1988).

outline how shame (*aischunē*) can lead to the discovery of a new truth about the self (both individual and collective), but also to show why Socrates' shaming refutations (*elenchea*) often failed to achieve this goal with his interlocutors, and why an interlocutor such as Callicles reacts so negatively to Socrates.

Finally, I argue that in order to understand the phenomenon of shame it is necessary to understand its dynamic, intersubjective, and (potentially) self-reflexive character.[11] As Charles Kahn puts it, the Socratic elenchus should be understood as protreptic rather than deductive because it can get a person to recognize moral concerns that he doesn't currently possess, but that are contained in certain public opinions or exemplified in Socrates' philosophic way of life or both.[12] If people could come to see that the morally virtuous life is good for them and that the person standing before them embodies the fulfillment of their deepest desires, then they would choose his way of life rather than the life they are currently leading. But *contra* Kahn I also argue that shame need not always link the person to external or heteronomous moral concerns embodied in the other doing the shaming because (as I will illustrate in the case of Callicles) shame can also get the interlocutor to recognize how these concerns are already at least partially operative *in his own way of life*.[13]

The self-reflexive recognition possible in shame arises from the fact that this emotion is a dynamic mechanism of socialization that allows the individual to internalize external norms of practice and to make some of these norms his own.[14] The other before whom one feels ashamed can be an internalized other serving as the repository of one's own admired or accepted ideals and exemplars, or it can be an external other before whom one feels ashamed.[15] For this reason, Socrates can use shame both as a tool to discover what the interlocutor

---

[11] McKim's (1988, 37) view of shame relies on an overly static view of the psyche: i.e., he argues that if there is a common moral truth that is discovered by Socratic elenchus, this must reside in the already existing but unconscious beliefs of the interlocutor. Thus his notion of the way shame can reveal moral truth ends up being very similar to Vlastos' less psychological but equally static solution to the problem of the Socratic elenchus.

[12] Kahn (1983), 115–17. The word "protreptic" comes from the Greek word *protrepein*, which means to "turn (someone) forward," "urge on," or "exhort." Paul Nieuwenburg also considers this central to Aristotle's conception of shame (*aischunē*) and its attachment to the reputable opinions (*endoxa*) believed by all or most or the wise. See Nieuwenburg (2004), 453–55. Cf. Yunis (2007) and Frank (2007) for an account of the protreptic character of the rhetoric of the *Republic*.

[13] This self-reflexive character of shame is nicely captured by Richard McKim's (1988) account of shame in the *Gorgias*. For accounts of the ways in which moral concerns are actually operative in the life of the self-professed immoralist, Callicles, and for the ways in which Socrates brings these to light in his refutation of Callicles, see Benardete (1991, 78–79); Stauffer (2002 and 2006); and section 2.3 below.

[14] Elster (1999, 145) argues that "the emotion of shame is not only a support of social norms, but *the* support." Cf. Sokolon (2006, 112) who argues that shame is a more expansive motivator of social action than anger because it is "connected to a wider group of individuals, including political leaders, teachers, or long-dead ancestors."

[15] Williams (1993), 80–84.

sincerely honors or admires (McKim's position) and to discover the deposit
of moral truth contained in popular views (Kahn's position). The phenomenon of shame thus points both inwards to what the individual desires and
believes, and outward to the world of laws and practices within which they
move and live. In fact, it is often only with the occurrent experience of shame
that we first discover that there is an inner and outer world, though unfortunately while recognizing the painful split between the two of them.[16] The dynamic character of shame also means that if there is a common moral truth
to be discovered by Socrates and his interlocutors this might reside not just in
the depths of their psyche or in popular opinions, but also in the very dynamics
of the conversation on display in the *Gorgias*. In other words, the moral truth
that is discovered in a shame situation can arise out of and point back to the
very communicative interaction that is only now taking place between Socrates
and his interlocutors.

The reason that shame (*aischunē*), both for the Greeks and for ourselves, can
sometimes refer to the occurrent experience of feeling ashamed, sometimes to
the character trait or "sense of shame," and sometimes to a set of practices that
exemplify a shaming (as in the case of the Socratic elenchus) stems in part from
the dynamic character of the emotion of shame itself.[17] Any particular act of
shaming has the potential to alter our sense of shame because it has the potential to introduce a new other into our very psyche. Thus certain interlocutors
might well be induced to feel ashamed of their way of life only because of their
encounter with someone like Socrates,[18] and this experience might then prompt
them to incorporate aspects of Socratic philosophizing into their own unique

---

[16] As Nussbaum (2004, 183) puts it, "When an infant realizes that it is dependent on others,
and is by this time aware of itself as a definite being who is and ought to be the center of the
world, we can therefore expect a primitive and rudimentary emotion of shame to ensue." See also
Morrison (1989) and (1996); and Broucek (1991). Konstan (2006, 303 n.45) notes that the "idea
of a divided self was perfectly familiar to Aristotle and his contemporaries."

[17] I do think that Plato uses *aischunē* to refer to both the occurrent experience of shame and to
the disposition or sense of shame in the *Gorgias*, even if (as Konstan (2006, 95) argues), Aristotle
uses *aischunē* to refer to the occurrent feeling of shame and uses *aidōs* to refer to the disposition
or sense of shame. The *Gorgias* does not use the term *aidōs* at all, yet it does use the term *aischunē*
in the same passage to denote both a sense of shame and the feeling of shame (*Gorg.* 487b).
Socrates makes his interlocutors feel shame, but he also appeals to their sense of shame in order
to get them to agree to certain premises. (This is primarily true in the case of Gorgias, even though
Plato purposely makes it unclear whether or not Gorgias actually ever does feel the emotion of
shame. Polus thinks he does, but Socrates remains ambiguous about whether it was his sense of
shame or his feeling shame that made him agree to certain premises [487b]). See section 2.1 below
for a full treatment of the Gorgias refutation.

[18] This is central to Alcibiades' description of the effect that Socrates has on him in Plato's
Symposium (*Symp.* 216a–b), and I would argue it was also true of the effect that Socrates had on
Plato.

other.[19] As will be seen below in the case of Polus, this dynamic character makes the logic of a shame refutation difficult to pin down precisely because the viewpoint from which we judge ourselves as well as the very referent of the judgment (i.e., our self) can change in the process of coming to learn something new about ourselves in and through being shamed by an other. Indeed, as I shall now argue, in the case of Gorgias if a person does learn something new as a result of undergoing Socrates' shaming refutation, then one actually changes from being a "false" or insincere witness to a "true" witness of the very things that are brought to light in the shaming refutation.

THE REFUTATION OF GORGIAS

The first refutation of the dialogue is directed at the rhetorician, Gorgias. The assertion of Gorgias that Socrates targets for refutation is his argument for the moral neutrality of rhetoric.[20] Gorgias himself describes his rhetoric as the art of persuasion "in law courts and in other mobs . . . and about those things that are just and unjust" (*en tois dikastēriois kai en tois allois ochlois . . . kai peri toutōn ha esti dikaia te kai adika*)(454b).[21] However, because his rhetoric is morally neutral, Gorgias claims he is not responsible for the behavior of his students whenever they use rhetoric unjustly (457b–457c). But Socrates then asks him a crucial question:

> . . . is it necessary to know, and must the one who is going to learn rhetoric know these things (the just and the unjust) before coming to you? And if not, will you, the teacher of rhetoric (*ho tēs rhētorikēs didaskalos*), teach him who comes nothing of these things—for it is not your work—and will you make him who doesn't know such things seem among the many

[19] This fact about *aischunē* in Plato is consistent with both Nieuwenburg (2004) and Konstan's (2006) argument that, for Aristotle, shame can attune a person to *endoxa* (i.e., reputable or honorable propositions held by all, the many or the *wise*) [my italics]. Cf. Aristotle, *Rhet.* 1384a17.

[20] Dodds (1959, 7); Kahn (1983, 115); Wallach (2001, 180); and Stauffer (2006, 16) all argue that unlike Protagoras, Gorgias did not profess to teach his students virtue (*aretē*). The evidence for this fact is provided by what Gorgias says in the dialogue (452e), by the external evidence found in his historical writings, and by Plato's *Meno* 95c. Both Dodds (1959, 10) and Gish (2006, 50 n.28) point out that Aristotle also characterizes Gorgias' rhetoric in this way in the *Sophistical Refutations*. *Contra* Murray (2001) and Weiss (2003, 205) who argue that Gorgias' rhetoric is inherently unjust and immoral.

[21] As Nichols (1998, 25) points out, the extant remains of Gorgias' speeches are mainly display, praise, or show pieces, characteristic of epideictic or ceremonial rhetoric and not the forensic rhetoric used in the law courts, concerning the just and unjust. However, Wardy (1996, 26–27) argues that these distinctions were only later formalized by Aristotle in his *Rhetoric*, and that the *Encomium to Helen* mixes a defense of Helen with a praise or celebration of the power (*dunamis*) of rhetoric and *logos*.

to know, and seem to be good although he isn't? Or will you be wholly unable to teach him rhetoric, unless he knows the truth about these things beforehand? (459e–460a)

In response to this question, Gorgias concedes that he will teach his students justice. This concession, in conjunction with his acceptance of Socrates' "knowledge is virtue" thesis (i.e., to know justice entails being just), leads to a contradiction with his earlier thesis because it leads to the conclusion that the student of Gorgias will never be unjust (*adikon*) (460b–461a).[22] The logical structure of the argument is as follows:

(1) *p*—Gorgianic rhetoric is a morally neutral art which (when taught) has no effect on whether its students make a just or unjust use of it (456c–457c).

(2) *q*—Gorgianic rhetoric is concerned with justice and injustice (454 b).

r—Gorgias himself knows what is good (*agathon*) or bad (*kakon*), noble (*kalon*) or shameful (*aischron*), just (*dikaion*) or unjust (*adikon*) (459d–460a).

s—If a student comes to Gorgias not knowing these things, Gorgias will teach him (460a).

t—If the student learns about justice, he will be a just man (460b).

u—The just man acts justly (460b).

(3) *q–v entail not p*—The student who learns about justice from his study of Gorgianic rhetoric will never make an unjust use of it.

Where does the phenomenon of shame enter into this particular elenchic argument? It is not that Gorgias is ashamed at being caught in a logical contradiction (whether this is so or not is left unclear by the dramatic fact that Polus leaps in before we are allowed to see Gorgias' reaction to the contradiction that Socrates has revealed [461b]). Rather, Gorgias is shamed into accepting two premises—that he knows the just, noble, and good things (premise *r*) and that he will teach his students these things if they don't know them already (premise *s*)—and these two premises ultimately lead to a contradiction with his earlier thesis about the moral neutrality of rhetoric.[23] To signal that this is in fact the case, Plato has Polus, Gorgias' student and defender, leap into the discussion at this point and accuse Socrates of just this kind of psychological manipulation: "Or do you think—because Gorgias was ashamed (*ēischunthē*) not to agree further with you that the rhetorical man also knows the just, noble, and good things (*ta dikaia . . . kai ta kala kai ta agatha*), and if he came

---

[22] For criticisms of Socrates' "knowledge is virtue" thesis, see Irwin (1979), 126–27. For a defense of this doctrine, see Black (1958), 364 and Dodds (1959), 218.

[23] See Kahn (1983), 79–84; Dodds (1959), 216. *Contra* Irwin (1979), 125.

to him not knowing these things, that he himself would teach them, and then from this agreement perhaps some contradiction came about in the speeches . . . —for who do you think would utterly deny both that he knows the just things and that he would teach others" (461b–c)?[24]

When Socrates asks Gorgias whether or not he will teach his students justice, Socrates knows that as a foreign teacher of rhetoric Gorgias must take into account the fact that the Athenian public does not want its youth or potential leaders to be corrupted. Although Gorgias believes that his rhetoric is morally neutral and that the rhetorician cannot make his students just, he asserts that he will teach them justice, so that he himself will avoid the wrath of Athens. Thus Socrates skillfully manipulates Gorgias' sense of shame, that is, his sense of how the Athenian community will view his remarks, in order to get him to utter an insincere belief.[25] Moreover, the argument works in an *ad hominem* fashion: it is because of his profession as a foreign teacher of rhetoric that he feels the intense pressure to assert that he will make his students just.[26] The fact that neither Polus nor Callicles feel so constrained is evidenced by their willingness to admit the cause of Gorgias' shame (461b, 482c–d), and to praise the life of tyranny (470d–472d, 483a–484c).

Of course, Gorgias' insincerity poses a potential problem for the success of Socrates' elenchic argument by the very standards that Socrates himself had initially set out for it. In other words, Gorgias' insincerity would seem to make him a "false" witness to the truth of what Socrates is asserting. Socrates seems unable to provide even the one witness that he claimed was necessary for the success of his dialectical arguments (472b–c). In addition, Socrates himself seems to have called in many "false" witnesses of good repute (471e), i.e., the Athenian public, to get Gorgias to agree to the crucial premise in the first

---

[24] Gish (2006, 62) notes that Gorgias' shame is also signaled by his uncharacteristic silence, which lasts for most of the remaining discussion. *Contra* Nichols (1998, 138), who thinks that Polus' interruption indicates that he feels shame for Gorgias who was probably only silent out of prudent caution and not shame. The real ambiguity here, as I noted above in n.17, is not whether Gorgias feels shame or is merely prudent, but rather whether he actually feels shame or is motivated instead by a sense of shame. That Gorgias might be silent out of prudence does not preclude the fact that this prudence can be intertwined with a kind of shame before the internalized other of the prudent person. Cf. Aristotle, *Rhet.* 1384a17.

[25] Kahn (1983), 115. Gorgias' concern for his public reputation is also noted by Lewis (1987), 200. I agree with Lewis (1987, 200 n.10) that this concern for reputation does not necessarily mean that Gorgias is unconcerned with the truth, and indeed it is consistent with his desire to really know the truth about what kinds of things please his audience.

[26] Kahn (1983), 79–80. The close connection between shame (*aischunē*) and character (*ēthos*) is true both for individuals and collective entities, even though it is considerably more complex in the case of the latter. See Abdel-Nour (2003) for an account of why shame and not guilt is more apt to bring about real transformation on the part of a nation's collective identity. For the opposing view and for criticisms about the use of collective shame in feminist-democratic politics, see Locke (2007), 157–59.

place. At this point, his style of refutation seems similar to the rhetoric he accuses Polus and many other Athenians of practicing in the law courts "when they provide many witnesses of good repute for the speeches that they make" (471e).[27] The only difference seems to be that Socrates is more adept than either Gorgias or Polus at using the tool of shame to get his opponents to agree to things they do not really believe. However, I now want to suggest a number of reasons why the refutation of Gorgias should not be regarded either as conclusive evidence in support of Socrates' conclusion, or as an imposition of conventional views upon a "false" or insincere witness.

The first is that, *contra* Vlastos, Socrates does not assert that he has proven his thesis to be true and Gorgias' thesis to be false.[28] At the end of the refutation, he states only that the conclusion—the student of rhetoric will never be unjust—is what follows from the premises upon which he and Gorgias have agreed (461a) and he suggests that further conversation is necessary in order to examine these things adequately (461a–b). I think this assertion reveals that Socrates is aware of the provisional character of this conclusion and of the fact that it will require further testing and discussion with Gorgias and the other interlocutors. It also reveals that Socrates has not been duped by Gorgias' assent into thinking that he has adequately provided Gorgias as a "true" witness to his conclusion.

But this does not mean that the conclusion is false, or that there is no worthwhile point in getting Gorgias into such a position. Instead, it might mean that Gorgias is only now open to learning something new. Indeed, the dialogue opens with Gorgias complaining that he has not been asked "anything new for many years" (448a). As we shall see below, Gorgias does not run away after his refutation, but stays around to witness Socrates' arguments with Polus and Callicles, and jumps in at a number of crucial points to further the discussion (463a, 463d–e, 497b, 506a–b).[29] These interruptions illustrate the way in which Gorgias moves from being a "false" to a "true" witness of Socrates' conclusions in the course of the dialogue.[30] It is Gorgias who interrupts the conversation between Polus and Socrates twice to get Socrates to clarify what he means by

---

[27] See Todd (1990); Thür (2005), and chapter 4 below for a discussion of the role of witnesses in Athenian law courts.

[28] Vlastos (1983a and 1994a) does not actually address Gorgias' refutation in his article and instead draws his conclusions about the role of the elenchus in the *Gorgias* from his examination of the refutations of Polus and Callicles. I think this is partially responsible for his overlooking the fact that the interlocutors don't always "overtly" or explicitly believe every premise upon which Socrates gets them to agree.

[29] Dodds (1959, 313); Kastely (1991, 100); Weiss (2003, 200); Stauffer (2006, 121); and Gish (2006, 66) all note the importance of Gorgias' interruptions for a full understanding of the dialogue.

[30] *Contra* Dodds (1959, 313) who sees Gorgias' intervention at 497b as simply calling attention to the importance of Socrates' refutation of hedonism, and Kastely (1991, 99) who thinks that Socrates has alienated all three of his interlocutors by the end of the dialogue.

calling one kind of rhetoric a form of flattery (*kolakeia*) (463a, 463d–464a). It is also Gorgias who gets Callicles to continue to submit to Socrates' painful refutation twice so that he (Gorgias) and the others might have the possibility of fully understanding what Socrates has to teach them about the relationship between the pleasant (*to hēdu*) and the good (*to agathon*) (497b), and the resulting need for moderation (*sōphrosunē*) or punishing correction (*kolazesthai*) intemperance (*akolasia*) (506a–b).[31] These interruptions indicate that Gorgias is learning something both about himself and about a kind of rhetoric that consists of restraining rather than inciting or simply ignoring the lowest desires of one's audience. Moreover, Gorgias' interruptions illustrate the fact that whether Socrates' use of shame has a beneficial effect upon his interlocutors depends, in part, on how they react to this phenomenon.[32] In Section 2.3, I will show that the refutation of Callicles provides ample evidence of the kind of negative reactions that can be elicited by the feeling of shame. But before turning to this lengthy encounter I want to address Socrates' refutation of his second interlocutor, Polus.

THE REFUTATION OF POLUS

Immediately after Gorgias' refutation, his student Polus jumps into the discussion and tries to defend his teacher and his teacher's doctrines against Socrates' shaming tactics. In this section, the discussion gradually moves from an examination of the moral neutrality of Gorgianic rhetoric to Polus' explicit praise of the life of the tyrant Archelaus (470d–471d).[33] In this speech Polus focuses

---

[31] Weiss (2003, 200) argues that Gorgias' interruptions suggest that an alliance between him and Socrates has been formed to get ill "patients" like Callicles to submit to the painful medicine of Socratic refutation. Stauffer (2006, 121) argues that Gorgias' interventions are important, but more for what he is learning about Callicles' deep moral commitments than about himself. I think both of these arguments are partially right, but they overlook the fact that Gorgias explicitly says he wants Callicles to continue submitting to Socrates refutation "*for our sake too*" (*hēmōn heneka*) (497b; see also 506a–b). It is Polus and Callicles who continue to go along with Socrates' refutations to gratify others (462d, 497c, 505c), but Gorgias, like Socrates, is there to learn something new about himself. Cf. Gish (2006), 66, esp. n.82.

[32] The more positive reaction that Gorgias has in comparison to Callicles also depends, in part, on the fact that Gorgias isn't made to stay in the limelight as long as Callicles is. I thank the members of my graduate seminar on the *Gorgias* at Harvard for alerting me to this fact. This is partly why Plato's noble rhetoric, exemplified in the myth at the end of the *Gorgias*, encapsulates the teaching of the dialogue in an imagistic and memorable form. Even if the acute pain of a public shaming may make one focus only on the painfulness of the experience and not the content of the shaming, there is always a possibility that when the person is no longer in the limelight they will actually be less inclined to hide from what has been revealed in the painful and very public shaming. See chapter 4 for a further elaboration of this point.

[33] Many commentators have noted that the movement of the dialogue from Gorgias to Polus to Callicles corresponds to an ever-greater praise of tyranny: see Dodds (1959), 266–67; Benardete (1991), 38; Kastely (1991), 98–99; Gish (2006), 64–65; and Stauffer (2006), 83.

on the external goods that the tyrant obtains through force and then turns to the bodily and external evils that the unsuccessful tyrant must suffer (473c–d). This latter unfortunate person is tortured, castrated, impaled, has his eyes burned out, and is also forced to watch his wife and children suffer the same fate (presumably before his eyes are burned out), and Polus uses this speech to argue that it is better to do injustice than it is to suffer it. In the next part of the refutation, however, Socrates gets him to admit that it is more *shameful* to do injustice than it is to suffer it (474c), and from this concession Socrates is finally able to prove his own thesis, that it is in fact worse to do injustice than to suffer it (475c).

Polus' refutation reveals just how difficult the question of sincerity and insincerity becomes when one actually addresses the complexity and dynamical character of the communicative situation between Socrates and his interlocutors. The problem can be seen if we examine McKim's and Kahn's views of the refutation of Polus. When Polus argues that doing injustice is more shameful than suffering it, Kahn asserts that he is being insincere and simply tailoring his remarks to conventional Athenian wisdom.[34] Hence, he is uttering out of shame what he really believes to be false. McKim on the other hand thinks that the only other alternative is to say that Polus is uttering out of shame what he really (though at this point unconsciously) believes to be true.[35]

These interpretations, however, still leave out a number of possibilities that might characterize Polus' situation. First, a person can utter something that is true about certain aspects of their life and false about others. Second, the person might actually be of two minds or confused about something, that is, they might take two different perspectives on one and the same action. Finally, the person might be in the process of learning something new about himself or about the other person with whom he is conversing, while not fully understanding all of the ramifications of what he is asserting. Reading the Polus section gives many commentators the impression that Polus is being sincere, but is also honestly confused and perplexed by what he actually considers admirable and shameful.[36] This, however, is not the same thing as lying about these matters. By overlooking the genuine perplexity that is evident in the Polus refutation, McKim and Kahn end up oversimplifying the communicative situation within which a phenomenon like shame can occur.

[34] Kahn (1983), 117.

[35] McKim (1988, 40) first describes this as what differentiates Socrates' understanding of shame from Callicles': "Whereas Callicles says that men assert out of shame what they really believe to be false, Socrates thinks that they assert out of shame what they really believe to be true." He then goes on to apply this understanding of shame in his explanation of the Polus refutation.

[36] See for example Dodds (1959), 11–12; Kastely (1991), 100; Benardete (1991), 40–41; and Stauffer (2006, 64–75).

If, however, we see shame not so much as maintaining the boundaries between a static psyche and a static political world, but rather as dynamically constructing and constantly renegotiating what occurs on either side of the boundaries, then the logic of a shame refutation becomes very difficult to pin down.[37] The perspective from which we might make a judgment about ourselves as well as the referent of the judgment (i.e., who we are) can change in the process of coming to learn something new about ourselves in our engagement with others.[38] I believe that it is this possibility that allows one to understand the communicative situation between Polus and Socrates as well as the definition of the shameful and beautiful that Socrates gets Polus to accept. It is not so much that Polus is lying or being insincere when he comes to an agreement with Socrates about the shamefulness of the life of tyranny, but rather that he has become perplexed about his own views on this topic and is on the way to learning something new about himself, about the tyrant, and about the very activity of Socratic philosophizing that he is now experiencing.[39]

Plato himself explicitly signals this perplexity or uncertainty in the dialogue by the different responses that Polus makes to the various steps of Socrates' argument: the first three times that Polus responds to the argument he uses the terms *panu ge* ("certainly") twice and the term *ananke* ("necessarily") once (475a). However, by the end of the argument he uses the terms *eoiken* ("it looks that way") twice and *phainetai* ("it appears") twice (475c–e) in response to Socrates' conclusions.[40] Finally, at the end of the dialectical encounter between Polus and Socrates, when Socrates asks Polus whether he agrees with all of the conclusions they have reached about rhetoric, Polus exclaims: *Atopa men, ō Sōkrates, emoige dokei, tois mentoi emprosthen isōs soi homologeitai.* ("To me, Socrates, they seem strange indeed; but perhaps you make them agree with the things said before" [480e].) Here it is important to note that the word translated as "strange" is *atopon*, which literally means "out of place," but also has the connotations of extraordinary, strange, paradoxical, unnatural, disgusting, foul, marvelous, and absurd.[41] The Attic Greek word captures the

[37] Commentators who have noticed the complexity and dialectical "trickery" of this argument include Dodds (1959), 30; Adkins (1960), 280; Santas (1979); Kahn (1983), 93; and Vlastos (1995).

[38] See Markell (2003) for an account of how a politics of acknowledgment welcomes this kind of uncertainty about a future thick with surprise, and places it at the heart of our intersubjective relationships.

[39] As Guenther (2008,4) puts it, the experience of shame "*intersubjectifies*; it attests to an irreducible relation to others in the midst of one's own self-relation." That this dizzying and disorienting feeling of shame is often at the heart of our encounters with the new is well attested to in the works of Jean Paul Sartre and Hannah Arendt. Cf. Zerilli (2005); and Tarnopolsky (2007b, 288–89, 306–7).

[40] Cf. Stauffer (2006), 75; Kastely (1991), 97.

[41] Liddell and Scott (1996), 272.

many different levels, both cognitive and affective, at which Socrates' way of life astounded and perplexed his Athenian audience and literally turned their world upside down.[42]

In order to see how the refutation works, it is necessary to restate this argument in detail and to insert the survey of examples from which Socrates derives his definition of *to kalon* (the fine/beautiful/noble) and its opposite, *to aischron* (the foul/ugly/shameful):[43]

(1) *p*—Suffering injustice (*adikeisthai*) is worse (*kakion*) than doing injustice (*adikein*) (474c).

(2) *q*—Doing injustice is more shameful (*aischron*) than suffering injustice (474c).

r—All fine/admirable/beautiful things (*ta kala panta*) are called this because they are either beneficial (*ōphelimon*) or pleasant (*hēdu*) or both (474d).

(Derived from the following survey of examples:)

r .a. Beautiful bodies are beautiful because of their use (*chreia*) for some purpose or because of the pleasure (*hēdonē*) that they give to the beholder (474d).

r .b. Shapes and colors are beautiful because of some pleasure (*hēdonē*) or benefit (*ōphelia*) or both (474e).

r .c. All voices and things relating to music are beautiful for the same reason (474e).

r .d. All laws and practices are beautiful because they are beneficial (*ōphelimon*) or pleasant (*hēdu*) or both (474e).

r .e. All sciences are beautiful for the same reason (475a).

s—The shameful (*aischron*) is defined by the opposite of the beautiful (*kalon*), which is pain (*lupē*) and badness (*kakia*) (475a).

t—If doing injustice (*adikein*) is more shameful than suffering injustice (*adikeisthai*), then it exceeds suffering injustice (*adikeisthai*), in pain (*lupē*), or in badness (*kakia*), or in both (475b). (From *s.*)

---

[42] Nietzsche's initial discussion of Socrates in the *Birth of Tragedy* (section 13) captures these qualities extremely well. He describes Socrates as worthy of "astonished veneration" and "awed amazement," but also as a "demonic power," a "monstrosity per defectum!" and an "enigmatical, unclassifiable, and inexplicable" figure. See Nietzsche (1967), 88–89.

[43] It is, of course, important to point out that my summary is not the way Plato himself actually presents his doctrine, and indeed Polus' expressions of perplexity punctuate the refutation and dramatize the dynamic effects that these ideas have on Polus' understanding of himself and the world around him. When commentators of the *Gorgias* only see Plato's doctrine in terms of this kind of logical argument, they fail to see what Plato is trying to dramatize in the dialogue. Similarly, Gorgias' refutation is punctuated by important signs of hesitation on his part (458b–c, 458d) and by the uproar of the crowd witnessing his refutation, which convinces him to continue conversing with Socrates (458c). These dramatic elements are also at play in the Callicles refutation as I will show in my treatment of it in section 2.3.

u—Doing injustice (*adikein*) does not surpass suffering injustice (*adikeisthai*) in pain (*lupē*) (475c).

v—So doing injustice (*adikein*) cannot surpass suffering injustice (*adikeisthai*) in both pain (*lupē*) and badness (*kakia*) (475c). (From *t*.)

(3) *q–v entail not p*—Therefore doing injustice (*adikein*) must surpass suffering injustice (*adikeisthai*) in badness. In other words, doing injustice (*adikein*) is worse (*kakion*) than suffering injustice (*adikeisthai*) (G. 475c).

(4) *not-p*—"What I was saying was therefore true, that neither I nor you nor any other human being would welcome doing injustice (*adikein*) rather than suffering injustice (*adikeisthai*); for it happens to be worse (*kakion*)" (475e).

There are actually three elements of Socrates' refutation of Polus that make it logically problematic, but for that reason, psychologically telling.[44] The first is that Socrates never fully specifies in all of the examples whether it is the agent, the patient, or the spectator who is judging the object to be useful/beneficial (*chrēsimon/ōphelimon*) or pleasant (*hēdu*). (I shall refer to this henceforth as the equivocation of perspective.) His first two examples, i.e., beautiful bodies, shapes and colors, seem to point to the pleasure of the spectator. But his next example also points to the pleasure of the agent performing the music as well as the one listening to it. His examples of laws and practices seem to point primarily to the participants, i.e., the agent enacting or exercising the laws, and those subject to them. Finally, the example of the sciences also seems to point primarily to the participants—i.e., the teacher or student who is engaged in the activity—and it seems strange to speak of a spectator to this activity.

The logical problem with this argument is that Socrates claims to have proven that doing injustice is worse *for the agent* than suffering injustice is *for the victim*, but he ends up only proving that doing injustice is worse *for X* than suffering injustice is *for X*, where *X* might be the agent performing the acts of injustice but might also be the community beholding his acts of injustice.[45] Socrates has not proven the stronger conclusion that doing injustice is worse *for the agent* because his definitions of the beautiful and shameful are indeterminate about whether it is the participants (the agent or victim) or the spectator (the community) who judge the act or thing to be useful/beneficial (*chrēsimon/ōphelimon*) or pleasant (*hēdu*), harmful (*kakon*) or painful (*lupēron*). In order to be logically valid the perspective would have to be fixed throughout the argument and when it is consistently fixed, it becomes clear

---

[44] Cf. Kahn (1983), 92–97; McKim (1988), 45.

[45] Bodds (1959), 249; Vlastos (1991), 144; Santas (1979), 239; and Kahn (1983), 91–92.

that Socrates' inference (see 3 and 4 above) is not logically entailed by the premises he gets Polus to accept.[46]

Instead, what Socrates does is to get Polus to agree to his definition of the beautiful (i.e., as the useful/beneficial [chrēsimon/ōphelimon] or the pleasant [hēdu] or both [r]) by considering the uses or pleasures experienced by spectators of beautiful bodies, colors, shapes, etc. However, he then gets Polus to concede to premise u (i.e., doing injustice [adikein] does not surpass suffering injustice [adikeisthai] in pain [lupē]) by considering the relative pain of the two agents or participants to an act of injustice. Thus, even if it is the case that suffering injustice is more painful to the victim of injustice than doing it is to the doer, this does not mean that Socrates can then conclude that doing injustice must then be more harmful to the agent. Given the definition of the beautiful and shameful he is working with, he has not foreclosed the logical possibility that while it is more painful for the victim to suffer injustice it might only be more harmful for the community (the spectator) than for the agent to commit it.

The second problematic aspect is the fact that Socrates subtly moves from the sensuous pleasures and benefits of the body to the intellectual pleasures and benefits of the mind. (I shall refer to this henceforth as the equivocation of goods.) In the first three examples Socrates speaks of the sensuous pleasures and benefits of beholding beautiful bodies, shapes and colors, and of listening to music.[47] But the example "relating to laws and practices" (kata tous nomous kai ta epitēdeumata) (474e) is more difficult to categorize. In fact, one of the central issues of the Gorgias, and of this refutation in particular, is justice (dikē/dikaiosunē): what it is, and whether it is better to do it or to suffer it. If justice consists of obeying laws that specify the punitive practices of punishment (timōria), then it would seem to be bad and painful for the victim's body even if it is beneficial for the body of the community as a whole (i.e., in terms of protection or prevention). However, if it consists of the practice of moderating their immoderate (akolaston) desires through chastisement and punishment (kolasis)[48] or helping others by disabusing them of false beliefs in the process

---

[46] Vlastos (1991, 142–43) tries to show this by consistently making the spectator the judge of whether something is painful or pleasant to behold. This demonstration is less successful than the ones by Dodds (1959, 249) and Santas (1979, 239) that rely on consistently making the community the judge of the usefulness or harmfulness of beautiful acts. Cf. Mackenzie (1981), 241–44 for a slightly different version of the equivocation of perspective.

[47] This is consistent with his definition of the beautiful in the Hippias Major, where he stipulates that only the pleasures of sight and sound (and not those of taste, touch, and smell) are considered beautiful (Hipp. Maj. 302e).

[48] Over the course of the dialogue the word for punishment changes from timōria (472d–e) to kolasis (476e–479b), and this change reflects the paradigm shift Plato is attempting to make from retributive to rehabilitative punishment. This shift is even more dramatic in the myth at the end of the Gorgias where Socrates moves from talking about retribution (timōria) at 525b to talking

of the Socratic elenchus or of suffering these kinds of practices, then it would seem to be *good and either painful or pleasurable or both* for the victim's body and mind.[49] Finally, the example of the sciences or instruction (*mathēsis*) makes the intellectual character of the possible benefit and/or pleasure even more explicit.

The third problematic aspect of Socrates' definitions of the beautiful and shameful in this refutation arises from their disjunctive (or at least potentially disjunctive) character: the beautiful is the pleasant or the beneficial or both; the shameful is the painful or the harmful or both. (I shall refer to this henceforth as the equivocation of disjunction.) This is unique because it is the only instance in the early Socratic dialogues where Socrates himself puts forth definitions that fail to meet one of the primary criteria he uses for defining kinds, properties, or characteristics.[50] This is the criterion that the kind, property, or characteristic being defined be common to all instances of it. Socrates' disjunctive definitions of the beautiful and shameful thus fail to meet this criterion. To be more precise, they sometimes fail to meet this criterion, even though Socrates' definition allows for the possibility that in some instances the shameful will be both painful and harmful and the beautiful will be both pleasant and good.

Various commentators of the *Gorgias* have picked up on one or more of these logically problematic characteristics of the dialectical encounter between Polus and Socrates in order to find fault with Plato's logic, without ever considering that what Plato might actually be doing is pointing to the different kinds of psychological forces that are brought into play when two very different

---

about rehabilitative punishment (*kolasis*) at 527b–c. *Contra* Stauffer (2006), 173 and Mackenzie (1981), 236–37, who both see the myth as making concessions to non-Socratic and retributive arguments. For a fuller treatment of the theme of punishment in democratic Athens and the Platonic paradigm shifts, see Allen (2000b).

[49] Socrates himself claims that he finds refutation both pleasant and good: "And of what men am I one? Those who are refuted with pleasure if I say something not true, and who refute with pleasure if someone should say something not true—and indeed not with less pleasure to be refuted that to refute. For I consider it a greater good, to the extent that it is a greater good to be released oneself from the greatest evil than to release another" (458a). See Elster (1999) and Konstan (2006) for an account of how one and the same emotion can contain both pleasure and pain in Aristotle's view of the emotions (*pathē*).

[50] According to Santas (1979, 104), "Socrates believes that an adequate definition must answer the following four things: What is the kind (characteristic, property) which (a) is the same (common) in all F things, and (b) is that by reason of which all F things are F, and (c) is that by which F things do not differ and (d) is that which in all F things one calls 'the F'?". *Contra* Santas, who considers the *Gorgias* an early Socratic dialogue, I think it is precisely because the *Gorgias* is a transitional dialogue dealing with the psychological and logical aspects of the Socratic elenchus that Plato's definitions of the beautiful and the shameful do not conform to the same logical strictures as the early dialogues.

worldviews or conceptual schemas collide.[51] While McKim and Kahn address this oversight, they explicate the psychological aspects of the refutation only in terms of its *ad hominem* character and overlook the fact that the refutation itself contains a very interesting definition of the shameful that reveals a number of interesting characteristics of shame. Also, while they both notice the equivocations I mentioned above (i.e., the equivocation of perspective and the equivocation of goods), they don't see these as revealing important features about the phenomena of the beautiful (*to kalon*) and the shameful (*to aischron*) in human life.

In contrast, I think the equivocation of perspective reflects the unique and dynamic character that the fine/beautiful/noble (*kalon*) and the ugly/shameful/ignoble (*aischron*) had for the Greeks and continues to have for us today. The experience of beauty and shame involves simultaneously looking in two directions at once: inward to the self who acts in the world, and outward to the world shared with others who gaze upon us.[52] The spectator who criticizes the self in shame or who praises the self in beauty can be appropriated into the very ideas or self-images by which one then actively creates and passively perceives the world. So there is always the possibility that the spectator and the agent/patient can become one and the same, even though there is also the possibility that the spectator's perspective will not be appropriated into our psyche. In the occurrent experience of shame we entertain the spectator's gaze upon the self as a criticism of this self and thus feel the gap that then opens up between the old self that we were and the new self we might now become. The experience is thus a "disinterested" one because we are *in between* this old and new self and are in the process of transforming the very interests and preferences that we had prior to our recognition of the gaze of the other.[53]

We do not, though, have to assent to the judgment of the spectator and transform ourselves in accordance with this other, because we can also hide

---

[51] See n.37 above for a list of these commentators. Vlastos (1991 and 1995) has argued that Socrates (and indeed Plato himself) equivocates on the perspective of the judgment of the beautiful or shameful because he does not have a fully developed notion of the beautiful, and by this he means the Kantian notion of a disinterested pleasure in apprehending something that is in no way related to one's own desires or interests. According to Vlastos, if Plato had such a notion of the disinterested pleasure of apprehending that is the "true" hallmark of aesthetic judgment then he would have consistently retained the spectator as the referent for the judgment of the beautiful and shameful. However, as I show in this section, Vlastos' solution fails to do justice to the real depths of Plato's insights about the phenomena of the beautiful and shameful in human life.

[52] Arendt's notion of judgment, derived in part from the Greek experience of politics, also involves this bidirectional and dynamic character. As Zerilli (1995, 164–65) argues, Arendtian judgment reveals "who one is" at the same that it reveals the "world," and both of these creations do not exist prior to the communicative interaction.

[53] Zerilli (2005, 176–77) argues that the unique perspective or position from which political judgments take place is one of *outsideness*: "It is this third perspective that Arendt has in mind when she said that imaginative visiting involves not the mutual understanding of 'one another as

from, transform, or contest this other or simply hold it in abeyance even while acknowledging its weight as an other.[54] Polus, however, enters the conversation with Socrates as a person who *is* apt to be a slave to public opinion,[55] and for this very reason the distinction between the agent and the spectator tends to collapse in his case. As Polus tells Socrates at 462c, *he* (Polus) thinks that gratifying or flattering public opinion is a *kalon* (fine/beautiful/noble) pursuit.[56] Thus, *contra* Kahn, I think that Polus is being sincere when he agrees with Socrates that doing injustice is more shameful than suffering it. Socrates just gets him to consider how the actions of the tyrant, which Polus vividly described in his Archelaus speech (470d–471d), would be viewed by the Athenian community that Polus so admires and wishes to gratify.

Instead, it is Socrates who considers it ignoble flattery to turn away from a concern with one's own beauty in order to gratify other people. At 465b, Socrates tells Polus that flattery is like the practice of cosmetics: "it is evil-doing, deceitful, ignoble, and unfree, deceiving with shapes, colors, smoothness, and garments, so as to make them, as they take upon themselves an alien beauty, neglect their own beauty that comes through gymnastic."[57] Polus, on the other hand, considers gratification noble because he takes the spectator's rather than the agent's perspective of his own actions. This is precisely why Socrates begins with two wholly other-directed examples of beauty in his refutation of Polus: in the case of beautiful bodies, shapes, and colors, the judgment of beauty is determined solely by the benefit or pleasure that the user or beholder gets from the beautiful being. In these examples the material beauty of the body or shape is not presented as being either good or pleasant to the being that exemplifies it. In this respect, it is similar to the flattering practice or "alien beauty" of cosmetics: it is directed to the gratification of the beholder and not to the good of the one who wears the makeup. (The examples of shapes and colors is, I think, explicitly inserted to remind the reader of this earlier discussion of the "alien beauty" of cosmetics which deceives with shapes and colors at 465b).

---

individual persons', but the understanding that involves coming to 'see the same world from one another's standpoint, to see the same in very different and frequently opposing aspects'."

[54] See Calhoun (2004) for an account of the ways in which we can feel shame even when we don't agree with or want to conform to the opinions held by the one doing the shaming.

[55] Cf. Kahn (1983), 95; and Benardete (1991), 41–44.

[56] See Benardete (1991, 32) for an account of how Polus' knack for gratifying is used by Socrates to launch an attack on rhetoric without launching a direct attack on Gorgias. This account supports my argument that what Plato primarily attacks in the *Gorgias* is flattering rhetoric and not Gorgianic rhetoric.

[57] Monoson (2000, 223–36) argues that in Book 8 of the *Republic* Plato uses the image of the multicolored cloak (*peplos*) (which was the central symbol of the Panathenaic festival and was presented to the cult statue of Athena) to suggest the possible ways in which the festivals of democracy can be deceiving rather than enlightening if the spectator does not actively critique and judge the patterns being presented to them.

Why then does Polus accept Socrates' definition without raising this objection? He does so precisely because this corresponds to Polus' experience of the noble and shameful in his own life and to his brand of rhetoric that is aimed at flattering the audience's desires and prejudices. In other words, Polus' sense of shame is wholly attuned to his audience and its objectified public images of the citizen and the tyrant. This spectator view of human action was evident not only in Polus' estimation of his own actions but also in his judgment of the actions of others. His speech on Archelaus was grounded, not in any personal experience of tyranny, but rather in a projection of the conventional views of justice and injustice onto the external actions of a person.[58] In this speech the just and unjust were totally conventional: Archelaus was a slave by birth, and therefore to remain just, according to Polus, he should have remained a slave (471a). It was Socrates and not Polus who said that he would have to talk with Archelaus in order to determine whether or not he was just and happy, and therefore whether his actions should be considered just or unjust (470d). Polus and not Socrates is deeply conventional: his opinion of what is noble and just in others comes from the city's customs and laws rather than from his own insights into the person's motivations gained via a rational dialectic with that person. In acquiring these opinions, Polus has internalized an external authoritative standard and he expresses the opinions of the city in his judgment of himself and others. Polus thus exemplifies the "alien beauty" of cosmetics, or what I will elaborate in the next chapter as flattering shame. He is oriented to gratifying and preserving the existing public opinions about tyrants and he does so by expressing two popular but inconsistent moral attitudes in his Archelaus speech: "admiration for success, power, and wealth, no matter how obtained, [and] condemnation of unjust or criminal acts."[59]

I now want to turn to the equivocation of goods in order to show how this works in the Polus refutation and how it illustrates other important aspects of the beautiful and the shameful. Here I think that McKim nicely elucidates the direction in which Socrates *tries* to move Polus even though he (McKim) is overly optimistic about the extent to which Polus is capable of following Socrates' move. McKim argues that the refutation works by getting Polus to recognize the nonmaterial benefits of the soul that can wean him from his envy of the tyrant, Archelaus, and the material benefits that are obtained by Archelaus' successful injustice. In other words, he assumes that the subtle transition from

---

[58] As Benardete (1991, 42) aptly puts it, "The real tyrant is wholly opaque to Polus; he replaces him with an imaginary figure whom he can envy for his happiness and denounce for his injustice." See Frank (2007, 455–56) for the ways in which the tyrant's outward appearance can dazzle and deceive those who act like children and judge only from outward appearances.

[59] Kahn (1983), 95. Stauffer (2006, 62, 117–18) astutely argues that this ambivalence about unjust acts characterizes both Polus and Callicles. According to him, they both wish that virtue and justice would make one happy and secure even though they fear it cannot do this, thus turning instead to a less than fully sincere praise of the life of tyranny.

the bodily to the nonmaterial goods of the soul is noticed and fully appreciated by Polus. Thus, when Socrates asks him to consider the relative pain and harm of doing injustice, he is not only able to consider the pain of the sufferer, but has been

> primed to think in terms of another category familiar to but neglected by him, nonmaterial harm . . . He must, then, feel it to be "harmful" to the agent in some sense other than the material damage he inflicts upon his victim—in other words, that it causes the agent nonmaterial damage. In Socratic terms, Polus already believes that it is detrimental to the health of the agent's soul—and that such soul-harm outweighs the material benefits of committing injustice, since otherwise he would feel it to be admirable by virtue of being on balance beneficial.[60]

McKim thus thinks that the refutation works as a transparent didactic tool: Polus has a conversion experience and recognizes the nonmaterial harm caused by the tyrant's acts of injustice. Indeed, McKim even goes so far as to state, "Clearly, he [Polus] can never really have believed that committing injustice, with its harm to our soul-health, is preferable to the merely material ills of suffering it."[61] But I think that this overlooks Polus' genuine concern for the goods of the body and the external goods that the tyrant obtains through force, and I don't think that Polus now considers the tortures of the unsuccessful tyrant he described earlier as *merely* material ills.

Thus while I think that Socrates does want to wean Polus from these material goods or at least suggest to him that there are other nonmaterial goods (alluded to by Socrates' suggestion about the beauty of the sciences), the dialogue itself suggests that this conversion attempt has been less than successful. As I mentioned earlier, Plato alludes to this by signaling Polus' hesitation and skepticism in his response to Socrates' conclusions. Polus is confused and perplexed by Socrates' arguments rather than fully convinced by them. Moreover, McKim's solution suggests that Polus ends up with the kind of indifference to material and external goods that is characteristic of Socrates' philosophic way of life. I don't think that Socrates (or Plato) believes that *this* kind of consensus has been or could be achieved between Polus and Socrates.[62] Instead, I think that the refutation is aimed at a much weaker form of consensus, and that Plato is trying to show what this weaker consensus might be and why Socrates still fails to achieve it (as is evidenced by Polus' unresolved perplexity and confusion.)

The first thing that it is important to notice is that Polus preaches tyranny but doesn't practice it. Polus is a student of rhetoric and of his teacher Gorgias,

---

[60] McKim (1988), 47.

[61] McKim (1988), 47.

[62] Cf. Stauffer (2006, 74–75) who shares my view that McKim is overly optimistic about Polus' conversion to a Socratic form of life.

not a student of violence and the tyrant Archelaus. Polus wants the esteem and honor that he gets from gratifying his audience *more* than he wants the goods he would obtain through killing and torturing them, but he has not fully reconciled these desires in his own life.[63] He desires a certain type of nonmaterial good that depends on speech and not force. In this sense his own life does (at least weakly) embody the Socratic principle that doing injustice is worse than suffering it because Polus himself doesn't do the very acts of injustice which he attributes to the tyrant (i.e., killing, stealing, and torturing). Instead, he devotes himself to the practice of rhetoric that requires some kind of mutuality between the speaker and the audience and some kind of devotion to the pleasures of listening and talking to others. The equivocation of goods that is characteristic of Socrates' definitions of the *kalon* (fine/beautiful/noble) and *aischron* (ugly/shameful/base) is thus both an attempt to wean Polus from his envy of the material goods that the tyrant obtains through force, and an illustration of the fact that the *kalon* (fine/beautiful/noble) pursuits are linked to the nonmaterial pleasures of speaking and listening, watching, and being watched by others. However, *contra* McKim, this does not mean that Polus converts or is capable of fully converting to the Socratic way of life. Instead, Socrates (and through him Plato) attempts to show that the two different ways of life are at least weakly linked together by their devotion to the activity of speech and their mutual opposition to brute force.[64]

This however, still leaves the problem of Polus' perplexity and the disjunctive character of the beautiful and the shameful. I now want to explain how these two things are linked together. As I mentioned above, Socrates' definitions of the beautiful and the shameful in this section are only *potentially* disjunctive (and thus also potentially conjunctive): The beautiful is the useful/beneficial (*chrēsimon/ōphelimon*) or the pleasant (*hēdu*) or both; the shameful is the harmful (*kakon*) or painful (*lupēron*), or both. Again, it is Polus who thinks that gratifying or flattering one's audience is a *kalon* (fine/beautiful/noble) pursuit, but as Socrates tells Polus at 465a, this kind of activity, like cosmetics and cookery, "guesses at the pleasant without the best (*tou hēdeos stochazetai aneu tou beltistou*)." In this instance, the *kalon* activity of delivering speeches

---

[63] *Contra* Kastely (1991, 100) who thinks that Polus exemplifies an ethos of "exclusively external goods." As Nieuwenburg (2004, 460–61) argues (with respect to Aristotle's treatment of shame), the person who has a sense of shame that attunes him to reputable or honorable propositions (*endoxa*) and who desires esteem is morally superior to a person who has no shame and who admires things like money, because the former is at least potentially able to acquire a sincere desire for the common good.

[64] Similarly, at the beginning of the *Phaedrus*, Socrates explicitly points out that he and Phaedrus are "fellow Corybantic revelers" because they are both lovers of all kind of speeches (*Phdr.* 228c). This, however, does not preclude the fact that there are vast differences between them in terms of how each one listens to and judges the speeches that they hear, and these differences become progressively clearer over the course of the dialogue.

is only pleasant (and not beneficial) because it flatters the audience's existing prejudices and beliefs without ever suggesting how or why they ought to change. The audience is pleased to have its own prejudices soothed and Polus is honored by them for doing so. And this occurs even when these popular prejudices themselves contain an ambivalent attitude toward tyranny: the tyrant is secretly admired for getting what everyone wants, but is publicly condemned for doing precisely this.[65]

Notice too, that if the *kalon* (fine/beautiful/noble) is identified solely with the *pleasure* of recognition, then the corresponding notion of the *aischron* (shameful/ugly) is identified solely with the *pain* of misrecognition (e.g., loss of esteem or respect). For Polus and his audience it is painful *and therefore* "*shameful*" to be shown that they don't live up to these images that they endeavor to project to one another. As I will argue in the next chapter, in flattering shame the painfulness of a shame situation is equated with its shamefulness, and one's sense of shame then subsequently orients the person to avoid these kinds of painful situations (e.g., Socratic refutation) even when they might be benefited by them. The flattering rhetoric that Polus preaches thus aims at ensuring that the occurrent experience of shame, which is always in some sense painful, is absent from any public deliberations.

In contrast to this, Socrates thinks that his elenchic activity of refuting and being refuted is equally pleasant for the person performing it and the one suffering it, but that it is actually a greater good for the person who suffers it (458a). This is because having false opinions about the best life is the greatest evil for human beings (458b), and thus being released from them is a greater good than releasing others. When Socrates attains knowledge of his own ignorance he is benefited by being released from falsehood and he is pleased at the insight into human life that this gives him. Thus for Socrates the pleasant and the good do correspond in the *kalon* (fine/beautiful/noble) experience of elenchic refutation. (Note, too, that in this sense Socrates hopes to become a "patient" of the very people he incessantly questions, because he hopes that they in turn will help to release him from his own false opinions. The activity of Socrates' shaming elenchus requires the willingness of both parties to reciprocally take up the position of doctor and patient. If this is the case, then it should not be surprising that Plato himself would have performed such a service to Socrates in his own dialogues by actually disagreeing with and shaming his own teacher. I shall turn to this possibility in my account of Platonic respectful shame in chapter 4.)

But this correspondence requires a certain activity on the part of the person who is being benefited or refuted in this way, that is, it requires that the person reflect upon his or her own life and the ways in which it differs from the false

[65] Benardete (1991), 44.

opinion previously held. The correspondence of the beneficial and the pleasant in the experience of the *kalon* thus requires a certain kind of reflexive activity on the part of the patient and is not guaranteed by simply being shamed by Socrates. The fact that Socrates' definitions of the beautiful and the shameful are potentially disjunctive or conjunctive reflects the fact that they are not virtues for Plato, but rather are the psychic mechanisms by which we come to have certain virtues or vices and thus become certain types of people. They have a part to play in both the education and the corruption of our psyche in its ongoing interactions with the world of others.[66] The question of whether shame becomes a virtue or vice depends in large part on how we try to fill the gap between the self and the other that opens up for us. Their disjunction or conjunction is an achievement and not a given in human life, and Polus' state of perplexity and confusion is evidence of this very fact. If Polus were to see the connection between his love of speechifying and the benefits (to himself and the city) that a truly noble rhetoric would offer, and if he were to begin to engage in this other kind of rhetoric, then he would be able to truly apply the conjunctive definition of the beautiful to his own activities. Instead, he exemplifies the definition of the shameful (characteristic of flattering shame) wherein painful (*lupēron*) activities are considered to be shameful (*aischron*). Socrates, on the other hand, makes it clear that he calls only bad things shameful (*ta gar kaka aischra kalō*) (463d), and thus leaves open the possibility that pain might be a necessary and beneficial aspect of a noble rhetoric.

In chapter 4, I will show how Plato attempts to redress this perplexing character of the Socratic shaming elenchus by offering the interlocutors a positive and concrete image of the new way of life that might become possible to them if they were to change their life in accordance with the insights Socrates attempts to show them. But I now want to turn to the refutation of Callicles, to examine the most negative kind of reaction elicited by Socrates' shaming refutations.

[66] Thus although I agree with Nieuwenburg's (2004, 463) argument that shame can have a role to play in making us more sincere deliberators who develop a genuine concern for the common good that was originally not part of our pre-deliberative preferences, I disagree with him that shame always has this "direction of fit" toward the common good. This is because we can develop a sense of shame that focuses on the painful rather than the beneficial aspects of the occurrent experience of shame and that then compels us to hide from the beneficial truths that come to light in the shame experience. Konstan (2006, 96) suggests that Aristotle treats *aidōs* as a virtue like courage or moderation in the *Eudemian Ethics*, and he mentions that the Stoics treated *aidōs* as a healthy sentiment whereas *aischunē* was classified as a vicious emotion. However, Konstan (2006, 99–104) goes on to show that *aischunē* was not treated as a virtue by Aristotle, even if *anaischuntia* (shamelessness) was probably a vice. This is similar to how Plato treats shame (*aischunē*) (and for that matter, *aidōs*) in his works. Shame is not a virtue for him, even if both *anaischuntia* and *anaideia* (shamelessness) are vices. More importantly, as I show in chapter 3, a certain form of shame (*aischunē*) can itself be at the heart of the vice of flattery.

The Refutation of Callicles

The refutation of Callicles is considerably longer than the one directed at Gorgias or Polus. In fact, it accounts for more than half of the dialogue. What is so interesting about the Callicles refutation is the fact that Socrates presents a number of different arguments to try to persuade Callicles to retract his indiscriminate hedonism thesis.[67] As Nichols (1998, 144) points out, this is quite a contrast with the Polus section where "Socrates criticizes Polus's several rhetorical approaches, insisting on his own dialectical argumentation alone; [whereas] here Socrates himself tries several means of persuasion on Callicles." This, of course, makes sense if, as I argued in the last chapter, the "Socrates" of the *Gorgias* becomes progressively more Platonic over the course of the dialogue. What we see in the Callicles section is not just a more Platonic Socrates who espouses certain Pythagorean doctrines and myths; rather we also see (1) how the Socratic shaming elenchus reveals what both Callicles and Socrates consider to be honorable or shameful ways of life, (2) what effects the Socratic shaming elenchus has on a person like Callicles, and (3) what types of arguments prove to be more (or less) appealing to a person like Callicles. In other words, the Callicles section reveals Plato's own deepening reflections on the psychology of shame, and on the salutary and pernicious results of his teacher's shaming elenchus.[68]

The first argument consists of an extremely ascetic myth that likens human beings to leaky vessels (493a–d). Here, the soul of the person engaged in the hedonistic pursuit of maximum pleasure is compared to a leaky vessel that continually needs to be replenished.[69] Socrates argues that the best life would be the life of minimal desires where the vessel has few or no holes, and thus does not need continual replenishment. After making this argument he asks Callicles, "Well, am I persuading you somewhat and do you change to the

---

[67] It is important to note that Callicles begins with a defense of immoderation and hedonism, which is not necessarily the same as the doctrine of *indiscriminate* hedonism that Socrates gets him to agree to in their conversation. For a discussion of the differences between these doctrines, see Klosko (1984), 128–34; Gentzler (1995), 37–38; and Stauffer (2006), 104–5, 109. Although I agree with Benardete (1991) and Stauffer (2006) that the philosopher might be the greatest and most prudent hedonist, I disagree with them if this is meant to suggest that the philosopher is shameless or without any desire for the noble (*kalon*) pleasures of order, fit, symmetry, harmony, honor, victory, or esteem. The philosopher's shame (*aischunē*) is harmonized with his desire for the truth and this fact may make it appear as if he is shameless, but this is only because his shame (*aischunē*) is not slavishly attuned to the conventions of his city. For more on this point, see chapter 3 below.

[68] Kaufer (1978); Klosko (1983); and Cooper (1999), chapter 2 all argue that the psychology of the *Gorgias* points ahead to the more complex psychologies of the *Republic* and/or the *Phaedrus*.

[69] For the Pythagorean origins of this myth, see chapter 1 n.37.

position that the orderly are happier than the intemperate? Or even if I tell myths of many other such things, will you nonetheless not change anything?" (493d). Callicles then asserts that he will not change in response to such arguments (493d). As if to test this point, Socrates proceeds to tell another similar myth and asks, "In saying these things, do I somewhat persuade you to grant that the orderly life is better than the intemperate, or do I not persuade you?" (494a). And Callicles once again utters, "You do not persuade me Socrates. For that man who has filled his jars no longer has any pleasure" (494a).

Socrates then drops this line of argument altogether and proceeds to his "catamite" (*kinaidos*) argument. I want to suggest that he does this because he has discovered that the life of the ascetic holds no appeal for Callicles.[70] If Callicles does not honor ascetics, then he will not feel ashamed to learn that his hedonistic thesis is inconsistent with such a life.[71] Instead, Socrates must appeal to the ideals of action that Callicles himself looks up to and admires when constructing his praise of the life of hedonism and *pleonexia* (greed or taking more than one's share), and he knows what these consist of from the initial speech that Callicles makes when he bursts onto the scene (481b–485d). Here Callicles praises the life of courageous warriors and political leaders and condemns philosophers for being inexperienced in "human pleasures and desires" (484d). Thus Socrates' next line of argument tries to show Callicles how his hedonism thesis is inconsistent with *these* ideals.

Accordingly, just before making this argument Socrates tells Callicles, "Now continue just as you began, and do not hold back through shame (*apaischunēi*). Nor, it would appear, must I hold back through shame (*apaischunthēnai*)" (494c). The argument involves showing Callicles that the hedonism which he espouses would lead to the conclusion that the life of a stone-curlew (*charadrios*),[72] or a life devoted to itching and scratching, or the life of a catamite (*kinaidos*) would all belong among the best and happiest. This is because such people are continually experiencing the desire to scratch and the pleasure of satisfying this urge (494d–e). Callicles then responds, "Are you not ashamed (*ouk aischunēi*) Socrates, to lead the arguments into such things?" (494e). To which Socrates responds that he is just following Callicles' own argument—that the pleasant and the good are the same—to its logical conclusion (494e–495a).

---

[70] As Dodds (1959, 299) points out, the belief that the ascetic ideal amounted to a kind of death-in-life was a popular opinion.

[71] Stauffer (2006, 107–8) also points to the fact that the myth of the jars is not used to persuade Callicles but to show that such an image would never persuade Callicles, although he thinks that this is because a myth about the afterlife holds no appeal to Callicles.

[72] Dodds (1959, 307); Nichols (1998, 87 n.107); and Stauffer 2006 (110) all note that the stone-curlew (*charadrios*) is a bird that eats and excretes at the same time.

Callicles' outburst reveals that it is he and not Socrates who feels shame when investigating these things wherever they may lead.[73] Socrates is less susceptible to the conventional standards regarding these things than someone like Callicles, who had earlier claimed that the best life is lived only according to the standards of nature (484a–b).[74] As I argued in chapter 1, the life of the catamite was considered to be a form of homosexual love incompatible with the active life of an eminent statesman. Thus, "what Callicles is being asked to count among the logically possible constituents of the *aretē* (virtue) and happiness of superior men is the pleasure taken from an experience which is not only regarded as unmanly and humiliating but as legally depriving the person in question of his citizenship rights and his chance at a political career."[75] Socrates knows that it is precisely the life of the active citizen and statesmen that Callicles admires as the best and most honorable, and so he picks the one example that is most at odds with this ideal according to the conventional standards of democratic Athens.

The way that Callicles subsequently responds to this "shameful" example is also interesting because it reveals that there can be competing feelings of shame within the same individual. In the next passage he says, "In order that the speech should not contradict me, if I assert that they are different, I assert that they are the same" (495a). To this assertion Socrates responds, "You are corrupting the first speeches, Callicles, and you would no longer be sufficiently examining with me the things that are, if you're going to speak contrary to how things seem in your own opinion" (495a). At this point, Callicles is more concerned with how the immediate witnesses to this debate (his fellow interlocutors as well as the crowd witnessing the entire discussion) will view his defeat at the hands of Socrates than he is with how he himself views the life of a catamite.[76] His shame is turned outwards to how he will be seen if he loses a round to Socrates rather than to his own view of catamites and political

---

[73] Dodds (1959, 307); Kahn (1983, 105–6); Stauffer (2006, 110); and Gish (2006, 65 n.78) also note that it is Callicles and not Socrates who feels the shame at these examples. *Contra* Klosko (1984, 136), who claims that Callicles has no shame.

[74] This means that Socrates is unabashed but not shameless. For a full defense of this distinction, see chapter 3 below.

[75] Kahn (1983), 106–7.

[76] Stauffer (2006, 116) similarly notes Callicles' desire to remain consistent and avoid refutation by Socrates, although he does not link this to Callicles' awareness of the audience witnessing the refutation. Lewis (1986, 205) notes that there are two types of shame operative in Callicles at this point: he is ashamed of his shame because he claimed that he was not susceptible to feeling shame at merely conventional standards, and he is ashamed of the indecent consequences of his indiscriminate hedonism thesis. The suggestions by Stauffer and Lewis might also be correct, but this actually strengthens my point that there can be competing feelings of shame within the same person. There might be two or three different internalized or external others before whom one feels shame, and each of these others might not share the same opinion concerning what is shameful about your situation.

leaders. Socrates' assertion shows that he suspects Callicles of no longer sin-
cerely engaging in the search for the truth about how one ought to live, but
only trying to say things that will prevent him from losing this particular
argument under the watchful gaze of a crowd of others.

The other possibility, of course, is that like Socrates, Callicles is truly devoted
to the logic of the argument and to seeing where it will lead. And I believe that
Socrates' next line of questioning is meant as a way of testing whether or not
this is the case. Here Socrates tries to show Callicles that his hedonism is not
just shameful but logically incoherent. The argument consists of showing that
pleasure and pain do not really work "like an ordinary pair of conceptual
opposites, since they do not logically exclude one another over a given terrain."[77] To use Charles Kahn's summary of the argument:

(1) Good (fairing well, happiness) and its opposite are not found simul-
    taneously in the same subject, and do not cease together.
(2) Pleasure and its opposite (pain) are found simultaneously in the same
    subject, and cease together (e.g., the pleasure of drinking lasts only
    as long as the pain of thirst).
(3) Therefore, pleasure is not the good.[78]

Callicles does not respond to the conclusion of this argument at all.[79] In fact,
he tries to squirm out of it in the middle by asserting, "I don't know what
sophisms you are making, Socrates" (497a). Instead, Gorgias—who has been
a silent witness to the entire discussion since his own refutation—jumps in
and says, "Don't Callicles; but answer for our sake too, so that the arguments
may be brought to an end" (497b). Callicles then complains to Gorgias, "Socrates is always like this, Gorgias. He asks small things, of little or no worth,
and refutes them" (497b). And in response Gorgias tells Callicles, "But what
difference does it make to you? It is not at all your honor involved here, Callicles. Submit to Socrates' refuting however he wishes" (497b). Callicles then
reluctantly agrees to go on with the questioning, because "it seems good to
Gorgias" to do so (497c).

Callicles' failures to respond to this line of questioning, and his utterances
that such questions are worth little or nothing, thus establish the fact that a
life devoted to logical investigation has little or no appeal to *him*. (The fact
that Gorgias jumps into the argument and urges Callicles to continue suggests
that Gorgias *is* interested in what Socrates is trying to show him with this
particular refutation of Callicles.) As Gorgias himself explains, Callicles does

[77] Kahn (1983), 107.

[78] Kahn (1983), 107.

[79] McKim (1988), 42; and Kahn (1983), 107. See also Stauffer (2006, 113) and Irwin (1979,
202), who both note that Callicles goes further than simply ignoring this argument and actually
resorts to abuse for this silly talk.

not honor the philosophic type of life and thus does not feel any shame at being shown that his thesis is logically incoherent.[80] What Socrates does next involves, once again, appealing to the type of life that Callicles honors most and showing him that his hedonism is inconsistent with such a way of life.

As I mentioned above, Callicles' initial speech revealed that he honors the life of the brave and courageous warrior and leader (483c–484c). Thus Socrates' final line of argument is meant to show Callicles that his hedonism is inconsistent with this way of life and he does this by getting Callicles to admit that cowards actually experience more pleasure in fleeing from battle than courageous men do who bravely face their death (498a–c). This concession, in conjunction with Callicles' indiscriminate hedonism (i.e., the pleasant is the good), leads to the conclusion that cowards are actually better individuals than courageous men (499a–b). Callicles' admiration for courageous warriors will not allow him to admit this, so instead he retracts his hedonism with the statement, "As if you thought that I or any other human being did not consider some pleasures better and others worse!" (499b).[81] Interestingly enough, it is Callicles and not Socrates who makes the assertion that all human beings consider some pleasures better than others. In other words, Socrates finally gets his most recalcitrant "witness" to agree to the thesis that he has been trying to establish.

Unfortunately, however, this agreement proves to be temporary.[82] When Socrates proceeds to elaborate the consequences that follow from this—that just punishment is better for the soul than intemperance—Callicles pleads with Socrates to release him from the argument:

> I don't know what you are saying, Socrates, so ask someone else . . . How violent you are, Socrates. But if you're persuaded by me, you'll bid this argument farewell, or else you'll converse with someone else . . . Couldn't you go through the argument yourself, either speaking by yourself or answering yourself? (505c–d)

In response to this, Socrates tells Callicles that the argument should be carried through to its conclusion, but that "if you don't wish it, then let's bid it farewell and go away" (506a). Before Callicles is allowed to scurry away, however, Gorgias jumps in once again, and says, "But it doesn't seem to me, Socrates, that we should go away yet; rather you should finish going through the argu-

---

[80] As Stauffer (2006), 91, 121 points out, Callicles' hostility to philosophy was displayed in his desire, expressed in his first speech, to kick and beat Socrates.

[81] A number of commentators have noted this important retraction on Callicles' part. See Stauffer (2006), 115; McKim (1988), 22–23; and Kahn (1983), 108–11.

[82] Although Vlastos (1983a) uses Callicles' assertion that all human beings regard this thesis to be true to make his case that Plato is pointing to *logical* problems with the Socratic elenchus, he does not notice that Callicles' inability to hold onto this thesis shows the *psychological* problems with the Socratic elenchus. It is unable to fully persuade someone like Callicles.

ment" (506a–b). Callicles then agrees to proceed, but finishes the dialogue as an extremely reluctant witness to the things that Socrates expounds. The conclusion of the dialogue thus begins with the very different reactions of Socrates' two remaining verbal witnesses, Gorgias and Callicles.[83] I will return to the implications of these responses below, but before turning to this task I want to offer a number of remarks on the different aspects of shame evidenced by the Callicles refutation.

THE MECHANISMS OF SHAME

The refutation of Callicles reveals a number of important things about the mechanisms of shame, especially in terms of the other before whom one feels shame and the different kinds of relationships between the self and the other that are possible in shame. The first is that the other who witnesses the person's shameful action or behavior can be either an actual or an internalized and imaginary one.[84] This is important to note because it overcomes the simplistic view of shame as an emotion that works only in small or primitive face-to-face societies like ancient Athens, or that it is only ever a matter of saving face in front of an actual audience.[85] When Callicles is first ashamed at the image of the catamite (*kinaidos*), his feeling of shame arises out of the gap that he now recognizes between his indiscriminate hedonism thesis, which entails such a way of life, and his admired and internalized other of the Athenian statesman and leader. One part of himself (the part that honors courageous leaders) looks down upon the other part that believes in indiscriminate hedonism and that now comes to light as a catamite (*kinaidos*). Here the experience of shame involves the experience of being seen inappropriately by an other but this other is in fact internal to his self or psyche.

Then, when Callicles refuses to retract his catamite thesis, he does so because his shame is provoked by the immediate audience that is witnessing his discus-

---

[83] Cf. Gish (2006), 67.

[84] Williams (1993, 81) articulates this distinction in response to the "silly mistake" of supposing that "the feeling behind every decision or thought . . . governed by shame is literally and immediately the fear of being seen." Later he describes the imagined other as the internalization of the gaze of "a watcher or witness" (1993), 219. Both Elster (1999, 146) and Sokolon (2006, 111) note that Aristotle specifically says that one can feel shame at the "imagination of disgrace" (*Rhet.* 1384a). I think the imaginary other can be further differentiated into a realistic or a fantastical other, and this distinction becomes important in the next chapter.

[85] Dodds (1951, 17–18) uses the notion of face-to-face societies to distinguish "shame cultures" from "guilt cultures." This is a distinction that he borrows from the anthropologist Ruth Benedict's book *The Chrysanthemum and the Sword*. This oversimplistic distinction between shame and guilt cultures (and the concomitant tendency to see shame cultures as more "primitive" than guilt cultures, or shame as a more primitive emotion than guilt) is one of the main targets of my own and Williams' (1993) treatments of shame. For an extended discussion of this issue, see chapter 6.

sion with Socrates. Once again his shame involves having an inadequacy in his self revealed to an other but now this other is the actual audience that is witnessing the fact that Callicles is about to be shown up or refuted by Socrates. At this point his regard for this external audience temporarily cancels out or at least overwhelms the shame that had made him feel contempt for the life of a catamite. (That this is only temporary is evidenced by the fact that Socrates once again appeals to the internalized other of the courageous warrior and leader in his final refutation of Callicles.) In other words, Callicles, like most human beings, is motivated by a desire for reputation (*doxa*), esteem, or honor (*timē*) from other people around him and for self-esteem, and he feels shame (*aischunē*) when his actions or beliefs are found to be discordant with either of these two others.[86]

Callicles' final shame-refutation reveals another interesting aspect of the other that can be involved in shame. This is that shame "need not be just a matter of being seen, but of being seen by an observer with a certain view."[87] In the refutation immediately preceding the last one of the Callicles section, Callicles does not feel ashamed when Socrates tries to show him that his hedonistic thesis is logically problematic. This is because he himself feels contempt for philosophy and the whole way of life devoted to such "silliness and drivel" (486c). As he tells Socrates in his opening speech, he avoids those dark corners

---

[86] Cairns (1993, 100) points out that this was also true of *aidōs* in Homeric society. Elster (1999, 332–417) argues that any explanation of social behavior has to take into account the ways in which the desire for esteem and self-esteem can pull in opposite directions, and can work against one's material interests (e.g., Callicles' desire for esteem from the crowd and for self-esteem from his internalized ideal of the courageous warrior pull him in different directions, and they both pull him away from hedonism). Elster (1999, 417) adds that the role of the desire for esteem and self-esteem in self-deception still remains a theoretical puzzle for social scientists. The notion of flattering shame that I discuss in chapter 3 illuminates a form of collective self-deception in democratic polities that was as prevalent in Plato's day as it is in our own.

[87] Williams (1993), 82. Williams (1993, endnote 1, 221–22) further differentiates the second half of this distinction by arguing that this more discerning other can be a respected or disrespected observer or simply one with whom we agree or disagree, or both. And here he argues that this distinction is important for modeling the ethical operations of shame. Calhoun's (2004) otherwise interesting account of moral shame overlooks these subtleties in Williams' account. Cf. Wollheim (1999, 153–54 and 256 n.7) who corrects Taylor's (1985) tendency to conflate internalization with identification in her account of shame. Wollheim (1999) argues that we only feel shame when we have identified with the internalized other; however, I think this reflects his Freudian interpretation of shame as concerned only with the ego-ideal. I would argue that *aischunē* for the Greeks can be felt both for an internalized other and an other with whom we have identified, though it is likely to be more intense in the latter case. (See Arist. *Rhet.* 1383b3, 1384a15–b23.). I think Calhoun's (2004) account of moral shame makes a convincing case that this is also true for us today. She argues that we can feel shame at racist or misogynist comments made by another person simply because these are norms we have probably internalized from our still racist and misogynist societies. In such cases, we are ashamed of the collective self to which we belong, and which we may now feel we have not done enough to actually change. Cf. Abdel-Nour (2003) for an account of how shame works in the context of these kinds of collective and complex selves.

where the philosophers whisper together with three or four lads (485d–e). It is Socrates (and perhaps now Gorgias as well) who feels compelled to wander into these corners and to investigate all things to their logical conclusions. The other that Callicles does look up to and has internalized is the specific attitude embodied in the heroic *ēthos* of the courageous warrior and political leader. And it is this other that Socrates calls in as a witness to get Callicles to admit that his indiscriminate hedonism is too shameful even for him to admit. At this point, Callicles retracts his thesis because it is felt to be inappropriate from the perspective of the wise and courageous other that he admires. In other words, the other that Callicles has internalized and identified with has a substantive content that contains more than the fear of censure by an anonymous other. It is also not just an idiosyncratic representative of his own bizarre desires and fantasies. It is linked to specific social attitudes and expectations that sanction some actions and condemn others.

This fact explains why it is too simple to dismiss a shame refutation as *ad hominem,* i.e., directed simply to the hopes and desires of a particular individual. The hopes and desires of each individual are linked to the reasons for action embodied in the generalized ideals and character (*ēthos*) of their society, and the specific groups into which that individual has been socialized. This is why Socrates is able to predict that Callicles will twist himself up and down in the argument in order to stay in tune with his beloved people or fellow citizens (*dēmos*) (481d–e): Callicles ends up contradicting himself precisely because the Athenians he so loves and admires hold contradictory beliefs about the best way of life. In the deft hands of Socrates, shame (*aischunē*) becomes a psychological weapon that gives one insights into what motivates a particular individual *and* into the reasons for action embodied in a particular culture. This is precisely why what looks like a private conversation between Socrates, a number of different interlocutors, and a small audience is actually an intensely political dialogue containing Plato's own reflections on Athenian democratic practices.

The twists and turns in the Callicles refutation point to other important facts about the complex nature of shame. The first is that sometimes a person will assert out of shame what they believe to be true and sometimes they will assert out of shame what they believe to be false. In other words, to be shamed into telling a lie and to be ashamed of the truth are two different things. For this reason the accounts offered by Charles Kahn and Richard McKim end up being too one-sided. Both of them offer fruitful insights into the mechanisms of shame. But they focus either on the way in which shame causes the interlocutor to utter insincere remarks (Kahn), or the way in which shame causes the interlocutor to acknowledge the truth he believes deep down (McKim). What they both fail to see is that the recognition of the gaze of the other, so characteristic of the occurrent experience of shame, can compel someone in either of these two different directions. It can either prompt them to insincerely mimic or flatter the viewpoint of this other, or to sincerely entertain and respect the judgment of the other in order to learn something new about themselves and to obtain a different vantage point on their assertions and actions. In the next chapter I develop these distinctions by articulating the differences between flattering and respectful shame.

As I pointed out earlier, Gorgias seems to be shamed into insincerely professing to teach his students to be just because he knows that the Athenian public would condemn the moral neutrality of his art. Similarly, immediately after the catamite argument, Callicles is momentarily shamed into holding on to his indiscriminate hedonism thesis, because he is worried that the immediate audience is about to see him shown up by Socrates. In both cases, the interlocutor feels that a certain inadequacy about themselves has been or is about to be revealed to an other, and in both cases the interlocutor utters an insincere reply as a way of concealing or hiding this inadequacy from the other or audience whose censure or ridicule they fear.

In the other refutations of Callicles, however, the situation is somewhat different. In the catamite and coward/fool arguments, Callicles' hedonism thesis is now revealed as unacceptable and untrue for him. Thus he eventually retracts this thesis as being false and replaces it with the thesis that some pleasures are better than others. And his remark that he *and all other human beings* really do think that some pleasures are better than others is not an insincere remark, but rather a new insight into his own reasons for action that Socrates has shown him (499b). In this moment of recognition, there is then a common truth that is agreed upon by Callicles and Socrates, as Callicles comes to the painful but potentially beneficial realization that Socrates' thesis better accounts for his own actions. And the teaching about moderation—that certain pleasures need to be restrained—with which Socrates ends the dialogue, is justified by the moral truth that he and Callicles have agreed upon: that some pleasures are better than others.

Finally, I believe that the different responses of Gorgias, Polus, and Callicles to their shame-refutations reveal the importance of the moment of reaction to this phenomenon. The refutation of Callicles vividly illustrates the well-known fact that the primary experience of shame is painful, but this does not mean that such a phenomenon is necessarily harmful or pernicious. This is because shame is not a virtue in the way that justice, piety, temperance, and courage are. Instead, as I argued above, it is one of the mechanisms of socialization by which we come to be virtuous (or vicious) people. Children learn what it is to be just or temperate by the ways in which their behavior is judged appropriate or inappropriate by those around them, but whether or not it will become anything more than a psychological weapon of conformity depends upon how the person reacts to it. Just as it requires some action on the part of the patient to achieve the benefit of health, so it requires some sort of action on the part of Socrates' interlocutors to be benefited by his elenchic method. In the case of someone like Callicles the reaction to the occurrent experience of shame is to hide from the insights that Socrates is trying to show him and to squirm out of the conversation (505c–d).

However, in the case of Gorgias the reaction to this feeling of shame is to remain as a silent but attentive witness to what Socrates is attempting to discover about his subsequent interlocutors. When Gorgias does reenter the dialogue at 497b and 506a–b, he does so to get Callicles to continue talking with Socrates so that the argument might be brought to a conclusion. As I suggested above, this might mean that Gorgias *is* interested in what Socrates is trying to show him with his refutation of Callicles. Again, when Socrates first met Gorgias at the beginning of the dialogue, Gorgias complained that "no one has yet asked me anything new for many years" (448a), and he also stated that he was worried about his students' unjust use of the rhetoric that he had been teaching them. Here he tells Socrates, "It is just, then, to hate, expel, and kill the one who uses it not correctly, but not the one who taught it" (457c). Then, in the Polus and Callicles sections, Gorgias watches while Socrates refutes their arguments for the life of tyranny and injustice and replaces these with a noble rhetoric aimed at restraining and moderating the individual and the city. I believe that Gorgias' repeated pleas to Callicles to continue conversing with Socrates reflect the fact that he is learning something new from this very new "Socrates" and is now interested in the noble rhetoric that the new "Socrates" preaches. As a teacher of this kind of rhetoric, Gorgias would be able to protect himself from the moral condemnation of Athens which he fears, and which Socrates mobilized against him to shame him into accepting the premise that he would teach his students to be just.[88] But if Gorgias does learn this new rhetoric from Socrates and does begin to teach it then he would no longer be a "false" witness to the very premise that had originally defeated him. In learning something new from Socrates he would move from being a "false" to a "true" witness of Socrates' assertions. And he would also now be in tune with the opinions of the many, or Athens, about the need for moderation and justice. Thus, these conventional opinions would no longer appear "false" or hypocritical to him. In the next chapter, I will develop this suggestion further by showing how the very activity of shaming which Socrates espouses links up with the important Athenian democratic ideal of *parrhēsia* (frankness, freedom of speech) that he (and Plato) actually fear is *not* present in the case of flattering rhetoric. And I will thus show how shame plays a role not just in the responses of Socrates' interlocutors, but also in the politics of shame embodied in certain Athenian political ideals and practices.

---

[88] Nichols (1998, 133), Weiss (2003, 199–201), and Stauffer (2006, 41) all suggest that Gorgias might well be interested in learning this kind of noble rhetoric from Socrates, although both Weiss (2003, 205–6) and Stauffer (2006, 180) go on to doubt that Gorgias himself would have actually practiced it. Stauffer's (2006, 181–82) suggestion that it might well have been Plato who masters this alliance is consistent with my argument about Platonic respectful shame, although we disagree on the content of Plato's noble rhetoric. For our differences, see chapter 4 below.

Chapter Three

PLATO ON SHAME IN DEMOCRATIC ATHENS

IN THE LAST CHAPTER I examined the role of shame (*aischunē*) in the Socratic elenchus primarily within the confines of the discussion that occurs between Socrates and his three interlocutors. But I have not addressed the ways in which Plato's position on the salutary elements of Socrates' shaming elenchus actually bears upon the practice of Athenian democratic politics. This is a grave oversight because, as I mentioned earlier in chapter 1, the *Gorgias* abounds with references to famous Athenian democratic leaders such as Themistocles, Cimon, Miltiades, and Pericles (*Gorg.* 455e, 472b, 515e, 516d, 519a), and to specific democratic practices such as delivering speeches, voting, calling in witnesses to one's reputation, and ostracism (456a, 471e, 472c, 473e, 516d). In fact, the dialogue contains Plato's most explicit thoughts and harsh criticisms of the leaders, institutions, and practices of his native city. For this reason the *Gorgias* is often seen as Plato's own "Apology" in which he outlines his reasons for forgoing a career in Athenian politics in favor of opening a school of philosophy.[1]

This kind of interpretation of the *Gorgias* poses a second significant challenge to a project such as my own, which attempts to utilize Platonic insights into the nature of shame (*aischunē*) to help us think about issues in contemporary democratic politics. In this chapter I want to contest this interpretation of the *Gorgias* and offer a reformulation of Plato's relationship to democratic Athens with specific reference to the relationship between shame (*aischunē*) and the important Athenian democratic ideal of *parrhēsia* (frankness, freedom of speech) in order to recapture these Platonic insights for contemporary dilemmas. I turn to this relationship in particular because it is alleged by certain interpreters that Plato holds these as diametrically opposed, and that this opposition leads him to make his harshest criticisms of Athenian democratic politics.[2] So before offering my reformulation of the relationship between the

---

[1] See Dodds (1959), 30–34; and Kahn (1996), 52. As Dodds (1959, 32) puts it, "Apart from some short passages in the *Laws*, nowhere else in the dialogues has Plato told us *directly* what he thought of the institutions and achievements of his native city." Dodds attributes this notion of a Platonic "Apology" to Friedrich Schleiermacher in the introduction to his translation of the dialogue. Plato's own account of his disillusionment with Athenian politics in the wake of the restored democracy's condemnation of Socrates is famously recorded in his *Seventh Letter*.

[2] The idea that shame and free or frank speech are opposed for Plato is held by Allan Bloom (1968) who reads Plato as revealing the flaws in any democratic political system, and by Arlene Saxonhouse (2006) who reads Plato as a democratic thinker who is concerned to combat the

two phenomena, I need to reconstruct some of the central aspects of the "Platonic Apology" allegedly offered in the *Gorgias* in order to make clear the strict opposition that I wish to contest.

THE CANONICAL VIEW OF PLATO'S CRITICISMS OF ATHENS

Even if, as I argued in the last chapter, Socrates' shaming of Gorgias (and perhaps even Polus and Callicles) opens them up to the possibility of discovering a new ethical truth about themselves and about their audiences, it is also true that he comes across as someone skilled in manipulating his interlocutor's shame to get them to say things that they don't fully believe or even understand. In fact, Plato even puts this supposed critique of shame (*aischunē*) into the mouth of his character "Socrates," who asserts of Gorgias and Polus: "They have advanced so far into the sense of shame that—on account of feeling shame—each one of them dares to contradict himself in front of many human beings, and this concerning the greatest things (*hō ge eis tosouton aischunēs elēluthaton, hōste dia to aischunesthai tolmai hekateros autōn autos hautōi enantia legein enantion pollōn anthrōpōn, kai tauta peri tōn megistōn*)" (487b). In each refutation Socrates seems to skillfully refute his opponent's thesis by getting that individual to consider how an Athenian audience would view his remarks. Socrates thus seems to come to light as a master of utilizing the psychological compulsion involved in the phenomenon of shame by manipulating his interlocutor's fear of disgrace or dishonor before others. That "might makes right" does not simply translate into the physical strength of the many over others, but also into the psychological strength of social conformity, which works through the sense of shame.

But if this is the case, and Socrates truly is the popular speaker that Callicles accuses him of being (494d), then Plato would seem to be dramatically illus-

---

imperialistic tendencies of democratic Athens. In his commentary on the *Republic* (which for him reveals the same Platonic teaching as the *Gorgias*), Bloom (1968, 336) argues that Thrasymachus' blush reveals his shame and thus the fact that "he has no true freedom of mind, because he is attached to prestige, to the applause of the multitude and hence their thought." Bloom's interpretation associates shame with a conformist enslavement to convention in opposition to the truth. Similarly for Saxonhouse (2006, 76), "It is the philosophers' stripping away that which we desire to hide from the gaze of others that brings on shame and it is the playwrights' casting aside the shame that would inhibit their uncovering of the nature of our existence who can reveal, *hē alētheia*, that which is true. It is in this sense that shame opposes Socratic philosophy, for instance, in the activity dedicated to the pursuit of truth." See also Saxonhouse (2006), 193, 212. Her interpretation associates shame (*aidōs*) with a kind of covering, and *parrhēsia* or shamelessness with a kind of uncovering or exposing. This, however, overlooks the fact that while the older term, *aidōs*, is linked to the notion of a covering mantle (Konstan, 2006, 296 n.17), the more classical and democratic term, *aischunē*, (especially in its connotations of dishonor or disgrace), is closer to the very notion of uncovering that she wants to link to *parrhēsia* and even to truth (*alētheia*).

trating just why democratic rhetoric, whether just or noble, is worth nothing in regard to the truth. Such democratic rhetoric works through the love of honor and applause and the fear of disgrace rather than through a love of truth and a fear of untruth.[3] By skillfully manipulating their sense of shame, Socrates is able to get his interlocutors to contradict themselves because he gets them to assert what they do not believe to be true, but rather only what they think convention requires of them.[4] Thus, according to this canonical view, Plato's rejection of a life in Athenian democratic politics depends on the fact that it deals only with appearances, with the images that one must project to the many, who are like children demanding pastries and sweets instead of beneficial medicines (464d, 518b), or to the few, who demand a hypermoral rhetoric that presents justice in a flattering light.[5] Finally, according to this view, Plato's whole philosophy rests on the fundamental distinction between appearance and reality, convention and nature, and shame comes to light as precisely that emotional barrier to truth that prevents people from seeing beyond the conventions of their own society. The search for reality and truth can take place only between a few close philosophic associates in those spaces outside of politics where shame is discarded and replaced by philosophic *erōs*. (Hence the private setting of the *Republic* and *Symposium*, or the setting of the *Phaedrus* outside the walls of democratic Athens.)[6]

DISRUPTING THE CANON

Of course, if this is Plato's criticism of shame (*aidōs/aischunē*), then he is not really articulating anything that would be novel for either his contemporary audience or modern readers of his text. By Plato's time the notion that shame (whether *aidōs or aischunē*) could dispose one to be overly concerned with one's external reputation (*doxa*) or honor (*timē*) in the eyes of others was a significant theme both in Greek tragedies and oratorical speeches. Euripides'

In this chapter I contest this opposition between shame and truthful speaking, and with it the suggestion by both Bloom and Saxonhouse that Socrates is shameless.

[3] Cf. Bloom (1968), 336. According to Bloom, it is the philosopher alone who is truly shameless because his way of life involves questioning all laws and conventions. As I show in this book, while it is certainly true that flattering shame ties one to conventions and is at the heart of a dangerous kind of conformity, it is not true that all types of shame are slavishly linked to convention and opposed to the truth.

[4] Kahn (1983), 115.

[5] For Benardete (1991) and Stauffer (2006, 121, 182), the true philosopher would see beyond the noble and hyper-moral rhetoric that Socrates uses to embellish his way of life in order to protect himself from the likes of a noble and aristocratic youth like Callicles.

[6] Benardete (1991) suggests that the private setting of the *Phaedrus* outside the walls of Athens allows for a very different presentation of the character of the philosophic life than the one that is on display in the hyper-moral rhetoric of the *Gorgias*. I follow Stanley Rosen (1993) in thinking

Hippolytus examines shame (*aidōs*) more than any other tragedy, and one of its themes, articulated in Phaedra's great speech (lines 373–430), is that it can dispose one to take pleasure in and base one's conduct on the external rewards and sanctions of honor and disgrace in opposition to what is truly noble (*kalon*).[7] At 385–87 Phaedra states, "There are two sorts of *aidōs*; the one is not evil, the other a burden on the *oikos* (household). If the right measure were clear, then there would not be two things having the same letters."[8] Similarly, in his *Electra*, Euripides favorably contrasts the shame (*aischunē*) of the Farmer, which consists of a proper regard for others, with that of Electra and Orestes, which is ultimately selfish and concerned only with their prestige in the eyes of, and ultimately at the cost of, others.[9] Sophists and orators such as Antiphon and Democritus also take up this problem with a form of shame (*aidōs/aischunē*) that is overly concerned with external sanctions, honors, and conventions.[10] And for modern readers this characterization of shame as concerned with one's reputation in an ultimately selfish way resonates with a neo-Kantian disparagement of this emotion for being nonmoral, egoistic, and heteronomous.[11]

However, the real problem with the canonical interpretation of Plato is not that it lacks novelty or that it is completely wrong. And I do not want to turn the canonical Plato on his head and argue that he was actually an avid supporter of Athenian democracy or that he advocated dishonoring and disgracing others as part of a philosophic hazing ritual necessary to become a disciple of Socrates. Nor do I want to argue that contemporary democracies require more of this type of shame, which leads to conformity or to an excessive concern with one's own honor or esteem. I believe that the *Gorgias* does illustrate what Plato took to be serious difficulties with the Athenian democracy in which he lived, and with the kind of shame (*aischunē*) that motivated at least some of his contemporaries. But the canonical view oversimplifies what for Plato amounts to a much more complex understanding of the place of shame (*aischunē*) in political life. To summarize what I shall develop in much more detail below, Plato thinks that:

---

that the erotic, moral, and poetic character of philosophy comes through in all of Plato's middle dialogues, and here I would include the *Gorgias*.

[7] For a careful and extensive analysis of the different meanings of *aidōs* in Euripides' *Hippolytus*, see Williams (1993), 95–97 and Cairns (1993), 314–42.

[8] This follows the translation by Goldhill (1986), 135. In the *Phaedrus*, Plato argues that the rhetorical art must be able to collect and divide the disputable things like love (*erōs*) and madness (*mania*) (*Phdr.* 262d–265b). It is this art that he practices on shame (*aischunē*) in the *Gorgias*.

[9] For a fuller treatment of *aidōs/aischunē* in this play, see Cairns (1993), 270–72.

[10] See Antiphon, fr. B 44 Diels-Kranz; Democritus, fr. B 181 DK. For a treatment of these orators, see Cairns (1993), 360–70.

[11] For a critique of Kant's views on shame from an ancient Greek perspective, see Williams (1993), 75–102.

(1) Shame (*aischunē*) is a necessary but dangerous motivational force underlying both democratic deliberations and philosophic discussions.

(2) The Athenian democratic ideal of *parrhēsia* (frankness, freedom of speech) articulates the structure of shame (*aischunē*) necessary to these two forms of deliberation.

(3) A corrupt form of shame (*aischunē*) leads to a corrupt democratic politics and that a healthy form of shame (*aischunē*) provides the conditions for a healthy democracy and philosophy.

Before proceeding to develop Plato's own complex views on shame (*aischunē*) and *parrhēsia* (frankness, freedom of speech), I need to reconstruct the rich Athenian democratic context within which his argument is situated. As I mentioned in my Introduction, a number of political theorists and classicists have recently begun to examine the ways in which Plato's dialogues actually utilize or develop various Athenian democratic ideals and institutions, often alongside or even *within* his criticisms of Athenian life and politics. By first reconstructing various aspects of the Athenian "democratic imaginary" or "normative imagery," and then juxtaposing these to Plato's (or Socrates') account of his own philosophical practice, a new reading of Plato's treatment of democracy becomes possible.[12] Such a strategy shows that there are significant similarities between Socratic dialectic and the preliminary scrutiny (*dokimasia*) and final accounting (*euthunai*) that Athenian citizens had to undergo before assuming office and stepping down at the end of their tenure.[13] It also shows that while Plato notoriously attacks certain democratic institutions such as the ideal of freedom (*eleutheria*) in Book 8 of the *Republic*, or the institution of majority rule in the *Gorgias*, he does so because they have taken on a debased form wherein freedom becomes license and majority rule becomes rule by a mob (*ochlos*).[14] In their debased forms, both of these phenomena actually then

---

[12] For recent scholarship that focuses on the connection between specific aspects of Athenian democratic culture and Plato's depiction of philosophy, see Saxonhouse, (1996), 87–114; Saxonhouse (1998), 273–84; Euben (1994), 208–14; Euben (1997), chapters 8 and 9; Wallach (1997), 377–91; Wallach (2001); Monoson (2000); and Foucault (2001), 20–24, 77–107. I borrow the phrases "democratic imaginary" and "normative imagery" from Monoson (2000), 9 and 12. She borrows the term "normative imagery" from Nicole Loraux, *The Invention of Athens* (Cambridge, MA: Harvard University Press, 1986).

[13] Euben (1997), 91–108. Similarly, Saxonhouse (1996 and 1998) argues that the gentleness and variety so characteristic of Athenian democracy are also integral to Plato's own practice of philosophy.

[14] For the notion of freedom as license see *Rep.* 8.557d; for freedom as anarchy see *Rep.* 8.560e. Cf. Sokolon (2006, 113), who argues that licentiousness is regarded as shameful for Aristotle and that, even though this includes the involuntary action of being violated sexually, he makes it clear that it is more shameful to deliberately choose licentious actions. My account of the difference between true and false witnesses in the *Gorgias* corresponds to the notion of a thoughtful multi-

threaten certain other ideals or institutions, which are in fact shared by Platonic philosophizing and Athenian democratic politics.

In this vein, and for the purposes of this chapter, there are important similarities between Plato's depiction of philosophic activity and the Athenian practice of *parrhēsia* that was expected of anyone addressing the Athenian assembly.[15] And this connection between philosophy and the practice of *parrhēsia* is characteristic of Plato's depiction of philosophy in his early (*Laches*), middle (*Gorgias* and *Republic*) and late (*Laws*) dialogues.[16] It thus eludes being explained simply by the distinction between a democratic Socrates (depicted in Plato's early dialogues) and an anti-democratic Plato (elaborated in his middles and late dialogues). And it thus suggests that we see Plato not as an enemy to democratic Athens but as an immanent critic of a corrupt Athenian democracy calling this community "to its own best possible self without romanticizing what a rigorous pursuit of that best self would entail."[17]

The second strategy employed for this new reading of Plato's dialogues involves distinguishing between the representations of democracy and democratic leaders in the dialogues and the actual historical institutions and theories of democracy that were prevalent in Athens at the time. This strategy is especially important for understanding Socrates' criticisms of democracy and its slide into tyranny in Book 8 of the *Republic*, and Socrates' criticism of the democratic leaders Pericles, Cimon, Miltiades, and Themistocles, and the democratic citizen, Callicles, in the *Gorgias*.[18] In these instances the kind of "democracy" or "democrats" Socrates criticizes are in fact ones that fail to live up to certain ideals explicitly espoused by Athenian democratic discourse.[19] His criticisms of these "democrats" explicitly mention the Athenian practice of *parrhēsia* as a normative ideal shared by democratic debate and Socratic dialectic, which Socrates (and Plato) think aren't actually being practiced by those

---

tude that becomes a mob. As I also elucidate in this chapter, the ideal of *parrhēsia* meant that a citizen should have the courage to stand alone before the majority and speak his own mind.

[15] Monoson (2000), chapter 6; and Foucault (2001), 23–24. Monoson's work on *parrhēsia* is actually indebted to the lectures originally delivered by Foucault in 1983 at the University of California at Berkeley that were later published as *Fearless Speech* in 2001.

[16] Plato, *Laches*, 178a, 179c, 189a; *Gorgias*, 487a, 487b, 487d, 491e, 492d, 521a; *Republic*, 5.450c, 5.473c, 9.557a–b; *Laws*, 7.806c, 7.806d, 8.835c. For a fuller explanation of these passages as examples of *parrhēsia* see Monoson (2000), 155–70. For another description of *parrhēsia* in the *Laches*, *Laws*, and *Apology*, see Foucault (2001), 91–107.

[17] Monoson (2000), 13.

[18] For a fuller treatment of the *Republic* passages, see Monoson (2000), 172–77; for a fuller treatment of the *Gorgias* passages, see Euben (1994), 208–14. Dodds (1959, 355–59), Irwin (1979, 235), and Stauffer (2006, 153) all stress that Socrates' account of the Athenian leaders and citizens in the *Gorgias* is perverted and designed to put them in the worst possible light.

[19] In a related comment, Tarcov (1996, 7) points out that "what are often quoted as Plato's harshest criticisms of democracy actually occur in [his] account of the degeneration of democracy into tyranny rather than in the preceding description of democracy as such."

who profess to be democrats or friends of democracy.[20] Thus, Socrates and Plato come to light not as anti-democratic, but rather as sympathetic critics recalling their fellow citizens to the true practice of democracy. And the very things which Socrates sarcastically praises Callicles for possessing—wisdom, good-will, and frankness (*parrhēsia*) (487a)—are put forward as democratic ideals that are meant to counter the tyrannical impulses of "Calliclean democrats" who flatter the people (*dēmos*) in the hope of gaining power over them.

Following the first strategy, I shall reconstruct the Athenian democratic ideal of *parrhēsia* and highlight those elements that are common to this Athenian ideal and to Socrates' shaming elenchus as it is presented in the *Gorgias*. It will then become clear that Socrates' distinctions between flattering rhetoric and his own political art of justice rely on distinctions that were already being made by democrats in fifth and fourth century Athens. Plato's accomplishment in the *Gorgias* is not that he articulates an ideal of discussion that is *completely* alien to his Athenian audience, but rather that he shows how the cooperative ideals of justice and moderation can be made consistent with the more traditional heroic excellences of courage and self-assertion in the figure of the courageous and just *parrhēsiastēs* (frank speaker), Socrates.[21] In the *Gorgias* it is Socrates who consistently maintains the democratic ideal of *parrhēsia* because he alone is able to continue speaking frankly about his view of the good life, even when his views seem dissonant and strange (*atopon*) to most human beings (480e, 481c). This practice requires that one be free of the flattery (and what I shall articulate later in this chapter as flattering shame) that often motivates Socrates' interlocutors, who contradict themselves because they fear the dishonor, pain, and criticism that their views would elicit from an Athenian audience.[22] In contrast, Socratic respectful shame, exemplified in his shaming elenchus, requires participants who are willing to suffer the pain of critique in the ongoing and reciprocal investigation of their collective ideals.

Following the second strategy, I show that Socrates' attacks in the *Gorgias* are directed at supporters or leaders of democracies who dream of being tyrants, while falsely professing to be concerned with the common good. His critique then is leveled not just at the corrupt democratic practice of flattering rhetoric but also at the fantasies of those individuals who engage in this practice. If the feeling of shame involves the recognition that we don't actually live

[20] Monoson (2000), 176 ; Euben (1994), 211.

[21] Kahn (1983), 95–96. In chapter 4, I explore how Plato's use of myth at the end of the *Gorgias* actually encapsulates what is new and unique about the Socratic elenchus by utilizing older and more traditional Athenian images and motifs.

[22] At *Gorg.* 521a, Callicles tells Socrates that he should engage in flattery and gratify the Athenians in order to avoid the dangers of having his goods confiscated or of being put to death. In stark contrast, as Foucault (2001, 17–18) points out, danger and risk were actually integral components of the democratic ideal of *parrhēsia*, especially when the individual was speaking to the majority of other citizens.

up to the ideals or self-image we have of ourselves, it can also play a role in showing us that we don't live up to the corrupting image of the tyrant. A certain type of shaming might then have a positive role to play in preventing these democrats from becoming the tyrants they secretly or not so secretly admire.

As will be seen below, both Polus and Callicles think that they want to be tyrants but the life they have chosen and the fact that they continue conversing with Socrates reveals that they have not fully actualized this ideal *in their own lives*. Socrates' interlocutors might be speaking frankly or truthfully when they admit their admiration for the tyrant, but if they are themselves deceived about how much this ideal actually conforms to their own actions then they are in fact "false witnesses" for the tyrant.[23] Their words might correspond to their self-image, but this self-image might not correspond to their actions. If Socrates can get them to feel ashamed by some of the actions that the image of the tyrant entails, then he might get them to recognize the gap between their selves and this fantastical image. In this case, their occurrent experience of shame would be closer to what Socrates means by knowledge of one's own ignorance: knowing *that* you are not identical to the tyrant might be a necessary step toward knowing *who* you are.

PARRHĒSIA AS AN ATHENIAN DEMOCRATIC IDEAL

I will turn first then to an account of the Athenian practice of *parrhēsia* in order to reconstruct the rich democratic context of Plato's dialogue, the *Gorgias*. *Parrhēsia* is often translated as "outspokenness," "frankness," or even "freedom of speech";[24] but its literal meaning is closer to "saying everything."[25] More specifically, it referred to the practice of frankly speaking one's own mind, "especially uttering a deserved reproach."[26] *Parrhēsia* was an essentially democratic ideal for two reasons. First, "it forcefully articulated some of the meaning of the Athenian conception of freedom (*eleutheria*)," which was itself articulated in part through its *contrast* to tyranny, both in its Athenian and Persian forms.[27] Under tyranny one had to flatter the tyrant and could not

---

[23] Irwin (1977, 115) also notes the new kind of interlocutor that both Polus and Callicles represent in comparison to the interlocutors of the earlier dialogues. In these earlier dialogues, Socrates' project was to get his interlocutors to see that they are not as just as they think they are.

[24] Liddell and Scott (1996), 1344.

[25] Monoson (2000), 52; and Foucault (2001), 12.

[26] Monoson (2000), 52. Foucault (2001, 17–18) also emphasizes the element of criticism and the fact that the critic was always in a position of inferiority with respect to his interlocutor, e.g., when a citizen criticized the majority.

[27] Monoson (2000), 54. Cf. Kalyvas (2007, 416) for the link between classical conceptions of tyranny and the downfall of freedom.

speak one's mind without being put to death.[28] In contrast, *parrhēsia* was part of the democratic practice of holding those exercising power accountable through exposing lies and abuses of power, and demanding change.[29]

Second, *parrhēsia* expressed one of the substantive ideals of democratic assembly debate which ensured that the decisions rendered by the majority were wise and not simply democratically legitimate. In this respect it was a necessary complement to the more procedural ideal of *isēgoria*, which meant literally "equality of public address."[30] *Isēgoria* allowed all citizens to be actively engaged in the deliberative process by allowing them to present their view of the public interest for consideration by everyone.[31] At the same time, however, *isēgoria* also produced one of the greatest threats to the discernment of a public interest and the production of wise decisions. This threat consisted of "manipulative and deceptive oratory in the service of a speaker's personal ambitions rather than the public interest. By pandering to the whims and desires of the people, a clever orator could elevate himself to a position of leadership."[32] Indeed this danger of deceptive and flattering rhetoric was a major reason for the deep ambivalence that the Athenians exhibited toward the arts of rhetoric and sophistry.[33] Because the right to speak was an essential part of the Athenian political identity, learning to speak well was seen as crucial to becoming a successful citizen and leader. Yet the very art of rhetoric also supplied the means by which demagogues could rise to power by appealing to the interests, pleasures, and desires of the lower classes.[34]

The critical ideal of *parrhēsia* was thus utilized to counter this threat through its very opposition to deceitful and flattering rhetoric. An appeal to the ideal of *parrhēsia* was meant as a way of affirming the speaker's personal integrity, freedom of thought, commitment to speaking and exposing the truth, and to placing the public interest over personal interests and pleasures.[35] It also entailed a certain amount of danger and a degree of courage on the part of the speaker who risked suffering heckling, humiliation, fines, and even punish-

---

[28] As Tormey (2005, 69) puts it, "Tyrants cannot stand challenges to their power; they want all the power, and they want to monopolize it in such a fashion that no other individual or office can come to undermine or query their position."

[29] Monoson (2000), 55. According to Foucault (2001, 22, 86), *parrhēsia* evolved from the democratic practice of frank speaking between citizens both in the agora and in the assembly in the fifth and fourth centuries BC to the practice of advisors or counselors speaking frankly to their king with the later rise of the Hellenistic monarchies.

[30] Ober (1989), 296; and Monoson (2000), 56.

[31] Monoson (2000), 57; and Ober (1989), 296.

[32] Monoson (2000), 59. See also McClure (1999), 11–15.

[33] Gish (2006) argues that it was the Athenians' inability to distinguish Socrates from such deceptive sophists and rhetoricians that was partly to blame for his condemnation.

[34] Ober (1989), 189; and McClure (1999), 10–11.

[35] Monoson (2000), 60; Ober (1989), 296; and Foucault (2001), 14.

ment for offering unwise advice to or criticism of the assembly.[36] This danger was linked to the critical character of the truth, which was always "capable of hurting or angering the *interlocutor*."[37] Finally, *parrhēsia* implied a close connection between the speaker and his words.[38] Speaking with *parrhēsia* meant that a person's cares and convictions were on display, and it was not to be confused with "mere audacious speech, with playing the devil's advocate, or even with bold speculation."[39]

The practice of *parrhēsia* was, however, not simply linked to the virtue of the speaker, but also required a certain virtue on the part of the audience or hearer. "To the extent that the hearers willingly suffer criticism, reflect on their opinions and generally listen to others, *their* public-spiritedness (that is, their placement of the public good before that of personal pleasure) is on display as well as that of the speaker."[40] In other words, *parrhēsia* (like *aischunē* for Plato) was an intersubjective and reciprocal practice that implicated both the speaker and listener. Speaking with *parrhēsia* thus ensured that proposals before the assembly were rigorously scrutinized and criticized and that the will of the entire people (*dēmos*) was itself interrogated.[41]

PARRHĒSIA AND SHAME

What is striking about this presentation of *parrhēsia* is how much it resembles Socrates' own model of the true art of rhetoric that he professes to practice in the *Gorgias*. The term *parrhēsia* occurs six times in the *Gorgias* (487a, 487b, 487d, 491e, 492d, 521a), and is used to indicate the psychological disposition required of an interlocutor in order for Socrates to discover the "true things themselves" and "to make a sufficient test of a soul's living correctly or not" (486e–487a). In these very contexts, however, Socrates consistently and explicitly opposes it to shame (*aischunē*). Immediately after Callicles delivers his speech defending powerful and superior rulers, Socrates tells him that he will serve as a "touchstone" for Socrates to test his own soul because he possesses three things: knowledge, good-will, and outspokenness (*parrhēsia*) (487a). And he goes on to state that Gorgias and Polus proved to be inadequate interlocutors because they lack *parrhēsia* and are too sensitive or inclined to shame:

---

[36] Monoson (2000), 60; and Foucault (2001), 15–16.

[37] Foucault (2001), 17.

[38] Foucault (2001), 12.

[39] Monoson (2000), 62. Foucault (2001, 13, 77–84) points out that *parrhēsia* itself eventually takes on a pejorative sense where it does mean chattering or reckless and outspoken ignorance. Cf. Saxonhouse (2006), 129–45 for a discussion of the pejorative uses of *parrhēsia* in tragedies and democratic oratory.

[40] Monoson (2000), 61.

[41] Monoson (2000), 61; and Foucault (2001), 18.

... and these two foreigners here, Gorgias and Polus, are wise and friends of mine, but rather too lacking in outspokenness and too sensitive to shame (*endeesterō de parrhēsias kai aischuntēroterō mallon*), more so than is needful. And how could they not be? Since indeed they have advanced so far into the sense of shame (*aischunēs*) that—on account of feeling shame (*aischunesthai*)—each one of them dares to contradict himself in front of many human beings, and this concerning the greatest things. (487a–b)

As indicated earlier, the Athenian democratic ideal of *parrhēsia* required that a speaker frankly and boldly utter his own sincere thoughts on a subject instead of flattering or deceiving the audience by tailoring his remarks to their views. It thus seems directly opposed to the psychological disposition of shame (*aischunē*), which is attuned to the ways that an audience views one's utterances, and which can be an inhibitory emotion preventing one from saying anything that the audience will deem inappropriate or shameful. Indeed, Socrates' remarks about the way in which shame (*aischunē*) prompted both Polus and Gorgias to contradict themselves concerning how one ought to live suggests that shame is not just a hindrance to good political debate, but also to Socratic dialectic as well. One of the requirements of Socratic elenchus is that the interlocutors always be frank about what they really believe, and Socrates reminds Callicles of this when he (Callicles) is on the verge of uttering an insincere remark: "You are corrupting the first speeches, Callicles, and you would no longer be sufficiently examining with me the things that are if you're going to speak contrary to how things seem in your own opinion" (495a). Here, again, it is Socrates and not Callicles who extols the democratic practice of *parrhēsia*, but now for the purposes of engaging in a philosophical discussion.

However, I want to argue that this does not mean that Socrates or any person speaking with *parrhēsia* is altogether without shame (*aischunē*). Rightly understood, the ideal of *parrhēsia* articulates the structure of a kind of shaming and a sense of shame (what I will refer to below as Socratic respectful shame) that is *necessary* both for democratic politics and for Socratic elenchus, but is not *sufficient* to ensure that all parties to the debate discern a common interest or collective truth. As I mentioned earlier, *parrhēsia* requires that the speaker and the audience possess the courage either to utter a deserved reproach or to suffer the pain of critique, and as I showed in the last chapter, this kind of reciprocal relationship is integral to the shaming experience of the Socratic elenchus. In both cases one must be willing to suffer the pain of critique that is integral to the experience of being shown that you (i.e., either a person or collectivity) do not live up to the very ideals you have set for yourself. In the two cases, both parties to the debate must be able and willing to experience the *painful* cognitive-affective recognition of the gaze of an other that reveals a certain inadequacy in the self. But what can be *beneficial* about the experience is that it can reveal a common truth between the agent and patient, the speaker and audience: one can feel ashamed before an other *because* one shares with that other the judgment that one's behavior is a violation of some shared ideal or standard of propriety. Thus, the recognition inherent to the feeling of being ashamed before an other can consist in the acknowledgment that a deserved rebuke or reproach has been given by this other. And this kind of respectful shame is manifested in both the democratic ideal of *parrhēsia* and the Socratic shaming elenchus. In this way *aischunē* and *parrhēsia* can be intricately connected to the positive attempt "to reconstruct or improve oneself,"[42] either as an individual or as part of a collectivity.

What can endanger the discovery of this common truth and the project of reconstruction is the person's reaction to the experience. While the experience can be both painful and beneficial for the discussion participants, either party to the debate may fixate solely on the *pain* of critique as something bad to be avoided in the future. Their sense of shame will then inhibit them from any future situations in which they will have to feel this pain or make others feel it. A false consensus can then form wherein "debate" becomes a reciprocal exchange of pleasantries, such that neither party will ever have to endure the pain of critique. Instead of respectfully showing each other just how and why they have fallen below a certain ideal or exemplar of action, each party to the debate merely flatters the existing prejudices and opinions of the other in order to avoid the pain of rebuke. This is not to say that Plato advocates a politics of feeling bad rather than one of feeling good, for this alternative would itself only fixate on the pain of the shaming situation rather than the benefit that can come from it.[43] Rather, Plato wants the Athenians to avoid a politics of flattery where the person delivering the message and the audience receiving it aim only at the pleasant and not at the good (465a).

The Structure of Shame

Thus, the occurrent experience of shame, as this is articulated in the democratic ideal of *parrhēsia* and the Socratic elenchus, can lead to two very different reactions and two very different senses of shame: either the flattering shame that is involved in the kind of politics and rhetoric advocated by Polus and

---

[42] Williams (1993), 90.

[43] This also means that a Platonic politics of shame would not be consistent with the kind of shaming penalties that have recently been introduced to punish DUI offenders or sexual predators, such as making these people wear signs advertising their crimes to everyone who passes by. These kinds of stigmatizing shame penalties do seem to aim more at the *pain* and humiliation that these people will feel, than at any *benefit* either they, or those watching them, will receive from the spectacle. For empirical evidence that suggests that such penalties do not benefit either the shamed convict or the public, see Massaro (1997) and Nussbaum (2004).

Callicles, or the respectful shame that is required for Socratic self-knowledge. In order to make these distinctions clear, I first need to analyze more carefully some of the elements of the phenomenon of shame and also some of the ways in which shame words are used, both in English and in Greek.

The emotion of shame involves physiological and behavioral (i.e., affective) as well as cognitive elements.[44] The physiological and behavioral elements of shame can consist of a number of things: the feeling of pain, certain physiological symptoms (i.e., turning red or blushing), and certain behavioral responses (averting one's gaze, squirming awkwardly, bowing or veiling the head, etc.). The Platonic dialogues abound with examples of blushing and squirming interlocutors.[45] Although no one in the *Gorgias* is described as blushing, Callicles' response to Socrates' final line of questioning vividly illustrates the kind of painful squirming exhibited by someone who is feeling ashamed:

> I don't know what you are saying Socrates, so ask someone else . . . How violent you are, Socrates. But if you're persuaded by me, you'll bid this argument farewell, or else you'll converse with someone else . . . Couldn't you go through the argument yourself, either speaking by yourself or answering yourself? (*Gorg.* 505c–d)

But the emotion of shame involves more than just bodily responses, both for the Greeks and for ourselves. Indeed, it is difficult if not impossible to differentiate certain emotions by virtue of bodily changes, either in terms of the physiological experiences of the subject or in terms of the outward behav-

---

[44] This description of shame reflects what has come to be known as the "two components" or cognitive-affective view of emotions (Schacter (1962), 379–99; and Calhoun and Solomon (1984), 4), although, as Rorty (1980, 1–3) points out, the degree to which various emotions include these elements varies considerably. Elster (1999, 246–83) has recently complicated this picture of emotions by proposing a seven-component view that includes (1) qualitative feel, (2) cognitive antecedents, (3) an intentional object, (4) physiological arousal, (5) physiological expressions, (6) valence on the pleasure-pain dimension, and (7) characteristic action tendencies. (He adds the proviso that not all emotions contain all of these elements.) I would classify 1, 4, 5, and 6 as affective, and 2 and 3 as cognitive components of emotions. I am less inclined to include his seventh feature, characteristic action tendencies, within the experience of the emotion itself, and instead refer to this as the moment of reaction within a shame situation throughout this book. However, it might well be the case that while the moment of recognition and the moment of reaction are always analytically distinct, they are *sometimes* experientially intertwined in a shame situation.

[45] See for example Thrasymachus' blush (*Republic*, 1.350d), Charmides' blush (*Charmides* 158c), Clinias' blush (*Euthydemus* 275d), Dionysodorus' blush (*Euthydemus* 297a), Hippothales' blush (*Lysis* 204b), Lysis' blush (*Lysis* 213d), and Hippocrates' blush (*Protagoras* 312a). I agree with Gooch (1988) that not all of the red faces in Plato signify shame and in some instances are closer to humiliation. I also agree with him that some interlocutors clearly do feel shame without blushing. However, I disagree with him that Lysis' blush is only one of self-conscious recognition and does not involve shame.

iors observed by others.[46] A person can flush red, and experience a certain amount of pain when they are ashamed, embarrassed, humiliated, angry, or afraid. In order to differentiate these emotions, one needs to consider their cognitive element: the fact that they involve different appraisals or evaluations of different situations.[47] When we see someone flush red in front of a person wielding a gun, we might well ask, "Are you afraid of this person or ashamed or angry?" And their answer will involve giving reasons that refer to various circumstances or facts about the world to differentiate the emotion: "Actually it's not that I am afraid of him, I know the gun he is holding is fake, but I am angry because that's my gun and I told him not to touch it." (Alternatively, the person might reply, "No, I'm not afraid, I am ashamed because it reminds me of my own previous life as a mobster.") In order for someone to be afraid of a person wielding a gun, that person has to be in a certain cognitive state that involves specific intentional attitudes directed to circumstances in the world, i.e., that the gun is loaded, that guns can harm people, that the person intends to pull the trigger, etc.[48]

In the case of a self-reflexive emotion like shame the cognitive character is somewhat more complicated because the evaluation involved in the emotion also refers back to the self as this self is now seen by an other. To clarify this it is helpful to distinguish between the *cognitive antecedent* of shame, which involves some kind of gaze by an other and the *intentional object* of shame, which involves the judgment of a perceived inadequacy in the self prompted by the gaze of this other.[49] We might react to the feeling of shame by lashing out at the other, but we do so because this other has prompted the revelation of an inadequacy in our self, which then causes the reaction of lashing out. (In contrast, in emotions like anger or disgust both the cognitive antecedent and the intentional object refer to the other rather than to the self.) Although Jon Elster has argued that the cognitive antecedent of shame is the "contemptuous or disgusted disapproval by others of something one has done,"[50] I believe that shame in Plato's *Gorgias*, as well as in our own contemporary experiences,

[46] Cairns (1993), 7; and Redding (1999), 8.

[47] For the view that emotions involve cognitive elements such as evaluations, appraisals, and judgments, see Solomon (1980); Cairns (1993); Elster (1999); Koziak (2000); Nussbaum (2001 and 2004); Fortenbaugh (2002 [1975]); Hall (2003 and 2005); Konstan (2006); Sokolon (2006); Kingston and Ferry (2008); and Krause (2008). Indeed, Cairns (1993); Elster (1999); Koziak (2000); Nussbaum (2001 and 2004); Fortenbaugh ([1975], 2002); Hall (2003 and 2005); Konstan (2006); and Sokolon (2006) all explicitly go back to either Aristotle's or Plato's theory of emotions to argue for the importance of the cognitive (and political and social) features of the emotions.

[48] As Redding (1999, 11) puts it, "What at first seemed like a mere feeling or felt bodily state turns out to be a highly complex cognitive state involving conceptualizations and 'attitudes' intentionally directed to actual (in the case of beliefs) or desirable states of affairs in the world."

[49] I borrow the term "cognitive antecedent" and "intentional object" from Elster (1999), 249–73.

[50] Elster (1999), 149.

does not require the attitude of contempt or disgust on the part of the other.[51] Instead, it is usually prompted by a show of disapproval or criticism by this other toward what one has done.[52]

What I have just outlined very schematically refers only to the occurrent experience or feeling of shame. However, just like English-language users, the Greeks used emotion words in a dispositional sense as well.[53] Emotional dispositions are propensities to have occurrent emotions. So for example, a person who is quick to become angry is often referred to as "irritable" and a person whose anger, when triggered, is extremely strong is referred to as "irascible." But an angry person need not be characterized by either of these two dispositions, so occurrent emotions and emotional dispositions are distinct phenomena.[54] In fact, part of what is said about shame (aischunē) in the Gorgias often refers to the second-order disposition or sense of shame rather than to the occurrent feeling of shame.[55] The problem is that the second-order disposition can be expressed in ways that are identical to the occurrent experience. However, at this level, especially with painful emotions such as shame, the shame-word refers not to our feeling ashamed but to our disposition to avoid situations in which we feel shame.[56] Thus, one's sense of shame is supposed to enable one to avoid actions and situations that one judges to be shameful (aischron); accordingly, in the Gorgias Socrates consistently points out that he has avoided flattery because he considers it shameful (aischron) (465a, 522d).

These second-order dispositions are more likely to be described as character traits than feelings or emotions, and sometimes (though not in the case of shame) are designated by different words, i.e., irascibility or timidity rather

---

[51] In chapter 5, I argue that this is the kind of attitude on the part of the other that tends to produce the emotion of humiliation.

[52] In fact, even the admiring gaze of an other can cause a person to feel shame, if that person does not share the other's estimation that what she has done or is doing is admirable.

[53] Cairns (1993), 10–12. Cf. Calhoun and Solomon (1984), 24; and Rorty (1980), 2.

[54] I borrow this example and explanation from Elster (1999), 244.

[55] Konstan (2006, 99) argues that, for Aristotle, aischunē always refers to the occurrent experience or feeling of shame and not to the disposition or sense of shame. However, I believe that Plato does use aischunē in both the occurrent and dispositional sense in the Gorgias and that this is evident in the passage I quoted earlier: "They have advanced so far into the sense of shame (aischunēs) that—on account of feeling shame (aischunesthai)—each one of them dares to contradict himself in front of many human beings, and this concerning the greatest things" (487b). Plato is careful to have Polus (at 461b) and Callicles (at 482c–d) assert that their predecessors felt ashamed, but Socrates' own assertions about Gorgias and Polus' shame is more ambiguous about whether it was their sense of shame or their feelings of shame that caused them to contradict themselves. Plato also clearly seems to be talking about the habitual sense of aischunē when he says in the Republic that the tyrannical son "habituates himself to be like his father and to have no shame [aischunesthai] before or fear of his parents" (Rep. 8.562e).

[56] As Elster (1999, 244) puts it, "I might acutely desire never to experience shame but also desire to have a disposition to feel shame—in fact, the latter desire presupposes the former."

than anger or fear.[57] Quite often English users distinguish the second-order disposition from the occurrent emotion by distinguishing between the sense of shame and the feeling of being ashamed. Yet even here one might still use the same words "shame" or "ashamed" to refer either to the inhibitory disposition or to the occurrent emotion. Thus when we say, "Have you no shame?" the "shame" whose absence is being decried "is a second-order disposition regarded as a desirable character trait."[58] We might also say that "so-and-so felt ashamed to say what he thought in front of her" and we don't necessarily mean that the person felt the occurrent emotion of shame, but rather that he felt inhibited to say something that would have made him feel the occurrent emotion. These kinds of ambiguity can occur in the Greek as well, and indeed are part of what adds to the complexity of the *Gorgias*.[59]

This distinction between the occurrent and the dispositional is important because, as Aristotle argues in his *Nicomachean Ethics*, when we talk about a virtue (*aretē*) we are not talking about an emotion (*pathos*) or a capacity (*dunamis*), but rather a disposition (*hexis*) (Arist. *Nic. Eth.* 1105b–1106a). There is nothing virtuous about feeling anger or fear for Aristotle; rather one must feel anger in the right way, about the right things, toward the right people, etc. In this vein, I will argue that my own distinctions between flattering and Socratic respectful shame correspond to a vicious and a virtuous way of engaging with an other in order to discover (or to conceal) a truth about the self. For Plato, Socratic respectful shame is at the heart of a courageous truthfulness that is necessary for any healthy ethical and political deliberations.[60]

FLATTERING VS. RESPECTFUL SHAME

I now want to utilize a number of these concepts to articulate what I consider to be Plato's critique of the shame that is involved in the rhetoric of flattery. First, it is important to note that in order to develop a second-order disposition or sense of shame, an individual must first experience the occurrent emotion of being ashamed on at least some previous occasions. Parents do care for their children through shaming as well as loving, and anyone who has ever cared for infants can attest to the fact that they occasionally take great pleasure in

---

[57] Cairns (1993), 11; and Calhoun and Solomon (1984), 24.

[58] Cairns (1993), 11.

[59] As I argued in chapter 2, while Charles Kahn (1983) and Richard McKim (1988) offer important insights into the working of shame in the *Gorgias*, both of their accounts overlook these ambiguities of reference. I show how these ambiguities of reference are also overlooked or oversimplified in contemporary accounts of shame and civility in chapter 5.

[60] Cf. Nieuwenburg (2004) for an excellent account of the crucial role that shame plays in Aristotle's notion of the virtue of truthfulness. Konstan (2006, 95) points out that in Thucydides *aidōs* is related to the virtue of modesty, whereas *aischunē* is related to the virtue of courage.

doing the most shameful, i.e., disturbing and tyrannical things.[61] Yet in the instance that they are rebuked for engaging in these shameful activities their pleasure is replaced (or at least accompanied by) the painful recognition of this disapproving gaze of the parent. Moreover, the pain and awkwardness the child feels in shame is not a result of direct physical punishment, but rather the psychological punishment of disapproval and criticism. As human beings, it is simply a fact that we react to and feel very intensely how we are judged or viewed by others. The blush is itself the physiological manifestation of this recognition of the gaze of the other.[62] Even if we are aware of no inadequacies in our self but walk into a room where everyone turns and expresses disapproval, it is incredibly difficult not to feel embarrassed or ashamed. Similarly it is extremely hard not to feel good about ourselves if we walk into a room and everyone looks on at us admiringly. And this good feeling can occur even if we were thinking disparaging thoughts about our self upon entering the room. Indeed, human beings can and often do orient their lives to pursue the pleasures of recognition, admiration, and honor and to avoid the pain of criticism, disapproval, and dishonor. Our sense of shame can thus come to orient us to avoid disapproval or criticism *as such* rather than orienting us to avoid the actions that were originally judged to be bad and thus worthy of

[61] While this might seem to conflate two different things, i.e., feeling ashamed at something we discover about ourselves and experiencing a shaming at the hands of another, it is unlikely children would ever be able to make the first kind of discovery if they didn't ever experience the second kind of action by an actual other. *Contra* Massaro (1997) who argues that cultural critics who valorize shame confuse the noun, "shame," (which for her refers to a sense of shame that is important for showing us our limits and curbing infantile grandiosity [660–61]) with the verb, "shaming," (which for her is always an uncertain and dangerous thing to do to another person because we can never predict with certainty what impact it will have on the person, and it can even make a person want to kill himself [655]). So while she agrees that a sense of shame is important for all individuals, she thinks that shaming is always dangerous. However, her view tends to equate all acts of shaming with the kind of humiliating shame penalties that she is right to criticize elsewhere in her article, but even a loving parent will sometimes, intentionally or unintentionally, shame their child, and this is probably necessary for them to overcome their tyrannical and destructive impulses.

[62] Here I agree with the first part of Arlene Saxonhouse's (2006, 183) treatment of Hippocrates's blush in the *Protagoras*, i.e., that it is the "unique human response to the gaze of another," but I disagree that the blush is also simultaneously the desire to "be unseen, to hide." For me, the desire to hide or cover the self is characteristic of one possible reaction to the moment of recognition within the occurrent experience of shame (*aischunē*), but the occurrent experience of shame itself (manifested by a blush) is not equivalent to this hiding/covering reaction or desire. Jon Elster's treatment of shame seems closer to my own in that he distinguishes between the "cognitive antecedent" of shame that involves the awareness of the gaze of an other and the "action tendencies" of shame, which primarily involve hiding. However, it is never clear in his account how hiding could really be the primary action tendency of shame if, on his own account (Elster (1999, 145, 154), shame is also the most painful and thus important emotion for making us conform to social norms. This suggests to me that the "action consequence" of transforming the self must be equally prevalent.

criticism.[63] This is precisely one of the things that happens in the case of flat-tering shame: one fixates on the *pain* that is inherent to the cognitive-affective recognition of the gaze of an other that reveals a certain inadequacy in the self, and it is this painful recognition that becomes the "shameful" situation that one tries to avoid in the future.

I believe that it is this feature of shame (*aischunē*) that Socrates critiques in the flattering model of rhetoric and politics. Here the democratic orator pur-sues his own interests by flattering others in order to gain power over them. The goal seems to be the avoidance of the occurrent experience of shame on the part of both the orator and the audience. The orator is never to say any-thing that will cause his audience displeasure or dishonor as a way of ensuring their support and thus satisfying his own desires. But in order to do this suc-cessfully, his *sense of shame* must be attuned to what his audience considers shameful and admirable, so that he can tailor his speech to their views and gain their admiration. (Flattering shame, then, does not refer to the occurrent emotion produced in the audience or experienced by the orator, but rather to the disposition or sense of shame that reciprocally motivates both the audience and orator to avoid ever saying anything that might be painful to their respec-tive audience, even when this involves the truth.) Like a chef who offers chil-dren pastries instead of bitter medicines (464d–e), the orator offers the audi-ence flattering images of themselves so that they never have to hear anything that is painful or displeasing to them. By taking on the perspective of one's audience, this audience becomes the final arbiter of what can and cannot be said. The speaker must attempt to conceal any "deficiencies or deviations from the group ideal before this third person," and in order to do so he "addresses [himself] directly to the onlooker and is oriented to the objectified public image."[64] The speaker's sense of shame thus attunes him to the view of the other, but in such a way that this other can never again reveal any inadequacies or criticisms of his self. Nor is he (the speaker) oriented to revealing any inade-quacies in his audience. Instead, both parties to the debate engage in the plea-sure of reciprocal recognition as such. In the end it is exactly this kind of flattering rhetoric that Callicles urges Socrates to pursue in order to preserve himself in an imperialistic democracy like Athens (521a).[65]

[63] Douglas Cairns (1993, 2–3, 455) points out that the Greek verbs *aideomai* and *aischunomai*, occurring with an accusative referring to another person or persons, could mean either "I feel shame before" or "I respect," or some combination of both. However, Cairns points out (1993, 3) that in the case of the "I respect" usage "the concentration on the self and one's own status is prompted by and focuses on consideration of the status of another ... And the possibility of criticism from the other is either absent or deeply buried." However, in the "I feel shame before" usage of either term, the status of the other is "*significant simply as a possible source of criticism*" (my italics).

[64] Straus (1979), 223.

[65] For the link between flattery, demagoguery, and tyranny in the tyrannical democracy de-scribed by Aristotle in the *Politics*, see Abizadeh ([2002], 2008), 74 and Tarcov (2005), 133. Tarcov

In contrast to this model of politics and discussion, Socrates' allusions to the example of medicine (464d–465d, 480c) remind us that the structure of care involved in the relationship between a doctor and patient may require painful or bitter procedures or pills,[66] and the analogy that Socrates wishes us to draw from this is that caring for the health of someone's soul may similarly require the painful cognitive-affective mechanism involved in the feeling of shame. One of the central debates in the *Gorgias*, which is made most explicit in the confrontation between Socrates and Callicles, is whether the pleasant and the good are identical and whether the pursuit of maximal pleasure is indeed the best way of life for human beings. Insofar as *Socrates* argues against the equivalence of the pleasant and the good, the painful and the bad, it is certainly not the case that shame is a bad thing *because* it is painful. In fact, it is Socrates' interlocutors in the *Gorgias* who draw this conclusion. They equate the pleasure of recognition and esteem with the good and the pain of critique and dishonor with the bad. Instead, when the Platonic Socrates describes the rhetoric of justice to Polus, he describes it as a form of rhetoric that does not take into account what is painful:

> For speaking in defense of one's own injustice, therefore, or that of parents or comrades or children or fatherland when it does injustice, rhetoric will be of no use to us, Polus; except if someone takes it to be of use for the opposite purpose, supposing that he must most of all accuse himself, and then whoever else of his relatives and friends happens at any time to do injustice, and not hide the unjust deed but bring it into the open, so as to pay the just penalty and become healthy, and compel both himself and others not to play the coward but to grit his teeth and submit well and courageously as if to a doctor for cutting and burning—pursuing what's good and fine, *not taking account of what's painful*, and if he has done unjust deeds worthy of blows, submitting to beating; if worthy of bonds, submitting to being bound; if worthy of a fine, paying it; if worthy of banishment, going into exile; and if worthy of death, dying—himself being the first accuser both of himself and of others that are relatives, and using rhetoric for this purpose, so that, their unjust deeds having become manifest, they may be released from the greatest evil, injustice [my italics]. (480b–d)

The Platonic Socrates' description of the rhetoric of justice in this passage bears a striking resemblance to the kind of courage and daring required on

---

(2005), 133 notes that the demagogue is the one who flatters the *dēmos,* so it is them and not the demagogue who is the real tyrant.

[66] Again, the association of medicine and pain would have resonated much more with Socrates' Athenian contemporaries because their medical procedures involved such things as cutting and drawing blood without, of course, the benefits of modern painkillers.

the part of both the speaker and audience speaking with *parrhēsia*. Indeed, by making his character "Socrates" present his elenchic activity as a kind of courageous rhetoric for the benefit of one's fatherland, Plato explicitly draws a connection between the Socratic shaming elenchus and the Athenian demo-cratic ideal of *parrhēsia*. As was shown earlier, *parrhēsia* was intricately related to the practice of uttering a deserved reproach and entailed the risk of heckling, fines, and punishment. However, a rhetoric that consists of accusing oneself and one's friends is very different from one that consists of flattering oneself and one's friends. It requires that one remain open to the possibility that the other with whom one is conversing might actually show you something painful about yourself that you were unaware of, or had concealed from yourself in the past. In other words, it requires that one remain open to the possibility of being rightfully shamed out of one's conformity and complacent moralism by an other in the ongoing and mutual project of collective self-examination. Only by remaining open to this possibility do we come to truly respect this other and, through the insights of this other, to new possibilities of self-respect and self-understanding.

It is not surprising, then, that it is Callicles who thinks that philosophy is appropriate only during one's youth and that it should not get in the way of the more important education regarding the customs and pleasures of one's city (484c–485e). He ends up being the interlocutor least capable of submitting to Socrates' shaming refutations and least willing to learn anything new about himself or his city (505c–d). In contrast, Socrates' shaming elenchus and dem-ocratic debate both require participants who are willing to recognize the gap between themselves and their idealized images of themselves, and who can make this recognition the necessary first step toward the ongoing project of reconstruction and transformation. A Socratic respectful shame is thus neces-sary to constrain or inhibit the flattering shame that prompts participants to slavishly mimic the viewpoints of others, while concealing the fact of this slav-ish imitation both from themselves and from this other. And a person like Socrates might well be unabashed (lacking in flattering shame), without thereby being shameless (lacking in Socratic respectful shame).[67]

Indeed my typologies of flattering and Socratic respectful shame are in part meant to address a prevalent misconception about whether or not Socrates himself, and philosophers more generally, are or ought to be shameless.[68] By overlooking the possibility that a person who lacks flattering shame might still possess a robust sense of shame, my critics have accused me of overlooking

---

[67] For this distinction, see Straus (1979), 223.

[68] I fully address the prevalent and oversimplistic tendency to think about the complex human phenomenon of shame in terms of the binary distinction between shame and shamelessness in chapter 5.

Socrates' shamelessness.[69] However, I think that there are many instances in the early, middle, and late dialogues where Plato is careful to show us that Socrates is not shameless and to point out just what kinds of actions are shameless. Thus for instance, in the *Apology*, Socrates is careful to point out that his accusers are the shameless ones (*Apol.* 17b) and that he himself is eventually convicted only because he refused to *shamelessly* wail and lament and thus pander to the spectators in order to ensure his survival and acquittal (*Apol.* 38e). This, for Socrates, would have been an act of shamelessness and would have been completely discordant with his respect for philosophy. In Books 8 and 9 of the *Republic*, Socrates argues that the *tyrant* is the one who tries to become shameless by renaming shame (*aidōs*) "simplicity" (*ēlithiotēs*) (*Rep.* 8.560d–e), and mistakenly calling shamelessness (*anaideia*) "courage" (*andreia*) (*Rep.* 8.561a). In Book 10 of the *Republic* Socrates says that he himself does have a certain shame before Homer (*Rep.* 10.595b), and in the *Phaedrus* Socrates says that his first speech was shameless (*Phdr.* 243c), and that he must recant it in front of a person who is of noble breeding and gentle in character and before whom he does feel shame (*Phdr.* 243d). Finally, in the *Gorgias*, Socrates repeatedly tells Callicles that he would be ashamed of not being able to help either himself or his friends or relatives from committing an injustice toward human beings or the gods (509b–c, 522d).[70]

So I do think that there is an other before whom Socrates felt respectful shame and that this was, as he asserts in the *Gorgias* and the *Apology*, related to his love of philosophy (*Gorg.* 481d, *Apol.* 28d). As Socrates puts it in the latter dialogue, his obedience to the god means that he will remain in his philosophic station and not "take into account death or anything else compared to what is shameful" (*Apol.* 28d).[71] That Socrates had a certain shame before philosophy also means that he might well have felt ashamed before a noble and gentle character like Plato, whose own philosophizing was both

---

[69] See Green, (2005): 266–79. Bloom (1968) also suggests that the philosopher is shameless but not vicious because his insatiable desire for the truth and the pleasures of contemplation make him less attracted to the things like money or power that do pose a threat to the common good and that do motivate the tyrant. This kind of argument fails to account for the fact that Socrates and Plato do express shame before the activity of philosophy, before other philosophers, and before great poets like Homer, as I go on to show in this chapter. Aristotle also clearly states that a person will feel shame (*aischunē*) at things that are truly regarded as wrong in front of their acquaintances (Arist. *Rhet.* 1384b23) and will feel shame (*aischunē*) in front of one's advisors or teachers (1385a25), and there is no suggestion that this would exclude philosophers.

[70] I follow Oona Eisenstadt (2001) in thinking that because of this kind of shame, Socrates might well have felt ashamed of not being able to educate more of his fellow Athenians during his lifetime so that they would have been able to recognize his elenchic activities as just, and thus acquit him at his trial. See also Raymond Geuss' (2001, 30–31) helpful distinction between the shamelessness of Diogenes and the shame of Socrates.

[71] This translation is taken from "Plato's Apology of Socrates" in *Four Texts on Socrates*, trans. Thomas G. West and Grace Starry West, (Ithaca and London: Cornell University Press, 1984), 80.

similar to and different from his own (hence the above-mentioned *Phaedrus* passage).[72] For Plato and Socrates, the *agōn* of philosophic discussion and democratic debate did not consist of shameless self-assertion, but rather of a complex negotiation and contestation between the self and others, both real and ideal. Plato's accomplishment in the *Gorgias* is not that he creates a wholly new "Socrates" who only now feels shame, but rather that he creates a new "Socrates" who is able to suggest the ways in which his Socratic respectful shame is (and always was) similar to the democratic ideal of *parrhēsia*, which Plato fears is *not* actually being practiced by his other fellow Athenians.

PLATO *contra* TYRANNICAL DEMOCRATS

But is Callicles not as equally unabashed as Socrates in his frank praise of tyranny? I have tended to treat Callicles as the slavish flatterer of the *dēmos* that Socrates accuses him of being (*Gorg.* 481d–e). And I might thus seem to be overlooking his first speech about the powerful, unjust, and immoderate life of the tyrant who tramples on the conventions of the many. Here Callicles certainly seems to be courageously rejecting the democratic ideals of Athens rather than mimicking or flattering them. Thus, his speech could be seen as an example of democratic *parrhēsia* because he boldly asserts a critique of the *dēmos* and of the democratic principle of equality. However, I want to end this chapter by suggesting why this is in fact not the case. The problem is that Callicles is not really voicing a view that is alien to his Athenian democratic audience. As Socrates' remark at 492d suggests, Callicles' praise of tyranny is actually consistent with "what the others think but are unwilling to say." Callicles might be frank about his wish or dream of becoming a tyrant, but this wish may in fact have been shared by many other "democrats" who covertly admired the tyrant while condemning his actions as unjust. Callicles at his most shocking is still only flattering his beloved *dēmos*, and the moral indignation that the many direct toward the tyrant may be possible only because they envy the goods that he attains through his acts of injustice.[73] I believe that Plato felt this was indeed the case in the "democratic" Athens he so vehemently criticizes in the *Gorgias*.

But if this is the case, then the democratic desire for majority rule via a simple vote becomes problematic: "With so many confused about what it means to be a democratic citizen and about the criteria for distinguishing between democratic leaders and tyrants, voting to decide which way of life or

---

[72] I address the similarities and differences between Socratic respectful shame and Platonic respectful shame in chapter 4.

[73] For an alternative example of the transmutation of envy into indignation, see Elster (1999), 99.

policy is best amounts to moral and political suicide."[74] And this means that even though Socrates' own views on justice and on the correct procedure for conducting a debate seem strange and extraordinary (*atopon*) to both Polus and Callicles,[75] they might well be so only because they stand apart from this covert admiration of tyranny and tyrannical democracy. "Socrates' critique may be an effort to save his native city from a corrupting vision of itself . . . [and] Socrates' attempt to exorcise the glamour of tyranny and thus break the unholy alliance between the would-be tyrant and the many who surreptitiously envy him, even at their own moral and political expense, makes the philosopher an ally of democracy."[76]

Thus part of Socrates' distrust of the many, which he expresses in the Polus section, consists of the fact that *they* think that tyranny is the best life. What Socrates attempts to do in his shaming refutations of a "democrat" like Callicles is to show him that he doesn't fully identify with the tyrant because he can still be ashamed by some of the actions entailed by the tyrannical life of indiscriminate hedonism. Just as the elenchus is used in dialogues such as the *Euthyphro* and the *Crito* to show Socrates' interlocutors that they are not as just as they think they are, it is used in the *Gorgias* to show his interlocutors that they are not as unjust as they think they are.[77]

Moreover, as I mentioned earlier, in critiquing Callicles' particular brand of *parrhēsia* Plato is relying on debates that were all ready taking place in democratic Athens. By the fourth century BC a number of orators had begun to distinguish between a critical kind of *parrhēsia*, which was important for good democratic deliberation, and a kind of *parrhēsia* that was reckless and ignorant, and merely pandered to the desires of an audience drunk on their own lawlessness and lack of self-restraint.[78] This context is extremely important for understanding Plato's criticisms of democracy in both the *Republic* and the *Gorgias*. In Book 8 of the *Republic* Plato initially characterizes democracy as being a city filled with freedom and free speech (*kai eleutherias hē polis mestē kai parrhēsias gignetai*) (*Rep.* 8.557b). However, his harshest criticisms of democracy actually occur in the section where he describes democracy's slide into tyranny (*Rep.* 8.564a–569c). Here, Plato argues that the tyrant eventually does away with anyone who continues to speak frankly to him and to one another (*parrhēsiazesthai kai pros auton kai pros allēlous*) in order to fully establish himself in the city and to enslave the citizenry (*Rep.* 8.567b). His criticism of the tyrannical democrat thus focuses on the fact that he actually banishes

---

[74] Euben (1994), 209.

[75] Polus asserts this at 467b, Callicles asserts this at 481b–c.

[76] Euben (1994), 208.

[77] Stauffer (2006) sees this unrecognized attachment to justice, shared by both Polus and Callicles, as an important key to understanding the unity of the *Gorgias*.

[78] Foucault (2001), 77–87.

the good kind of critical *parrhēsia* from the city and kills anyone who continues to practice it. As Plato dramatically illustrates in the *Apology* and predicts in the *Gorgias*, the gadfly or critical frank speaker, Socrates, is eventually put to death by just such a tyrannical *dēmos* because he refuses to follow Callicles' advice to gratify and flatter them (521a–b).

In the later sections of the *Gorgias*, Plato articulates what lies at the heart of Callicles' own brand of *parrhēsia*, and his analysis illustrates why this kind of frankness amounts not just to flattery but also to a very dangerous type of ignorance. At 517b–c Socrates sarcastically praises Themistocles and Pericles for being "terribly clever" at supplying the Athenians with ships, walls, and dockyards, which were all potent symbols of Athens' imperialism.[79] But he accuses them of never "leading the desires [of the citizens] in a different direction" (517b). Callicles, the product of this imperialistic Athenian democracy, exemplifies this in his own praise of tyranny and indiscriminate hedonism, i.e., the pursuit of any and all desires, at 491e–492c. For Plato, the most problematic desire that lies at the heart of both Athenian imperialism and Calliclean indiscriminate hedonism is the desire for a godlike omnipotence and immortal glory that allows one to evade pain, suffering, and the ultimate danger, i.e., death of the self or of the polity. As I mentioned earlier, in flattering shame one equates the shameful with the painful and thus attempts to avoid all situations in which one ever has to feel pain and suffering, but since this is simply not possible for mortal and needy human beings, flattering shame can dispose one to construct a fantastical image of omnipotence as a way of satisfying this all too human desire. We can aspire to and be motivated by fantastical images and exemplars of action that simply cannot be predicated of our human experience of pain and suffering.[80]

This desire for omnipotence also requires a further clarification of the kinds of other that can be involved in shame. First, to recall some of the points I made in the last chapter, the other that prompts the self's judgment of its own inadequacy can be actual or imaginary and internalized.[81] And in either case, this other can be more than just the fact of being seen: it can be the repository of very specific attitudes, ideals, and behaviors.[82] Although Bernard Williams

---

[79] Cf. Nichols (1998), 37 n.29.

[80] Blitz (2005, 16), Bradshaw (2005, 176), and Newell (2005, 150) all argue that the tyrannical individual is characterized by his desire to be like a god and to transcend human finitude. This desire also characterizes the philosopher; however, the difference between the two is that the tyrannical individual wants to be like a god in having or possessing the good, which he equates with a kind of immortal life here on earth, whereas the philosopher strives to be like a god, which he equates with the eternal truth. In his unceasing striving for this truth, the philosopher never turns away from knowledge of his own finitude. In contrast to the philosopher, then, what the tyrannical individual has in common with a god is a *lack* of love of wisdom, and a *lack* of the desire to become wise (Bradshaw (2005, 176).

[81] Williams (1993), 81; Cairns (1993), 18; and chapter 2, n.84.

[82] Williams (1993), 82–83; and chapter 2, n.87.

tends to conflate the notion of an internalized and imaginary other in his first set of distinctions, I think it is important to distinguish these. What Plato illustrates in the *Gorgias* is that human beings can be attuned to both realistic and fantastical others and that either (or some combination of both) of these others might be internalized by someone living in an imperialistic democratic polity. The fantastical other that Polus and Callicles are attuned to consists of their fantasy of the omnipotent and godlike person who is free from all of the restraints, sufferings, and pain that are actually characteristic of human life.

For Plato, then, shame becomes a problematic emotion when it is linked to this kind of fantastical projection and desire for omnipotence, which hides rather than discloses our mortal and needy natures. At the end of the *Gorgias* Plato's Socrates criticizes the Athenian imperialistic democratic leaders Themistocles and Pericles for feeding precisely this fantasy of the Athenians by turning their attention *exclusively* to fortifying the city with countless ships, walls, and arsenals (517c).[83] Such projects, however, transformed Athenian democratic politics into a collective endeavor to secure mere life rather than the best life, and *all* deliberations were centered on the ultimately fantastical desire to preserve oneself and one's city from every possible kind of pain and danger, including death (511b–c). As I will show in chapter 5, Plato's alternative model for a more salutary form of democratic engagement involves acknowledging and coming to terms with, rather than avoiding and denying, the mortality and vulnerability that we share with others. And as I will now show in chapter 4, it also involves corrections to his teacher's overly adversarial method of democratic engagement.

---

[83] As Strauss (2005, 233) puts it, "Tyranny offers not merely repression but grandeur ... We contemporaries make a mistake if we measure freedom by a regime's ability to erect monuments, to patronize the arts, or to build protective walls."

Chapter Four

SOCRATIC VS. PLATONIC SHAME

SHAME AND DECEPTION IN PLATO'S *GORGIAS*

My account of shame in Plato's *Gorgias* so far has focused on Socrates' interaction with his interlocutors, both in terms of the ways in which some of their reactions to Socrates lead to what I have described as flattering shame, and the way in which Socrates' shaming elenchus exemplifies a kind of Socratic respectful shame. I have said very little, however, about the relationship between Socrates and Plato on the issue of either flattering or Socratic respectful shame; and thus about what Plato might actually be *criticizing* about Socrates by means of the drama in the dialogue. Shame may well be the crucial element in the Socratic refutations of the *Gorgias*, but was Socrates himself aware of the extent and ramifications of this psychological factor? Is there something about Socrates' comportment toward his interlocutors in the *Gorgias* that makes them react in the less than ideal ways that they do? Is the less skeptical and more constructive "Socrates," who progressively comes to light over the course of the *Gorgias*, a mouthpiece for a more mature Plato reflecting his own views upon, or corrections of, his teacher? Might this new "Socrates" exemplify something of a respectful and reciprocal shaming of Socrates, by Plato?

In chapter 1, I defended the affirmative answer to all of these questions by arguing that the *Gorgias* is one of Plato's transitional and middle dialogues containing his own reflections on and criticisms of his teacher, Socrates, and his own deepening understanding of the motivational sources of human behavior. In this chapter, I want to address these issues by considering the similarities and differences between the Socratic shaming elenchus and the myth that is presented at the end of the *Gorgias*. I believe that the myth at the end of the dialogue embodies, in the most vivid way, a number of these reflections and criticisms. And here it is not just the content of the myth itself that illustrates these reflections and criticisms, but the very move to myth as a communicative medium that must be seen as crucial for understanding what Plato is saying about the Socratic shaming elenchus in the dialogue.[1]

---

[1] As Annas (1982a, 119–120) notes, three of Plato's dialogues end with lengthy and elaborate eschatological myths that are relevant to the dialogue's main moral argument, and here she includes the *Gorgias, Phaedo*, and *Republic*. For my purposes, it is important to note that these all

More specifically, it is my contention that Plato's introduction of the myth at the end of the *Gorgias* must be interpreted in connection with his complex teaching about the role of shame (*aischunē*) in the Socratic elenchus and the kinds of reaction that this elenchus produces. Even commentaries that focus specifically on the role of shame in the *Gorgias* often fail to address the myth at the end of the dialogue altogether.[2] However, the myth itself abounds with some of the most powerful tropes of shame, and these vivid images would have resonated with Plato's Athenian audience no less than they do with his contemporary readers. As Bernard Williams has argued, being seen naked is a paradigm instance of the experience of shame both for the Greeks and for ourselves.[3] Similarly, one of the most memorable images of the *Gorgias* myth is the trial of the great kings and tyrants stripped naked and dead, revealing their whip scars of injustice, before the equally naked and dead souls of the three judges Minos, Rhadamanthus, and Aeacus (523c–525a).[4] As I shall argue below, these images are meant to vividly illustrate the effects on the soul of Socrates' shaming refutations, as well as the discrepancies between flattering shame and Socratic respectful shame. Socrates' shaming refutations involve the painful but potentially beneficial cognitive-affective recognition of the gaze of an other that reveals a certain inadequacy in the self. In the myth at the end of the dialogue this fact is quite literally "embodied" in the vivid images of the naked souls, standing before the discerning eyes of the judges, with their festering sores and whip scars of injustice revealed for all to see (524c–525a).

However, as I shall also argue, the fact that the myth illustrates the very elenchic method that is primarily on display in the earlier sections is itself

---

fall into Plato's transitional period (*Gorgias*) or middle period (*Phaedo, Republic*), where he begins to focus more deeply on the role of the emotions and the other *alogon* elements of the soul in psychosocial interactions.

[2] See for example McKim (1988); Kahn (1983); and Gish (2006).

[3] Williams (1993), 78. Konstan (2006, 103) argues that nakedness did not play as central a role in Greek shame as modern interpreters such as Williams tend to assume because "Greek males in the classical period exercised naked in public." Williams (1993, 78) may overemphasize the connections between nakedness and sexuality because he focuses primarily on *aidōs* and not *aischunē*, and one of the derivatives of *aidōs* is *aidoia*, a standard Greek word for the genitals. However, Williams (1993, 78) does suggest, in the same context, that nakedness is only a very vivid instance of the more basic experience of shame, which involves being seen inappropriately by an other. As Nussbaum (2004, 186) puts it, nakedness and sexuality (both for the Greeks and for ourselves) are probably only manifestations of a more primary experience, which she describes as a sense of inadequacy or failure to attain some ideal state (184). My differences with Nussbaum's account will become clear in chapter six.

[4] As Dodds (1959, 379) notes, the scars on the soul reappear frequently in many later writers including Plutarch, Epictetus and Tacitus, who all probably derived this memorable image directly or indirectly from Plato. The three judges all belong to various ancient mythological sources and were all renowned for their justice. However the particular form of the myth, which recounts what goes on in the underworld, was probably taken over by Plato from the Orphic form of poetry known as a *katabasis*, a poem describing a visit to the underworld. See Dodds (1959), 373–74.

indicative of Plato's own response to what he saw as certain limitations in the Socratic elenchus for dealing with the mechanisms of shame (*aischunē*). Myth has certain advantages over the Socratic elenchus because of its very imagistic and narrative form, and the myth at the end of the *Gorgias* represents Plato's most extended attempt in this dialogue to combine the advantages of Gorgias' epideictic display rhetoric with the painful forensic rhetoric of the Socratic elenchus.[5] The procedure of Socratic justice was able to diagnose or lay bare the errors in a person's way of life, but the painful character of Socrates' medicine sometimes ended up being a poison rather than a cure because it failed to be as therapeutic as it was diagnostic.[6] Instead, it is Gorgias who boasts of his ability to help doctors when he first meets Socrates (456b), and who reenters the discussion at a crucial moment to convince Callicles to carry on with or "submit" to Socrates' painful discussion, if only to gratify Gorgias himself (497b–c).[7] If Plato himself is able to combine the two types of medicine and rhetoric that Gorgias and Socrates practice, then he might be able to perform both operations through one mode of medicine/rhetoric. As Benardete puts it, "Medicine is both diagnostic and therapeutic. If rhetoric were comparable, it would diagnose and cure the sick of soul through the same kind of speeches it used in transmitting its teaching."[8] Thus, although the myth *illustrates* the experience of being ashamed before an other, it also *exemplifies* the comportment toward another that is characteristic of the second-order disposition of shame itself: that is, of how one approaches an other in an attitude of respect. In other words, I will argue that Plato's use of myth in the dialogues of his middle period reflects his own subtle corrections to what he saw as problematic in Socrates' ironic comportment toward his interlocutors in his elenchic refutations. The myth embodies what I shall call Platonic respectful shame, and this form of shame reflects a number of the corrections that Plato believed were necessary to overcome the negativity of Socrates' own brand of respectful shame.[9] Second, I want to argue that Plato's use of myth includes elements of

---

For the importance of this motif of *katabasis* (descent) in the *Republic*, see Segal (1978); Rosenstock (1983); and Seery (1988).

[5] Both Dodds (1959, 372) and Irwin (1979, 242) argue that it is probably Plato's earliest eschatological myth. As Irwin (1979, 7) points out, Socrates does use allegory and speaks about immortality in some of the earlier dialogues (specifically, *Apol.* 40c–41c and *Crito* 54bc), but he doesn't engage in the kind of detailed myth telling that occurs in the *Gorgias, Republic, Phaedo,* and *Phaedrus.* Cf. Annas (1982a).

[6] Benardete (1991), 14.

[7] See also Dodds (1959), 5; Nichols (1998), 133; Gish (2006), 66; Weiss (2003), 198–99; and Stauffer (2006), 31. Similarly, in Section 14 of his *Encomium of Helen*, Gorgias compares the effect of his *logos* on the mind to that of a drug (*pharmakon*).

[8] Benardete (1991), 14. Unlike Benardete, I think that the "sick of soul" includes Socrates as well as Callicles, who both need to be made more gentle if any kind of healthy relationship is to be achieved between the two of them (and by extension) between democratic Athens and Socrates.

[9] *Contra* Stauffer (2006, 177) who argues that the myth is not meant to be the primary model for Plato's new kind of noble rhetoric.

both the painful medicine of Socratic elenchus and the more pleasant medicine of Gorgianic rhetoric,[10] even though he disagrees with these two "doctors" about certain other elements of their remedies.

These last statements, however, might still seem to place me in the tradition of interpreters who treat shame, myth, and even Socratic irony (an element of the elenchus I have evaded up to this point) as modes of communication aimed at deceiving one's audience. Shame has often been seen as a major culprit in the rhetoric of deception. A person's sense of shame can dispose him to hide or conceal his true views from the monitoring gaze of his audience precisely because what is considered shameful or noble by this audience or other is not always identical to what the person himself considers to be true or false. It can also, and perhaps more problematically, induce self-deception: the person who mimics the audience's perspective can begin to think that this perspective correctly characterizes all of his own actions and thoughts. Indeed, in the last chapter I outlined some of the ways in which flattering shame can lead to these sorts of results. However, in this chapter I want to defend both Socratic and Platonic shame against the charges of deception, specifically as these two forms of comportment are exemplified in Socrates' famous irony and Plato's eschatological myths.

Socratic irony and Platonic myth have both been interpreted as forms of deception, or at least as forms of communication that hedge their truth claims, for reasons that imply inferiority on the part of the receiver of the message. Plato's myths have been seen as stories directed to those interlocutors who are unable to give up their own attachment to the conventional views of justice, even though these views may well have been refuted by the strictly rational arguments of the dialogue.[11] Similarly, Socrates' irony has been interpreted (both by his contemporaries and by his interlocutors in the *Gorgias*) as a form of deception or pretense that masks his own feelings of superiority or disdain for his inferior interlocutors.[12] Gregory Vlastos' own seminal article on Socratic irony (which I shall examine in more detail below) attempts to rescue it from these charges of deception, but he has no problem treating Platonic irony as a "use of words intended to convey one meaning to the uninitiated part of the audience and another to the initiated, the delight of it lying in the secret intimacy set up between the latter and the speaker."[13]

[10] See Wardy (1996, 28–30) for the argument that Gorgias' *Encomium of Helen* endeavored to produce pleasure in the listener through its use of novelty (*kainotēs*) and order or harmony (*kosmos*). Similarly, Plato's myth, which is meant to reveal the teaching of the dialogue in a new and novel form, goes beyond Socrates who prided himself on always saying the same things (482a–b, 490e).

[11] See for example Benardete (1991); and Stauffer (2006).

[12] Callicles angrily accuses Socrates of being ironical toward him at 489e. Aristotle treats irony as a vice in the *Nicomachean Ethics* (*Nic. Eth.* 1127a23).

[13] Vlastos is here quoting from the definition of irony in Fowler's *Modern English Usage*. See "Additional Notes: 1.3" in Vlastos (1991), 245.

Treating either Socratic or Platonic irony as forms of deception suggests that they are forms of flattery that are tailored to the viewpoint of the audience in much the same way that the flattering sense of shame allows the person to say only what will please and not pain his audience.[14] Here, the second-order disposition or sense of shame causes a person to utter an insincere or false remark because it makes them tailor their remarks to the audience rather than uttering what they really believe to be true.[15] One conceals one's meaning or viewpoint from the audience or other by mimicking the perspective of the other, and this stance thereby sets up a relation of superiority or disdain to this very other. In this chapter, I want to argue instead that Socratic and Platonic irony reflect two different kinds of respectful shame. Socrates' sense of shame disposes him to utter the truth to everyone he meets no matter how painful (*lupēron*) or strange (*atopon*) these views might seem to his interlocutors. Accordingly, he tells Callicles that he would not be ashamed of being struck on the jaw or being put to death by the city, *but he would be ashamed of being unable to render this painful but beneficial service to the city* (508d–509c). Socrates' sense of shame then disposes him to avoid what he considers most shameful, i.e., the flattering rhetoric that aims at the pleasant without the best. Out of respect for his interlocutors, Socrates utters the truth as he sees it. Yet, for this very reason, he ends up appearing strange, annoying, non-sensical, mocking, and thus ironical to the very Athenian audience he refuses to flatter.[16] As Callicles puts it, his ideas literally turn their worldviews upside down (481c).[17]

Similarly, Plato himself believes that Socrates' just rhetoric of shaming someone for their own benefit is necessary in light of the fact that the pleasant and the good are not identical and that a certain amount of pain is often

---

[14] Weiss (2003) and Stauffer (2006) both argue that the alliance between Plato and Gorgias involves flattery and thus the embellishment or covering over of the true message that Plato wants to convey to his more philosophic audience. Weiss (2003, 205) even goes so far as to suggest that it is an evil or wicked practice done for the sake of the good of protecting Socratic philosophy. It is a poison for the many in order to protect the philosophic few. I disagree. To borrow a phrase from Annas (1982a, 120), these interpretations tend to see the mythical or "aesthetic" aspects of Plato in a strictly "pejorative sense." Annas (1982a, 119) also notes the tendency of many commentators to see Plato's myths as tedious or as "holidays from serious thinking" because they seem to simply drive home a point already made in the "rational" part of the dialogue, but now "as an optional extra for those who like stories."

[15] Stauffer (2006) suggests that Plato's noble rhetoric is actually tailored to the viewpoint of Callicles whose "noble" understanding of the world ultimately contains contradictory beliefs about whether hedonism or courageous self-sacrifice is the best way of life.

[16] Polus accuses Socrates of being *atopon* (strange/extraordinary/out of place) at 473a and 480e. Callicles accuses him of being *atopon* at 494d, of driveling (*phluarein*) at 490c–d, 490e, and being ironical (*eirōnikon*) at 489e.

[17] As Irwin (1979, 169) puts it, "Instead of simply saying with Polus (480e) that they are absurd, he [Callicles] sees that if they are true, they imply radical criticisms of most people's beliefs and values."

integral to the recognition of moral truths. However, I believe that his revision to this kind of Socratic respectful shame reflects the additional consideration that certain pleasures might well be beneficial as part of the more curative aspects of a noble rhetoric. The pleasures of sight and sound, so integral to Gorgias' epideictic rhetoric, can be combined with the more painful and negative aspects of the Socratic elenchus to elicit a more positive reaction to the experience of being ashamed. Plato's attitude of respectful shame involves the insight that people must be met on their own ground and that the soul must be led not just by turning the eyes, but rather by turning the whole soul;[18] and the myth at the end of the *Gorgias* reflects the beginnings of Plato's own understanding of the role that a more imagistic and narrative logic might play in turning the whole soul of the interlocutor. To respect another person involves not just pointing out his past mistakes and errors (as is the case with the Socratic elenchus),[19] but also greeting them on their own grounds to then slowly lead them to new ways of seeing the world. In other words, what looks like an act of flattery or deceit might actually be indicative of the kind of relationship to one's audience that is integral to eliciting a change in their background disposition, i.e., their sense of shame. In the final section of this chapter, then, I shall consider Plato's introduction of the myth at the end of the *Gorgias* as indicative of this possibility and thus as exemplifying a respectful shame that combines the painful insights of the Socratic elenchus with the pleasures of certain sights and insights that are partially grounded in the experiences of his democratic audience, including Callicles.

But before turning to consider Platonic irony as a form of respectful shame, I will first examine the ways in which the myth illustrates the process and limits of the Socratic elenchus. I will then examine the differences between elenchus and myth and suggest how these differences reflect Plato's own attempts to go beyond the limits of Socrates' shaming elenchus. I will then treat Socratic elenchus and Platonic myth as different forms of irony. And finally I will examine how and whether these ironical stances constitute forms of flattering or respectful shame.

[18] In the *Republic*, the Platonic Socrates describes education as an art (*technē*) of turning around (*metastrephein*) or turning (*strephein*) the whole body and not just the eyes toward the light and away from the darkness (*Rep.* 518b–d). In the *Phaedrus*, the Platonic Socrates describes the rhetorical art (*rhētorikē technē*) as a "leading of the souls through speeches [*psuchagōgia tis dia logōn*], not only in law courts and whatever other public gatherings, but also in private ones. . . . " (*Phdr.* 261a).

[19] As Nussbaum (2004, 35) puts it, even though our emotions are open to rational persuasion, this does not mean that our emotions instantly change once they have been shown to be irrational or unreasonable. Elster (1999) likewise notes that there is a certain amount of inertia to our emotions. For Plato and Aristotle this is connected with the fact that they only become virtues for us after a long process of habituation. See Abizadeh ([2002], 2008, 71) for the argument that this aspect of the emotions (*pathē*) means they can provide an important supplement to abstract *logos* in the narrow sense by serving as a "repository of the uncodified wisdom of past experience."

The Myth as an Illustration of the Socratic Elenchus

The *Gorgias* myth recounts the trial that human beings must face at the end of their lives, which determines whether they will go away to the islands of the blessed or to Tartarus, the prison of retribution and judgment (*to tēs tiseōs te kai dikēs desmōtērion*) (523b). At the beginning of the myth, Socrates recounts the two specific reforms that Zeus makes to the trials of human beings held at the end of their lives as they prepare to enter the next life. The first reform is to take away their foreknowledge of their own death (523d–e). The second reform is to require that both the men on trial and the judges themselves be naked and dead (523e). These two reforms actually illustrate many of the more lengthy criticisms of Athenian trials and political practices that Socrates makes in his earlier discussions with Gorgias, Polus, and Callicles (471e, 475e–476a, 511b–513a).[20] Taking away the foreknowledge of death corresponds to Socrates' criticism of imperial Athenian politics. Such a politics, according to Socrates, amounts only to an elaborate preparation for saving and prolonging mere life: "For the true man, at any rate, must reject living any amount of time whatsoever, and must not be a lover of life. Rather, turning over what concerns these things to the god and believing the women's saying that no man may escape his destiny, he must investigate what comes after this: In what way may he who is going to live for a time live best?" (512e–513a). This need to reorient oneself away from the concern with mere life toward the concern with the best life is succinctly illustrated in the transition from the foreknowledge present under Cronos to the lack of this foreknowledge under Zeus.

Standing *naked* and *alone* before the judge with the whip scars of injustice evident on the soul corresponds to Socrates' assertion that his style of refutation is directed to the person himself rather than to the many witnesses that the person calls in his own defense (471e–472c).[21] A traditional Athenian trial was a contest (*agōn*) between two opponents in front of a very large panel of jurors (*dikastai*).[22] In the absence of modern techniques of forensic investigation and evidence gathering, the dikasts' decision had to be made primarily on the basis of the character of the accuser and accused.[23] In order to support

---

[20] See Irwin (1979), 243; and Edmonds (2009), 5–6.

[21] See Edmonds (2009), 6.

[22] See Ober (1989), 8, 45; Nichols (1998), 33, n.22; Edmonds (2009), 5; and Thür (2005), 159. Thür (2005, 159) points out that 201 to 401 jurors were needed for private suits and 501 for most public cases. Ober (1998, 8) argues that juries could be between 200 and 1500 citizens over thirty years of age.

[23] See Todd (1990), 30; Edmonds (2009), 4; Lanni (2005), 122; and Thür (2005,) 165. Lanni (2005, 121) points out that some form of discussion of character occurs in 70 of 87 popular court speeches. Both Todd (1990, 30) and Thür (2005, 165–166) stress that this was still balanced by a concern to find the truth about the matter of the case.

the case, litigants would call in witnesses who would try to establish their status and good reputation within the various familial and geographical networks of which they were a part.[24] Like *parrhēsia* in the democratic assembly, witnessing was seen as a privilege and entailed a certain amount of risk or danger (*kindunos*).[25] The risk involved was that of being punished for false testimony (*dikē pseudomarturiōn*), and the penalty, if convicted three times, involved the loss of citizenship rights (*atimia*).[26]

In contrast, Socrates had told Polus earlier in the dialogue that they must both "bid all these others farewell" and instead stand witness for each other (472c). Similarly, in the myth, Zeus reforms the trial procedures so that the person stands alone before the judge who now contemplates his soul bereft of all adornment and the support of witnesses: "And he who decides the trial must be naked, dead, and must with his soul itself contemplate the soul itself of each man immediately upon his death, bereft of all kinsfolk and having left all that adornment behind on earth (*erēmon pantōn tōn sungenōn kai kataliponta epi tēs gēs panta ekeinon ton kosmon*), so that the trial may be just" (523e). It is, not surprisingly, similar to the image of Socrates on trial that is so vividly portrayed in Plato's *Apology*: the solitary individual who refuses to bring forth his family and friends to support his cause (*Apol.* 34d–35c).

The *nakedness* of the person standing trial represents the experience of being ashamed before another that is so vividly portrayed in Socrates' lengthy elenchic encounter with Callicles. It is the experience of being exposed or unmasked by having the contradictions in one's views revealed both to oneself and to others.[27] Here the judge's examination of the whip scars, festering sores of injustice, and false oaths corresponds to Socrates' exposure of contradictions in the views of his interlocutors.[28] And the medical metaphor that is used throughout the *Gorgias* is extended into the myth to describe the way in which the judge diagnoses the unhealthy souls of the great kings and tyrants: "Rhadamanthus halts them and contemplates each one's soul, not knowing whose it is; but often, laying hold of the great king or some other king or potentate, he perceives that there is nothing healthy in the soul (*ouden hugies on tēs psuchēs*),

---

[24] See Todd (1990), 30; Edmonds (2009), 4; Lanni, (2005), 122; and Thür (2005), 165–66. Todd (1990, 27) points out that witnesses are cited on more than four hundred occasions in the one hundred forensic speeches he examines.

[25] See Todd (1990), 28; and Thür (2005), 162.

[26] See Thür (2005), 162.

[27] As Kastely (1991, 107) puts it, "Both judge and the one judged stand naked before each other. The issue is whether one has the courage to present oneself for the most telling of examinations, in which motives, purposes, and commitments will not be clothed or cosmetically enhanced, and equally whether one has the courage to conduct such an examination."

[28] Edmonds (2009), 8–9. Dodds (1959, 379) argues that "Plato here gives a new turn to the old and widespread popular idea that when ghosts appear they show the *physical* scars or mutilations which their bodies suffered during life. Cf. *Odyssey* II. 40 f."

but it has been severely whipped and is filled with scars from false oaths and injustice, which each action of his stamped upon his soul . . ." (524e–525a).

The fact that this exposure is painful yet potentially beneficial is then drama- tized in the discussion of the retribution (*timōria*) and just punishment (*dikē*) of curable and incurable souls. This section of the myth might be interpreted as Plato's attempt to supplement the teaching of the elenchic sections with the unproven premise that injustice will be punished and justice rewarded in the end.[29] But what Plato actually does is to use the retributive and punitive aspects of traditional Athenian eschatological myths to illustrate the painful cognitive- affective mechanism of shame that is involved in the Socratic elenchus.[30] So- cratic justice, like punitive punishment, is painful both for incurable souls and for those who might potentially benefit from Socrates' shaming refutations: "the benefit comes about for [the curable souls] through pains and griefs *both here and in Hades*, for it is not possible otherwise that they be released from injustice" [my italics] (525b–c). Socrates' proviso here (italicized in the previ- ous quotation) is significant, because it underlines the fact that the myth is meant to illustrate the painful effects of Socrates' shaming refutations *here and now*, not just in the afterlife.[31] And this admission about the necessity of pain is, I think, one of the starkest admissions by Plato that the Socratic elenchus involves a kind of painful and ruthless critique of one's previous way of life. It was no doubt an experience that Plato himself suffered at the hands of his teacher Socrates, and his "afterlife" was, no doubt, his turn from the imperial- istic politics of Athens to philosophizing. Accordingly, in the myth the one person whom the judges decide to send to the islands of the blessed is the philosopher (526c).

[29] Annas (1982a, 125, 138) reads the myth of the *Gorgias* in just this way. As she (1982a, 138) puts it, "Plato insists flatly that justice will bring rewards to the agent in the end, though without giving us any good reason to believe this." Stauffer (2006, 169) thinks that the myth is primarily about punishing injustice, at least partly in response to Callicles' frustrated assertion that injustice does seem to triumph in this world at 511b. Both Annas (1982a, 125) and Stauffer (2006, 167) note that it is not the kind of myth that will be convincing to someone like Callicles. However, this overlooks the fact that it is not just the content of the myth but rather its form as a memorable story that might eventually overcome Callicles' resistance to it.

[30] Mackenzie (1981, 233–39), Annas (1982a, 122) and Dodds (1959, 373–74) note the tradi- tional character of many of the motifs in the myth, but because of this, they assume that Plato is using these motifs in much the same way as they were traditionally used: to argue that justice will pay in the end, or in an "afterlife." However, I believe that the novelty of Plato's use of these motifs comes from the way that he uses an aspect of these traditional tropes, i.e., the painfulness of the experience of retribution (*timōria*) to suggest something quite different, i.e., that there is a certain amount of pain involved in giving up a mistaken way of life. *Contra* Mackenzie (1981, 233– 39) and Stauffer (2006, 173) who see the retribution (*timōria*) in the myth as Plato's concession to traditional and non-Socratic arguments.

[31] Edmonds (2009), 2. Cf. Annas (1982a, 124) and Irwin (1978, 248) who both argue against Dodds' (1959, 303, 375, 380–1) view that the myth presupposes a doctrine of reincarnation wherein the just souls benefit only in a subsequent lifetime.

A shaming refutation is painful precisely because the occurrent experience of shame involves the loss of, or at least a temporary setback to attaining, an other that one sees as valuable in some way.[32] Earlier, in his discussion with Callicles, Socrates had defined punishing (*kolazein*, not *timōrein* or *zēmioun*) as the activity of keeping a soul away from the things it desires (505b): just as a sick person must be kept away from the very sweets he desires and must instead be administered bitter or painful medicine, so the unjust person must experience the painful shaming of Socrates' elenchus to show them that they do not live up to the life they profess to admire. The punishments of the myth thus correspond to the pain involved in recognizing the gap between our self and this valued other in and through the very gaze of an other upon the self. Socrates' shaming refutations of Polus and Callicles involved showing them that they do not actually live up to the ideal of the tyrant and the life of complete injustice that they both openly professed to admire. Why this is a painful or tragic realization becomes clearer in Socrates' discussion with Callicles. Here, Socrates makes it clear that the greatest tyrant might well be the corrupt Athenian democracy itself that demands ever greater conquests to fulfill its limitless desires. Callicles' own deep erotic attachment to the Athenian *dēmos*[33] means that any recognition of this fact and of the need to moderate or restrain the desires[34] will be painful precisely because it means losing or turning away from the very forum that he loves so much.[35] At this very point, Callicles recoils from the discussion and tries to squirm out of talking with Socrates:

Soc. Now then, is keeping it away from the things it desires punishing?
CAL. Yes.
Soc. Being punished, therefore, is better for the soul than intemperance, as you were thinking just now.

---

[32] Cairns (1993), 19–21; and Morrison (1996), 208 n.2.

[33] Callicles' love for the Athenian *dēmos* is attested at 481d and 513c.

[34] After Socrates finally shames Callicles into admitting that some pleasures are better than others (499b) (and thus that the pleasant and the good are not identical), he embarks on a lengthy demonstration that the life of moderation and restraint of desire is better than the life of immoderation and limitless desire.

[35] Callicles' inability to turn away from the Athenian *dēmos* might also reflect the fact that this collective other, like most collective others, has both shameful and worthy aspects of its self. This is also consonant with Plato's endeavor to try to be more in tune with the worthy or admirable aspects of his Athenian democratic audience. In other words, *absolute disagreement* with a collective other, such as one's own polity, is rarely possible. This comes out in the fact that there is a steady progression over the course of the entire dialogue toward a "Socrates" who begins to articulate more clearly the positive doctrines that he shares with the moderate ideology of the Athenian *dēmos*: i.e., that suffering injustice is better than doing it, and that some pleasures need to be restrained. For more on this point, see chapter 5. The myth is only the most memorable and vivid example of the new more Platonic Socrates.

CAL. I don't know what you are saying, Socrates, so ask someone else.

Soc. This man here does not abide being benefited and suffering for himself this thing that the argument is about, being punished.

CAL. Nor do I care at all about the things you are saying, and I answered you these things as a favor to Gorgias. (505b–505c)

This very inability on the part of Callicles to take Socrates' bitter medicine is then encapsulated in the myth's discussion of incurable souls. That the myth includes incurable as well as curable souls is meant to illustrate, not only the limitations of a person like Callicles, but also the limitations of the shaming mechanism of the Socratic elenchus, especially when it is used on an interlocutor like Callicles. In chapters 2 and 3, I argued that any shame refutation or situation involves a moment of recognition and a moment of reaction, and in the previous paragraph I described Callicles' painful *recognition* of the gap between his new insight that some pleasures are better than others, and his love of the tyrannical and imperialistic Athenian *dēmos*. But Callicles' repeated attempts to leave or squirm out of the discussion with Socrates vividly illustrates the kind of *reaction* that an interlocutor can have when shown these very things. Even though Callicles momentarily retracts his indiscriminate hedonism thesis at 499b, and agrees with Socrates' definition of punishment at 505b, he repeatedly recoils from the painful discussion and refuses to accept these new insights in a manner that could make them part of his way of life. He does so because even though Socrates can momentarily get him to recognize a certain discrepancy between his admired others (e.g., the brave and courageous warrior and leader, and the indiscriminate tyrant), he cannot get him to give up the deepest erotic attachments that have structured his very soul:

CAL. In some way, I don't know what, what you say seems good to me, Socrates; but I suffer the experience of the many—I am not altogether persuaded by you (*pepontha de to tōn pollōn pathos—ou panu soi peithomai*).

Soc. Yes, for love of the people (*ho dēmou erōs*), Callicles, which is present in your soul, opposes me. But if we investigate these same things often (*pollakis*) and better (*beltion*), perhaps you will be persuaded (*peisthēsei*). (513c–d)[36]

---

[36] For a similar confession by Alcibiades, see *Symposium* 216a–c. Stauffer (2006, 146) notes the exceptional character of Callicles' assertion that he is somewhat attracted to Socrates' position; however, for him it attests to Callicles' ongoing *irrational* attachment to justice and nobility. I think Irwin (1979, 233) is closer to my interpretation in his argument that it shows that Callicles is not totally unreachable by rational arguments, especially if they were to be repeated and amended as they are in the *Republic*. *Contra* Benardete (1991, 93) who, as Stauffer notes, overlooks the dramatic significance of this remark and thinks that there is no real feeling behind it.

The painful medicine of the Socratic elenchus can diagnose the errors or contradictions in a person's way of life, but it does not have the power to fully cure and turn many souls, and I think that the quote above suggests at least three reasons for this.

This first one arises out of the limitations of the interlocutor's own soul and his reaction to Socrates' shaming elenchus. As I argued in chapters 2 and 3, Callicles was so attached to the pleasant feelings that arose from merging with his beloved but imperialistic *dēmos* that he was unable to truly care for what Socrates was trying to show him about this beloved other. Indeed, Socrates himself had actually predicted that Callicles would be unable to resist anything that this *dēmos* uttered and would twist himself up and down in the argument to conform to its wishes, desires, and demands (481e–482a). At the end of their discussion, Socrates tells Callicles that his love of this *dēmos* is precisely what has made it so hard for him to be persuaded by the argument.[37] Callicles' flattering sense of shame is so attuned to this omnipotent and tyrannical other that he is unable to cope with the pain that necessarily follows when he is shown exactly how this other is inconsistent with the momentary consensus reached between him and Socrates that some pleasures are better than others and that some pleasures need to be restrained.[38]

The second reason, however, arises more out of the limitations of Socrates' shaming elenchus itself, or to be more exact, the problem arises out of the fact that the dialectical method of the Socratic elenchus is insufficiently therapeutic. It can diagnose and lay bear the contradictions in a person's way of life and the norms that he uses to guide him in this life, but it cannot show this person how to change this life in accordance with the new insights gleaned from his interaction with Socrates. This is because it negates the person's pretenses and restrains their desires without replacing these with an image of the new way of life that might become possible if the person were to transform themselves in accordance with these painful insights. Indeed, by treating Callicles as a touchstone, i.e., a worthless metal to measure the worth of his own golden soul (486d–e), Socrates is as culpable in his lack of care toward Callicles as Callicles is ultimately culpable in not caring for anything Socrates has to say. Thus, in the myth, the incurable souls can only become examples to others "who see

---

[37] As Stauffer (2006, 147) points out, this love for the Athenian *dēmos* is attested to by Callicles' admiration for the Athenian statesmen Pericles, Themistocles, Cimon, and Miltiades who "he thinks served the Athenian *dēmos* well." He also notes that this love is an obstacle to his embracing an understanding of virtue that challenges or threatens this love. As Kaufer (1978, 71) argues, this statement by Socrates is an indication of Plato's deeper moral psychology that is beginning to be articulated in the *Gorgias*.

[38] As Kastely (1991, 105) puts it, "One's involvement with whom or what one loves does not easily lend itself to criticism, and it is natural to mistake criticism of a loved object as an attack on it."

these men suffering on account of their errors the greatest, most painful, and most fearful sufferings for all time, simply hung up there in Hades as examples" (525c). This passage is not meant to suggest that this is all that can be made of a person like Callicles, i.e., he can become a vivid example of just how much damage such tyrannical individuals can do either to their city or to philosophy. Rather it is meant to suggest that this might be all that the Socratic shaming elenchus was able to do with a person like Callicles.

Finally, as the above quote also makes clear, part of the reason why Socrates might not persuade Callicles is the insufficiency of the time that he is given to make his argument. As he puts it, "If we investigate these same things often and better, perhaps you will be persuaded" (513d). Callicles will probably not be able to remember the lengthy twists and turns of the argument that Socrates uses to refute his indiscriminate hedonism thesis, but he might well remember the vivid images of the naked and dead souls filled with the whip scars of injustice. In other words, Plato's use of myth remedies this very limitation of Socratic elenchus by supplying a reminder of some of the most important conclusions that have been reached in the conversation between Callicles and Socrates.[39] Accordingly, in the next section I will examine the differences between myth and elenchus in order to show how Platonic myth supplies this very supplement to the Socratic elenchus by virtue of its imagistic and narrative form.

Platonic Myth vs. Socratic Elenchus

The most obvious difference between the *Gorgias* myth and the dialectical encounters between Socrates and his interlocutors is of course their difference in length. To put it simply, the use of myth reflects two Platonic insights:

---

[39] Similarly Nichols (1998, 146, 149) suggests that writing down the Socratic lessons might also be a way of overcoming the time limitations brought to light in the *Gorgias*, and that this is what Plato argues for in the *Phaedrus*. It is also important to note in this context that the Greek notion of *nomos* meant not only conventions or laws, but also musical modes and customs, and that prior to the invention of writing Athenian leaders like Solon had the citizens sing the laws (*nomoi*) as a way of remembering them. In the *Phaedrus* Socrates explicitly talks about legislation as a writing on the soul. The myth of the *Gorgias* illustrates how a story about justice and injustice might be a kind of writing on the soul that can serve as a reminder of the conclusions established in the much lengthier elenchic part of the discussion. (The memorable character of myth might also overcome another limitation of the Socratic shaming elenchus: this is the fact that people are less likely to actually change their views under the intense gaze of a collective other. Recall that Socrates is shaming Callicles in front of a large audience, members of whom he does admire and want to impress. After this intense shaming is over, it might well be the case that in recalling the myth Callicles won't be as resistant to what Socrates showed him as he was during the heat of the discussion. This might also be one of the reasons why Gorgias had a more positive reaction to the Socratic elenchus: he was not shamed by Socrates under the gaze of the collective audience

that "a picture is worth a thousand words," and that "you have to see it to believe it."[40] That this is the case is, I hope, evident from my exposition of some of the elements of the Socratic elenchus that are illustrated by the single image of the naked, solitary, and dead souls of the *Gorgias* myth. As Danielle Allen has argued, Plato understood that "images could encapsulate sets of principles and symbolic orders and ... that people ... have to envision a particular before [they] can conceive of the abstract idea that is grounded in the particular."[41] The image of the naked soul nicely encapsulates both of these principles of exposition. First, it quite literally embodies the ailments of the souls of Socrates' interlocutors by envisioning them as whip scars and festering sores of injustice. The more abstract ideas that Socrates has attempted to establish with his interlocutors are now embodied in a number of vivid, concrete, and memorable images. Thus the principles of Socratic justice, which Socrates attempted to establish with his interlocutors through the twists and turns of a lengthy discussion, are now condensed and encapsulated in these mythic images. Although Socrates' interlocutors may not remember the intricate steps of proof or all of the conclusions established in this lengthy discussion, they can carry with them the image of the whip scars on the souls of the naked kings and tyrants.

While the imagistic nature of the myth can encapsulate whole sets of principles in a way that defies discursivity, the narrative character of myth works in a somewhat opposite fashion. It exploits the temporal sequence of narrative to bring out the relations between ideas.[42] The myth does this first by illustrating the differences between the traditional Athenian style of refutation and Socrates' style of refutation in the story of the shift from Cronos' system of trials to Zeus' reformed system.[43] It also does this by illustrating different aspects of the Socratic elenchus as different moments in a trial: the judgment is meant to represent the exposure of contradictions by Socrates, while the punishment is meant to reflect the painful nature of this very exposure.[44] In the occurrent experience of being ashamed these two moments are in fact part of what I have called the moment of recognition: the painful cognitive-affective recognition of the gaze of an other that reveals a certain inadequacy in the self.

---

for as long as either Polus or Callicles. Platonic respectful shame, exemplified in the myth, might be a way of overcoming this limitation of the searing character of the Socratic elenchus.)

[40] Allen (2000a), 149.

[41] Allen (2000a), 147.

[42] Both Annas (1982a, 140 n.15) and Edmonds (2009, 19) note that Plotinus was the first ancient commentator to understand this characteristic of Platonic myths.

[43] Edmonds (2009), 19.

[44] I have adopted this insight from Edmonds (2009), 19–20. However, my own analysis of the separate elements of the elenchus do not correspond exactly to his. I do not see the moment of punishment to be as curative as he does.

The myth also differs from the elenchic sections of the dialogue by attempting to introduce these radically new Socratic ideals of justice and dialectic on the basis of the old. It does this by introducing new ideas and principles within older and more traditional motifs. The proposed Socratic reforms of the Athenian trial and political procedures are placed within the traditional and authoritative Homeric tales of the afterlife and the transition of rule from Cronos to Zeus (523a–b).[45] The transition from clothed and adorned defendants to the naked and solitary souls is an attempt to resignify what is and is not shameful within the more traditional Athenian symbolic order. The traditional Athenian trial was meant to be a competition between two adversaries, one of whom would leave the courtroom shamed. "The public display of his shame would confirm the reevaluation of relative status positions that was effected by the punishment."[46] The traditional standard of the noble (*kalon*) and shameful (*aischron*) was simply success or defeat on the battlefield or in the courtroom no matter how this success was obtained.[47] Callicles' own views of the noble (*kalon*) and shameful (*aischron*) correspond to this traditional standard, but even a more "just" person like Crito expresses similar views. When Crito is trying to persuade Socrates to escape from prison, he thinks that Socrates' obedience to Athenian law is in fact incompatible with the virtue of a good and courageous man:

> For my part I am ashamed (*aischunomai*) for you and for us, your companions, that the whole affair concerning you will seem to have been conducted with a certain lack of manliness (*anandria*) on our part: the way the lawsuit was introduced into the law court, even though it was possible for it not to be introduced; the way the judicial contest itself took place; and now this, the ridiculous conclusion of the affair, will seem to have escaped us completely because of a certain badness and lack of manliness on our part, since we didn't save you, nor did you save yourself, although it was possible and feasible if we had been of even a slight benefit. So see to it Socrates, that these things be not shameful as well as bad both for you and for us. (*Crito* 45e–46a)[48]

The view of the shameful that Crito expresses here is very similar to the one that Callicles expresses in his first speech and twice in his discussion with

---

[45] For a more lengthy discussion of these traditional motifs, see Dodds (1959), 372–76; and Edmonds (2009), 18–19.

[46] Allen (2000a), 138. For the view that the competition for honor and the aim of reevaluating social relations and hierarchies could also be accompanied by a genuine desire to implement the rule of law and discover the truth about the case, see Lanni (2005) and Rubinstein (2005).

[47] This view is held by Adkins (1960). See Cairns (1993) for the opposing view that even in Homeric times the honorable (*kalon*) and shameful (*aischron*) covered the cooperative virtues of moderation and justice and not just the competitive virtues of courage.

[48] This translation is from *Crito* in *Four Texts on Socrates*, trans. Thomas G. West and Grace Starry West (Ithaca: Cornell University Press, 1984), 103.

Socrates (486a–b, 511a–c, 521c). Callicles tells Socrates that the philosophic way of life is shameful and bad precisely because the person who practices it cannot protect himself or anyone else from being tried unjustly, carried off to prison, and sentenced to death (486a–b). As Arthur Adkins points out, if one accepts *this* standard of the shameful then nothing could be more shameful than Socrates' life and death: "Socrates, having been poor, and hence a failure, all his life, had proved unable to defend himself in court as an *agathos* should, and by his death had left his family unprotected."[49]

Now, in his discussion with Callicles, Socrates embarks on a lengthy demonstration to prove that quite the opposite is the case. The most shameful thing is not to be struck on the jaw or killed by one's own city, but rather to be unable to help one's city to become more moderate and just (508d–509c). The *Gorgias* thus attempts to turn the more traditional Athenian view of what is shameful, which persisted into the classical age, on its head by portraying the philosopher who practices moderation and justice as the most courageous and noble person, who alone practices the true political art. And this entire lengthy and complex project is then encapsulated in the images of the myth at the end of the dialogue. The image of the one naked, solitary, and dead soul that is free of whip scars and festering sores represents the body of the condemned Socrates who is now resignified to represent a new image of the noble.[50] The traditional tropes of the shameful—nakedness, vulnerability, and death—now represent what is worthy of beholding by the judges rather than that which ought to be covered over or hidden from view.[51] The individual who, like Socrates, is willing to have his errors uncovered and his pretenses dissected in these elenchic encounters is now the bravest and most noble soul.

Moreover, this trope of nakedness as a kind of health of soul is not altogether alien to an Athenian audience: in their practice of gymnastics the Greeks exercised naked.[52] Also, as the Greeks well knew, gymnastic exercise involves pain, especially at the beginning of one's practice of such an activity. However, this pain is an integral and necessary step in achieving the higher pleasures involved in such an activity. Thus, their traditional image of the beautiful body, and of the toils necessary to achieve this beauty is now made to signify the beauty of

[49] Adkins (1960), 259.

[50] As Allen (2000a, 141) points out, envisaging the body of the condemned in discussions of punishment reflects Plato's own awareness that such images can be used to confirm or repudiate the fundamental principles of a regime's authority. Cf. Allen (2000b), 269.

[51] Konstan (2006, 95) argues that Plato's classical audience would have been aware of the subtle distinctions between *aidōs* and *aischunē*, and here the fact that *aidōs* is related to the metaphor of a covering mantle (Konstan, [2006], 296 n.17) would seem to be what Plato is trying to move away from in this myth. This also suggests that his persistent use of *aischunē* in the *Gorgias* is meant to get his audience to see uncovering as a necessary part of democratic deliberations.

[52] Socrates explicitly compares the beauty of gymnastics to the legislative activity of the true political art at 464b.

a soul whose errors and contradictions have been exposed through the painful process of Socratic elenchus.

But Plato's use of myth does not simply present new ideas in the guise of more traditional motifs; rather its very use in a written work represents a grafting of the newer form of philosophic and technical dialogue onto the more traditional form of myth itself.[53] As Jean-Pierre Vernant points out, *muthos* and *logos* did not originally stand in contrast to one another, but by the time of Plato's writings a number of oppositions between *muthos* and *logos* had been articulated.[54] *Muthos* had come to stand for the magical, marvelous, pleasant, and affective qualities of speech and oral pronouncements.[55] And it was precisely this magical quality of speech that the historical Gorgias was known for celebrating and famed for performing.[56] In contrast, *logos* (as exemplified by the written word) was meant to act "upon the mind at a different level from an operation involving mimesis or emotional participation (*sumpatheia*) on the part of the audience. Its purpose [was] to establish the truth following a scrupulous inquiry and to express it in a manner that should, by rights at least, appeal to the reader's critical intelligence alone."[57] By writing a myth which itself illustrates the process of Socratic elenchus, Plato attempts to combine the pleasures of listening and seeing a spectacle as a member of an audience (characteristic of the magical and affective/mimetic qualities of *muthos*) with the insights and rigors of demonstrative rationality (characteristic of the pains-taking analyses of *logos*) in a way which actually disrupts rather than affirms their strict distinction.[58] The interlocutors and audience of the *Gorgias* who came to feast on Gorgias' epideictic rhetoric end up getting a feast or spectacle whose vivid images portray the steps and rigors of elenchic analysis.

---

[53] In a similar vein, Gebauer and Wolf (1995, 45) argue that Plato's treatment of *mimēsis* in his dialogues "exploits the potential opened up to thought by the gradual introduction of writing over the preceding few centuries." While I agree with this statement, I disagree with them (1995, 26) that his critique of *mimēsis* represents an effort to "replace an image-based discourse, with its major tie to orality, with a conceptual one." Instead, I think that Plato's dialogues combine elements of both forms of discourse. Unfortunately, a full treatment of Platonic *mimēsis* is well beyond the scope of this book and I will treat this theme in another book. For an excellent treatment of the complexity and non-monolithic character of Plato's doctrine of *mimēsis*, see Halliwell (2002).

[54] Vernant (1988), 206. See also Annas (1982a), 120: "*Mythos* and cognate words originally mean no more than 'speech'."

[55] Vernant (1988), 206.

[56] Vernant (1988), 206. Cf. Wardy (1996), 40–41.

[57] Vernant (1988), 207.

[58] Annas (1982a) argues that it is precisely our contemporary tendency to see them as strict binaries that makes us treat Plato's myths as the simply playful and less serious parts of his dialogues. As she (1982a, 121) puts it, "In the case of his own 'mythical' stories Plato, so far from contrasting myth and reason, emphasizes both the obvious fact that we have a story, not an argument, and the less obvious fact that it is a *seriously meant* story: it is foolish to treat it as an old wives tale" (Cf. *Gorgias* 527a5–b2, *Republic* 621b8–c1, *Phaedo* 114d1–7, *Laws* 645b1–8).

I now want to treat these differences between Platonic myth and Socratic elenchus as indicative of Plato's own criticisms of and reactions to his teacher's characteristically ironic comportment toward others. In order to do this I will first analyze the ways in which Socratic and Platonic irony have been interpreted as forms of deception, that is, as forms of communication that conceal the truth. I will then analyze how Socrates' elenchic refutations in the *Gorgias* exemplify his ironic stance toward others and explain how this underlies the puzzling and perplexing character of Socratic respectful shame. Finally, I will try to defend Platonic irony, as this is exemplified by the *Gorgias* myth, from the charges of deception that have been leveled against it. Instead, I will treat it as a form of respectful shame that tries to go beyond the limitations of Socrates' own form of respectful shame.

Gregory Vlastos on Socratic and Platonic Irony

According to Gregory Vlastos, the intention to deceive was typical of the Greek words *eirōneia, eirōn,* and *eirōneuomai*.[59] Though this connotation of the word survived during Socrates lifetime, his method of questioning and discussing with others came to be seen as exhibiting something closer to our modern notion of irony: "Irony is the use of words to express something other than, and especially the opposite of, [their] literal meaning."[60] This definition encapsulates what Vlastos calls both "simple" and "complex" irony. In both cases, Vlastos argues that the intention to deceive on the part of the speaker is missing. Simple irony consists in the fact that the speaker intends exactly the opposite of what is being said. Telling someone on a rainy, miserable day that "the weather is utterly beautiful" is meant to convey just the opposite to the hearer, and this contrary meaning is transparent to both parties to the utterance. The purpose of such irony might be either humor or mockery, but not deceit, precisely because the speakers' irony makes his meaning transparent to the listener.

"Complex" irony is similarly free of the intent to deceive the listener, but this time not because the opposite concept or word is transparently intended, but rather because the speaker's irony signals to the listener that he intends to use the word to express something other than the literal meaning. "In 'complex' irony what is said both is and isn't what is meant: its surface content is meant to be true in one sense, false in another."[61] Here, irony might be used to pose a riddle to the listener who is then "left to solve it for himself."[62] It is

---

[59] Vlastos (1991), 23.
[60] Vlastos (1991, 21) is quoting from Webster's dictionary.
[61] Vlastos (1991), 31.
[62] Vlastos (1991), 22.

only by understanding Socrates' complex philosophical ironies, according to
Vlastos, that one can make sense of the Socratic paradoxes that come to light
in so many of Plato's early Socratic dialogues:

(1) Socrates disavows, yet avows, knowledge.
(2) He disavows, yet avows, the art of teaching virtue.
(3) He disavows, yet avows, doing politics.[63]

When Socrates disavows such things, often much to the chagrin and aggrava-
tion of his interlocutors, he is not doing so disingenuously or deceitfully.
Rather, he means that he does not teach or practice politics in the literal or
commonsensical way in which these things would be understood in democratic Athens at the time. His disavowal of teaching is not grounded in a lie,
but rather in the fact that he really doesn't teach in the conventional sense
where teaching involves transferring "knowledge from a teacher's to a learner's
mind."[64] Instead, he teaches by making his interlocutor aware of his own ignorance as a prelude to discovering the truth for himself.[65] Similarly, Socrates
can claim (*Apol.* 31d–e and *Gorg.* 473e) that he is not a political man and yet
claim, even within the same dialogue (the *Gorgias*), that he alone engages in
the true political art and is the only contemporary person to do politics (521d).
He can do so because when he disavows doing politics, he means the politics
of drafting proposals in the Assembly, whereas when he avows doing politics
he means improving the souls of his fellow citizens. According to Vlastos,
Socrates thus means and does not mean that he practices politics. The interlocutor is presented with a puzzle by Socrates' ironical assertions, and these ironies are not meant to deceive him but to get him to do the hard intellectual
work that would allow him to understand what Socrates means by his paradoxes. If there is any deception that occurs in the course of Socrates' arguments, Vlastos argues, this will be a case of self-deception. Here, Vlastos cites
the case of Alcibiades in the *Symposium* who is deceived into thinking that
Socrates wants to sleep with him. Alcibiades is deceived not by what Socrates
says about his love for Alcibiades, but by what Alcibiades wants to believe
about the nature of this love.[66] Alcibiades flatters himself that Socrates is as
conventional in love matters as Alcibiades' other lovers, and he (Alcibiades) is
thus in some sense self-deceived by his attunement to this conventional Athenian other of the lover.

---

[63] See Additional Note 1.1, Vlastos (1991), 237.

[64] Vlastos (1991), 32.

[65] Vlastos (1991), 32. In chapter 1, I argued that these very characteristics of the search for
moral truth point more to the art of medicine than the science of mathematics, and to the importance of the reaction of the individual in determining whether Socrates and his interlocutors will
reach genuine agreement on Socratic moral theses. Vlastos only begins to see this in his later
work, i.e., the very work that I address in this chapter.

[66] Vlastos (1991), 41.

Subsequently, in his additional note 1.2 to this essay, Vlastos contrasts Platonic with Socratic irony. Socratic irony leaves no doubt in the interlocutor's mind that the surface meaning is not the true or literal meaning, even though it does not provide the answer to the riddle of what the other, deeper meaning might be. The interlocutors know they are being presented with a riddle and it is left to them to solve it. But this, according to Vlastos, does not mean that Socrates' ironic utterances postulate a double audience, consisting of the uninitiated to whom the literal meaning is directed, and those initiates who comprehend the deeper, secret meaning of his utterances and who delight in the secret intimacy that this sets up between them and the speaker.[67] Though incorrect as a characterization of Socratic irony, this is, for Vlastos, an accurate description of Platonic irony. In dialogues such as the *Euthyphro, Ion,* and *Hippias Major,* Socrates is shown to ply ironies that are simply lost on his uncomprehending interlocutors, the deeper meaning of which is meant to be comprehended by the "initiates" or readers of the dialogue.

ALEXANDER NEHAMAS ON SOCRATIC AND PLATONIC IRONY

Alexander Nehamas rejects Vlastos' views of Socratic irony on the grounds that Vlastos' Socrates is altogether too transparent, honest, and knowledgeable. There is, according to Nehamas, a crucial element that is missing from Vlastos' depiction of Socratic irony: the element of uncertainty.[68] Socrates' professions of ignorance are sincere and not ironic, but this very sincere ignorance sets up a stance of irony toward all of his utterances. The ironist, for Nehamas, signals that his meaning is other than what he says, but he doesn't thereby imply that he, the speaker, sees the whole picture.[69] Instead, Socrates' irony involves an acknowledgment of his own uncertainty about the truth. Socrates does not intend to deceive with his ironical stance toward others, but rather attempts to register his own uncertainty and lack of clarity or transparency about the very issues under discussion.

Nehamas does, however, agree with Vlastos' view that Platonic irony involves elements of both deception and superiority.[70] In fact, he goes one step

---

[67] See Additional Note 1.2, Vlastos (1991), 245.

[68] Nehamas (1998), 52, 67.

[69] Nehamas (1998), 67.

[70] For an alternative and interesting view of Platonic irony in the *Gorgias* that does not involve deception of the readers but instead relies on their knowledge of the facts of the situation that Plato is describing see Klosko (1983, 585–86). Klosko's view of Platonic irony is close to the notion of dramatic irony, where the audience knows something that the characters in a play do not, and this discrepancy is an important part of the message of the drama. Klosko (1983, 586) also thinks that Platonic irony allows Plato to move beyond purely Socratic teachings, but his account of how this works is quite different from my own. He sees Plato as moving in a more authoritarian

further in his characterization of these two elements of Platonic irony. In dialogues such as the *Euthyphro* Socrates does ply his ironies on uncomprehending interlocutors who are deceived by his utterances, but for Nehamas these ironies are not then transparently comprehended by the reader of the dialogues. Instead, Platonic irony induces self-deception in the reader as it exhibits it in the characters. It does this by making the reader feel superior to the self-deceived "dunces" in these dialogues:

> And knowing better, what do we do? Mostly, we read this little dialogue and then we close the book, in a gesture that is an exact replica of Euthyphro's sudden remembering of the appointment that ends his conversation with Socrates. We too go about our usual business, just as he proposes to do. And our usual business does not normally center on becoming conscious of and fighting against the self-delusion that characterizes Euthyphro and that, as we turn away from the dialogue, we demonstrate to be ruling our own lives as well—*which is really the aim of this whole mechanism.* Socrates' irony is directed at Euthyphro only as a means; its real goal [is] the readers of Plato's dialogues.[71]

According to Nehamas, there is still a double audience posited by Plato's ironical stance, but here the "initiates" are even more exclusive than they are in Vlastos' characterization of Platonic irony. Nehamas thinks that the uncomprehending or self-deceived audience—the "dummies"—include both Socrates' interlocutors and most of the readers of the dialogue, and that the comprehending audience includes *only* Plato himself. To be able to recognize an expert in virtue requires that one be an expert oneself.[72] Even though nobody in the dialogues seems to recognize Socrates for the expert and just person he was, Plato, as author of the dialogues, suggests that he alone was capable of this with every word he writes. His very silence or absence from the dialogues, "which at first appears an act of humility, turns out to be a further ironical act of disdain."[73]

---

direction precisely because of the fate of Socrates. My own view is that the fate of Socrates at the hands of the restored (but still tyrannical) democracy made Plato move in a more democratic direction, but one that involved moderating and taming the tyrannical aspects of the *dēmos* and the overly agonistic aspects of his teacher, Socrates. Similarly, the musical education of *thumos* (spiritedness) in the *Republic* is meant to tame the harsher aspects of both the *dēmos* and the philosopher, Socrates.

[71] Nehamas (1998), 41. *Contra* Nehamas, I think this kind of self-deceptive move is only one possible response to Plato's dialogues induced by the ever present possibility of flattering shame, whereas Plato himself takes measures to overcome this move (on the part of his contemporary and future audiences) in his middle dialogues by presenting a more caring, less obnoxious, refutative Socrates.

[72] Nehamas (1998), 82.

[73] Nehamas (1998), 89. Nehamas' argument about Platonic irony is in line with Stauffer's (2006) notion of "noble rhetoric" as an embellishment for those unable to understand, and thus likely to harm, the philosophic individual.

Nehamas and Vlastos thus both think that Socratic irony is innocent of the intent to deceive, but that Platonic irony is guilty of this charge. For Vlastos, Platonic irony intentionally aims to deceive those interlocutors who accept the literal meaning without comprehending the truer hidden meaning and who aren't even aware that there is such a meaning. For Nehamas, Platonic irony induces self-deception on the part of the reader by getting them to feel superior to the stupid interlocutors who don't "get" Socrates, without themselves doing the further work necessary to truly understand him. And both Nehamas and Vlastos treat Platonic irony as a stance of superiority or disdain toward certain members of one's audience.

In contrast to this, Vlastos treats Socratic irony as a democratic or egalitarian way of posing a challenge or riddle to one's fellow interlocutors.[74] If Socrates' meaning is less than transparent to his interlocutors, this is because he knows that the only way to reach moral truth is to come to it by oneself.[75] There is always a kind of interpretive uncertainty or burden of freedom in any signifi-cant communication and Socratic irony merely exemplifies the recognition of this fact. For Nehamas, the uncertainty inherent in the stance of Socratic irony is even more radical than this because it exists not just between Socrates and the listener, but also between Socrates and himself. Nehamas' Socrates is much less dogmatic and certain about the truths that he has discovered than is Vlastos' Socrates. For Vlastos, Socrates is certain about the moral truths he has discovered via the Socratic elenchus, to the degree that such a method can establish certainty (with perhaps less rigor and demonstrability than mathe-matical truths). For Nehamas, Socrates' irony registers the fact that he is sin-cerely unclear or ignorant about what justice is, even though he is certain that he alone practices it. The most significant difference between their accounts lies then in the degree of uncertainty characteristic of Socratic irony. For Neha-mas, Socrates is protreptic but nondogmatic whereas, for Vlastos, Socrates is protreptic because he is dogmatic or certain about moral truth. They are, however, both convinced that Plato was dogmatically certain about moral truth and that he (Plato) was convinced that most people could not or would not exert the intellectual effort necessary to make these discoveries.

The difference in their estimation of Socrates' certainty lies very much in their disagreement about the place of the *Gorgias* in the Platonic corpus. For Vlastos, the *Gorgias* is an early dialogue, which portrays the historical Socrates who is not yet a mouthpiece for Platonic views.[76] For Nehamas, the *Gorgias* represents a middle work where Plato "abandons the project of presenting Socrates simply as he saw him and makes instead an effort to explain the

---

[74] This element of Vlastos' view is in stark contrast to commentators who think that both Socrates and Plato were equally anti-democratic throughout the dialogues.

[75] Vlastos (1991), 44.

[76] Vlastos (1991), 46.

phenomenon Socrates constitutes."[77] According to Nehamas, the reason Vlastos thinks Socrates is so certain about his possession of moral truth is that Socrates is already a mouthpiece for certain Platonic views by the time of the *Gorgias*. These views include Socrates' assertions that he is the only practitioner of the political art and that he has demonstrated certain moral truths with his interlocutors. If Vlastos had not included the *Gorgias* as one of the early dialogues containing an accurate depiction of the historical Socrates, then his democratic Socrates would have been more uncertain and thus more ironic than the one he presents.

For both men, then, Platonic irony is a rhetoric of deception, or at least it is for one of the two audiences that it posits: the inferior audience who takes the message literally and is therefore confused or misled by this message. Socratic irony is a rhetoric of concealment rather than deception, which indicates to the audience that its meaning is other than what is being said, without thereby making clear what this other meaning consists of. It is a stance toward others that recognizes and registers the uncertainty inherent in communication, both between the speaker and his audience and (in the case of Nehamas) between the speaker and himself. Plato's stance is much more certain or dogmatic, both about the truths he has discovered and about how the audience will interpret both levels of the message. Thus both Vlastos and Nehamas seem to draw the inference that the more certain you are about the truths you have discovered, the easier it is to control the specific interpretations of your utterances.

Socratic vs. Platonic Irony in Plato's *Gorgias*

As I asserted earlier, I consider the *Gorgias* to be a transitional dialogue between Plato's early and middle periods. Because of this I believe, *contra* both Vlastos and Nehams, that there are elements of both Socratic and Platonic views in the dialogue. The *Gorgias* displays aspects of the historical Socrates and also makes Socrates a mouthpiece for certain Platonic views and modes of communication, e.g., the positive doctrines that begin to be asserted at length in the Polus and Callicles sections and the myth at the end of the dialogue. While my Socrates bears a number of resemblances to the Socrates of both Nehamas and Vlastos, my Plato is much less dogmatic, disdainful, and deceptive than both of theirs.[78] In fact, I believe that the *Gorgias* reveals Plato's own view that Socrates' ironic stance toward others was inappropriate or insufficient for dealing with the uncertainties inherent in any communica-

---

[77] Nehamas (1998), 88.
[78] This is true also of my Plato in contrast to Benardete's (1991) and Stauffer's (2006) Plato.

tive interaction.[79] The elenchic sections of the *Gorgias* display a number of elements that were typical of Socrates' irony in order to show why Socrates was able to befuddle and even enrage his interlocutors. The myth at the end of the dialogue then vividly illustrates these limitations in the very act of attempting to transcend them.

In the elenchic sections of the *Gorgias*, Polus and Callicles both attest to the strangeness of Socrates' views (480e, 494d) and Callicles questions whether Socrates is serious or joking (481b–c).[80] Callicles tells Socrates that if what Socrates is saying is true, then their worlds would quite literally be turned upside down (481c). Here I think that Plato is both displaying Socrates' famous mode of comportment toward others, as well as the typical reaction to Socrates' strangeness and irony. In fact, there are two types of uncertainty that are articulated by Polus' and Callicles' assertions. First, they are uncertain about Socrates' truthfulness or sincerity, i.e., they don't know whether he is serious or joking. (In other words, *contra* Vlastos, they don't know whether they are being deceived or not, and this is part of the infuriating thing for them.) Second, their assertions about the strangeness of Socrates' views—that these views would turn their worlds upside down—means they are uncertain about how to apply these Socratic insights to their own conceptual schemas or worldviews. Socrates is *atopon*, literally "out of place," within their traditional Athenian conceptual schemas.[81] Both Polus and Callicles seem to realize that Socrates has shown them up and pointed to an inconsistency in their views, but they are given no clue *by Socrates* as to how this might fit into their lives. This, I think, makes the painful aspect of the shame experienced in the Socratic elenchus all the more acute. Shame quickly spirals into humiliation and anger when the person who is ashamed doesn't fully accept or grasp the standards by which they are being judged.[82] Socrates' interlocutors know that they have been "shown up" but they don't always fully grasp exactly how this has happened to them, and they certainly don't know what to do about it.

---

[79] I don't want to suggest that Plato felt he had overcome these limitations, because as I pointed out in chapter 2, the limitations of any linguistic utterance depend in part upon the way it is received and absorbed by the audience. I also don't mean to suggest that Plato felt he had fully overcome the first element of uncertainty in linguistic speech acts, i.e., that the intentions of the speaker are not always transparent, either to his audience or even to himself. The very act of writing dialogues on Plato's part might reflect this kind of uncertainty about his own psychological motivations, and might exemplify an attempt to bring to light and purge any lingering tyrannical impulses within himself. (I thank Robert Howse for this suggestion.) The final element of uncertainty lies in the fact that any speech act might generate meanings that are not limited to the context of either the speaker or the listener, especially when this speech act is put into the form of a written dialogue.

[80] Kastely (1991, 97) also notes how bizarre and outlandish Socrates' arguments appear to Polus and Callicles.

[81] Kastely (1991), 97.

[82] For the psychoanalytic notion of shame-rage spirals see Lewis (1971); Scheff (1987); and Tangney and Dearing ([2002], 2004), 162.

Paradoxically then, Socrates' own sense of shame, which prevents him from ever flattering the viewpoint of others, might well contribute to their anger and frustration.[83] His sense of shame is so attuned to the search for truth that it prevents him from ever uttering any pleasantries at all, and while this precludes Socrates from being guilty of deception or flattery, he might well be guilty of failing to acknowledge the experiences or sufferings of his victims in a way that might begin to assuage their pain and perplexity. Moreover, without giving his interlocutors any clue about the new terrain or "place" from which he spoke, his very difference from them comes across as superiority, mockery, or strangeness. To use Nehamas' appropriation of Søren Kierkegaard's description of Socratic irony, Socrates' comportment toward others involves an "infinite absolute negativity":

> Irony is "infinite" because it does not put in doubt the validity of this or that particular phenomenon of a culture but the culture as a whole. It is "negative" because it undermines what it opposes but is incapable of offering any serious alternative to it. And it is "absolute" because it negates what is actual by means of an implicit appeal to a future . . . of which the ironist remains unaware.[84]

Socrates' elenchus can puncture pretenses and pull the rug out from under one's admired others, but it does so without being able to replace them with any new others.

In contrast to this negative and painful stance toward others, Plato's use of myth in the *Gorgias* reflects a number of his insights into the ways in which the imagistic and narrative logic of myth can begin to open new spaces in the "topography [of] the mind,"[85] and thus to effect positive changes in the conceptual schema of one's audience. As I mentioned earlier, Plato's myth embodies the abstract principles of the rewards and punishments of Socratic justice in a number of vivid and memorable images. This practice reflects his awareness that it is important to give the audience a picture of the new way of life that would open up to them, if they were to transform themselves in accordance with the insights that come to light in the shaming situation. "Refashioning symbols shifts the conceptual possibilities available to an audience and the outer limits of what is conceivable for them."[86] Resignifying the body of the naked, solitary, and condemned Socrates as the vision of the one truly noble soul supplies the audience with a new other or ideal to replace the ones that Socrates has so relentlessly torn asunder.

---

[83] Kastely (1991, 98) shares my view that Plato is trying to show something about the inadequacies of Socrates' comportment toward others and not just the inadequacy of Socrates' interlocutors in the *Gorgias*.

[84] Nehamas (1998), 71.

[85] Allen (2000a), 149.

[86] Allen (2000a), 148.

Second, presenting these radically new ideas on the basis of older, more traditional motifs reflects Plato's awareness of the need to meet or greet one's audience on their own grounds before slowly leading or turning them toward the new. Platonic respectful shame requires acknowledging the place or terrain of the audience in terms of both the experiences they have suffered and the standards they now use to interpret these experiences. Moreover, aspects of these very experiences and standards are shared between the speaker and his audience. I think that Plato puts this insight into the mouth of his "Socrates" when he first meets Callicles. Here he tells Callicles, "If human beings did not have some feeling (*pathos*) that was the same—some having one and others another—but if some one of us suffered some private feeling different from what the others feel, it would not be too easy to point out one's own affection to the other" (481c–d). Moving between different conceptual schemas requires a principle of charity, of acknowledging the shared standards upon which any meaningful disagreement or difference can even be perceived.

This very aspect of Plato's respectful shame might seem very similar to what I have called flattering shame: mimicking the standards and views of one's audience in order to conceal the truth, either from them or from oneself. And I think this similarity has led interpreters of Plato, such as Vlastos and Nehamas, to interpret Platonic irony as a form of deception and a stance that postulates an inferior and a superior audience. But tailoring one's views to the audience need not always be done as a way of concealing one's own views from them. Instead, it may be a way of leading them onto a new path, and it might also be an acknowledgment of the fact that any new worldview always has a foothold in our old worldviews.[87] What I am suggesting is that, if the myth seems to convey two messages to two different audiences, it might well be that these two audiences are internal to one self, insofar as this self is considered dynamically in transition rather than statically.[88] Presenting new ideas on the basis of old motifs and conceptual schemas is Plato's way of facilitating his audience's conversion from the older to the newer schemas. And because any change to one's conceptual schema or mental topography simultaneously effects a change in the meaning that the actual topography of the landscape holds for one,[89] these conceptual changes might well underlie the possibility of a change in one's way of life. Just as the narrative character of myth presents the transition from the traditional Athenian political practices to the Socratic ones as different moments in a story, so it is now possible for Socrates' interlocutors to convert this myth or "old wives tale" into the story of their own life. Platonic respectful shame thus counters the absolute negativity of Socrates'

[87] I owe this insight to Sharon Krause.

[88] As I argued in chapters 1 and 2, shame is the psychological mechanism by which new others or norms of action are dynamically incorporated into the psyche.

[89] Allen (2000a), 144.

shaming elenchus with a more caring relationship between the "doctor" and the "patient," thus allowing for the possibility of a more positive reaction to the shame situation, and what Freud would call a more positive transference between the patient and doctor.[90]

Finally, Plato's use of myth reflects his insight that although a certain amount of pain is necessary to release one from injustice and error (525b–c), a certain amount of pleasure might also have its place in the curative aspects of a noble rhetoric. As I mentioned earlier, the very use of myth reflects Plato's own attempt to combine the pleasures of going to see a spectacle with the rigors of philosophical demonstration. As both Plato and Aristotle understood, even painful and terrifying spectacles give the audience a certain amount of pleasure. While Polus' use of Gorgias' epideictic rhetoric might have been guilty of flattery by offering the audience a feast of sights and sounds *without regard to their beneficial character* (465a), Socrates' painful rhetoric might well have been blind to the fact that an audience can be moved through pleasure as well as pain. Instead, Plato's respectful shame consists of combining the painful benefits of the Socratic elenchus with the pleasures of Gorgias' display (*epideixis*) rhetoric. The *Gorgias* thus ends with a spectacular portrayal of the painstaking but potentially life-altering practice of philosophizing.

---

[90] Freud himself would have found it difficult to find a better example of a failed transference than the one illustrated by Plato in the elenchic exchange between Callicles and Socrates. And Plato's version of respectful shame is meant, at least in part, to counter the problems he diagnoses in the relationship *between* Socrates and Callicles. For a treatment of the failed relationship between Socrates and Thrasymachus in *Republic* 1, see Tarnopolsky (2007a).

PART TWO

Plato's *Gorgias* and the Contemporary Politics of Shame

Chapter Five

PRUDES, PERVERTS, AND TYRANTS: PLATO
AND THE CONTEMPORARY POLITICS
OF SHAME AND CIVILITY

"Have you no shame?"
—quote from a Chicago gay marriage opponent

"We don't need any more shame!"
—quote from a Chicago gay-rights activist

The Contemporary Politics of Shame and Civility

In the previous four chapters, my discussion of shame has focused primarily on Plato's dialogue the *Gorgias*, and the three different politics of shame that are articulated therein: flattering, Socratic, and Platonic respectful shame. In this chapter I want to show how these three different politics of shame transcend their Athenian context, and can actually offer us helpful models for thinking about the contemporary politics of shame and civility. Specifically, I will show how Plato's insights into the complex and ambiguous workings of shame can address some of the conceptual confusions and oversimplifications in many of the contemporary theories of shame and civility. In fact, the epigraphs for this chapter illustrate the ambivalence and diametrically opposed stances that often surround shame, both in common parlance and in the theoretical debates about this emotion. It is as if *both* the supporters and critics of the politics of shame believe that the categories of "prude" and "pervert" supply an exhaustive classification of the phenomena they purport to examine. If a thinker believes that we need to reinstitute shame as a way of saving contemporary democracies from the disintegrating force of radical identity politics, then he tends to construe his opponents as a bunch of shameless perverts. On the other hand, if a thinker believes that collective deliberation in modern democracies is actually threatened by shame, then he tends to construe his opponents as a bunch of conformist prudes.

These categories, however, reflect what I take to be an oversimplistic view of shame, and it is an oversimplistic view that I think characterizes notions about the emotions and their place in contemporary politics more generally.

This is the view that emotions are either "naïve or incorrigible."[1] Shame is either considered an outdated, irrational or painful emotion that we need to avoid, and recourses to it are then considered naïve or prudish, or shame is considered to be an infallible guide to morality and civic order. In the first part of this chapter I will try to show how this misrecognition occurs in two important contemporary views of the place of shame in democratic politics. I choose these two thinkers because they are representative of the two sides of the debate now swirling around issues of shame and civility. The first view I will examine is the one articulated by Michael Warner in his book *The Trouble with Normal: Sex, Politics and the Ethics of Queer Life*. I will then turn to one of the most influential defenders of the politics of shame and civility, Jean Elshtain, as this position is articulated in her book *Democracy on Trial*. I believe that in these works both of these thinkers incorrectly characterize their opponents' and sometimes even their own position according to the oversimplistic opposition between shame and shamelessness. Yet this opposition actually fails to capture their *own* deepest insights into the place of shame in democratic politics. As I show in this chapter, both of these thinkers actually believe that a certain kind of shame is integral to the notions of respect and dignity and to the democratic right of resistance to authoritarian (Elshtain) or normalizing (Warner) regimes. The problem arises because neither thinker ever fully distinguishes between the good type of shame that they support and the bad type of shame that they oppose. Instead, they both end up mischaracterizing the subtleties of their *own* positions by retaining the oversimplistic distinction between shame and shamelessness. Expanding on Michael Warner's own formulation of the dilemma, I argue that the questions about the place of shame in contemporary democracies should not be how do we get rid of shame or how do we reinstitute it, but what kinds of shame are there and what should we do with these different types of shame?[2]

In the second part of the chapter and related to this last point, I argue that Plato's dialogue, the *Gorgias*, helps us to identify these kinds of confusions about shame, and provides a deeper understanding of the place of shame in democratic politics. It does so, first, by avoiding the simple opposition between shame and shamelessness, and second, by articulating three different kinds of politics of shame that can characterize our own contemporary democratic deliberations. My typology of flattering shame allows me to diagnose what is wrong with certain contemporary forms of democratic engagement and theoretical treatments of shame, and my typologies of Socratic and Platonic

---

[1] I am indebted to Iris Marion Young for suggesting this formulation in a response to my own work on shame. This is not the only way in which current debates about emotions are structured, only one of the most prevalent and problematic ones.

[2] Warner (1999), 3.

respectful shame allow me to show just how shame and respect can be intertwined in democratic deliberations. Thus I argue that, both for Plato and for us, shame does not necessarily exclude respect, but rather can work within a psychic and political structure of respect and dignity. Finally, I argue that even though shame does involve a certain discomfort and perplexity, one cannot simply equate these elements of shame with its perniciousness to democratic politics.

MICHAEL WARNER AND THE POLITICS OF SHAME

In Michael Warner's book, the "politics of shame" denotes the practice of diverting or avoiding the feeling of sexual shame by pinning it on someone else: the "queers," "deviants," and "perverts" who engage in these "dirty," "smutty" practices. Such a politics tries to silence or isolate these groups from the public, i.e., both from public recognition and from access to public resources, by asserting a norm of what is acceptable and then stigmatizing any deviant voices. According to Warner, everyone feels a certain unease or shame about sex, which then becomes political when people stigmatize, humiliate, injure, or simply refuse to recognize those "perverts" they construct as the repository of their own displaced and repudiated sexual shame.[3] One only has to think of the early responses to the AIDS crisis for a vivid example of how this phony moralizing works to place the blame on certain groups in a politics that combines misrecognition with the refusal of resources to fight the disease. Instead of seeing AIDS as a disease caused by unsafe sexual practices, it was first characterized as a plague that targeted "active homosexuals."[4] This kind of stigmatizing response amounts to something like, "If the perverts die, they deserved it." This kind of moralism thus "produces complacent satisfaction in other's shame."[5] Moreover, it makes it difficult for people to begin to talk about and reflect on the issues that matter most, e.g., What can we do to save lives? What kinds of practices put us at risk?

---

[3] Warner (1999), 3. According to Lauren Berlant (2008, 81), Eve Kosofsky Sedgwick's *Epistemology of the Closet*, published in 1990, was the first work to adapt an affective language to a political analysis, specifically on the issue of non-normative or queer sexualities. "What Sedgwick was saying was that a structural social relationship—enacted by stipulated and administrative laws and norms—was *shaming* . . . At the same time, the shame of being deemed a member of that population was said to produce a shamed *subjectivity*, which meant a subjectivity that felt a lot of shame."

[4] Densham (2006), 641. One of the primary goals of the ACT UP movement was to shift the paradigm for thinking about AIDS from the notion of a "gay plague" to the notion that AIDS is a disease caused by unsafe sexual practices.

[5] Warmer (1999), 7.

As Warner points out, this kind of shaming practice is not just detrimental but counterproductive because of the reaction on the part of those who have been stigmatized or shamed into silence in this manner.[6] It tends to make the desire to transgress the norm by which one has been stigmatized all the more appealing. People can begin to react by focusing on the thrill of these forbidden pleasures rather than reflecting on the risks they face or the reasons why something was forbidden in the first place. The other equally problematic reaction, according to Warner, is for those who have been shamed by such standards to try to avoid this shame by assimilating to the standard of the "normal" citizen, and to hide any deviances from this norm, both from themselves and from others. As Warner argues, the gay person who wants to become "normal" by embracing and assimilating to the standard of normalcy hopes to overcome the stigma of difference that separates him from this image. The problem with this kind of reaction is that, as Erving Goffman has argued, the only "normal" or "complete unblushing male in America [is] a young, married, white, urban, northern, heterosexual Protestant father of college education, fully employed, of good complexion, weight and height, and a recent record in sports."[7] In other words, all of us fall below this fantastical standard of the "normal" in important ways and trying to live up to such a norm condemns most of us to a life of shame about some aspect of our all-too-human selves.[8]

But Warner's argument for a queer politics that opposes the politics of shame does not entail that one get rid of shame altogether. As he puts it, "some shame may well be deserved."[9] What Warner really opposes is a particular kind of shame that works by stigmatizing and humiliating certain groups and individuals. The problem, however, is that he never clearly articulates what he means by an alternative queer politics that would try to find a certain dignity in shame.[10] And I think this oversight arises because he sometimes mischarac-

---

[6] Warner (1999), 198.

[7] I borrow this citation of Goffman from Nussbaum (2004), 173.

[8] Warner (1999, 70) here builds upon the notion of normalization that Foucault adapts from Canguilhem's work on statistical norms. These norms converge on some average even though *everyone* deviates from them in some context or other. It is for this reason that processes of normalization always work to continually produce various types of sexual deviancy, which they claim only to be discovering. Nussbaum (2004, 217–18) similarly argues that the problem with the "normal" is that it conflates two concepts: "On the one hand, there is the idea of statistical frequency: the normal is the usual, that which most people are or do. The opposite of 'normal' in that sense is 'unusual.' On the other hand there is the notion of the good or normative: the normal is the proper. The opposite of 'normal' in this sense is 'inappropriate,' 'bad,' 'disgraceful.' "

[9] Warner (1999), 5.

[10] After the publication of *The Trouble with Normal*, Michael Warner and many others participated in a conference entitled "Gay Shame," which was organized by David Halperin and Valerie Shaub at the University of Michigan, Ann Arbor, on March 27–29, 2003. The explicit aim of the conference was to explore the possibilities of constructing coalitional and transformative politics based on gay shame. The conference brought together academics like Warner who had begun to formulate the notion of a progressive or transformative politics of shame, as well as activists who

terizes his own position as an all-out opposition to the politics of shame. Thus, later in the work he talks about the need for "queers to be more articulate about the world they have already made, with all its variations from the norm, ... *with its ethical refusal of shame or implicitly shaming standards of dignity*" [my italics].[11] Then, in the final pages of the work, he speaks of the need to combat the moralistic response to AIDS prevention with a new kind of approach that "combats isolation, shame, and stigma rather than sex."[12]

His remarks at the beginning and the end of the book thus seem to point in two different if not contradictory directions. They amount to something like the following assertions: "Getting rid of shame is like trying to get rid of sex," and "We need to combat shame not sex." But Warner's position, which I will articulate more fully below, is actually far too complex to be captured by the simple binary of shame and shamelessness. And a similar problem occurs in Jean Elshtain's work *Democracy on Trial,* though in her case it arises out of her mischaracterization of her own position as kind of blanket support of shame.

Jean Bethke Elshtain and the Politics of Civility

Early in her book, Elshtain argues that by parading one's sexual proclivities in the public domain, the cross-dresser or sadomasochist harshly breaches the "boundary of shame" that preserves the distinction between the public and the private: "Paradoxically, in his quest to attain sanction for the *full* range of who he is, the cross-dresser or sadomasochist, the variations are nigh endless, puts his life on full display. He opens himself up to *publicity* in ways that others are bound to find quite uncivil, in part because a certain barrier—the political philosopher Hannah Arendt would have called it the boundary of shame—is harshly breached."[13] Instead, Elshtain argues that the best way for gays to preserve their lifestyles against dangerous intrusions by the state is to preserve what she calls the democratic distinction between public and private identities, commitments, and activities.[14] As she points out, the greatest dangers to democratic politics in the recent past came from precisely those regimes that politicized and essentialized the ascriptive characteristics of some people as a way of eliminating them altogether.[15]

---

had started an annual Gay Shame event in 1998 to protest the overcommercialization of the "gay pride" events around the world. A volume based on the conference, also entitled *Gay Shame,* and edited by Halperin and Traub, is due out from University of Chicago press in July 2009.

[11] Warner (1999), 192.

[12] Warner (1999), 218.

[13] Elshtain (1995), 54–55.

[14] Elshtain (1995), 39.

[15] Elshtain (1995), 45.

In contrast, the boundary of shame preserves the distinction between (and integrity of) the public and private spheres and thus preserves the rights and freedoms necessary for democratic citizenship.[16] If politics is to be preserved as a space of commonality and communication, where one's individual preferences and characteristics are transcended and transformed through rational argument, then we must avoid treating it as a space for merely voicing and recognizing personal and private grievances.[17] Ultimately, according to Elshtain, the trajectory of such a "politics of displacement" lies in an incommensurable, atomistic monadology of complaining voices. As she puts it,

> Shame—or its felt experience as it surrounds our body's functions, passions and desires—requires veils of civility that conceal some activities and aspects of ourselves even as we boldly and routinely display and reveal others when we take part in public activities for all to see . . . Flaunting one's most intimate self, making a public thing of oneself, is central to the politics of displacement, no matter who undertakes it—gay or straight; arguing for a position, winning approval, or inviting dissent as a citizen is something quite different.[18]

Following the Arendtian logic that one must conceal in order to reveal, Elshtain argues that only by placing certain aspects of ourselves in hiding can we then open ourselves up to the common space of appearances that involves both speech and action. And this entails for her that the bodily functions of sex must be hidden or covered so that we can deal with the more rational nonbodily traits that unite us as human beings.

What such a position overlooks, though, is the coerciveness that can arise out of this kind of civility or boundary of shame, and some of her remarks make it seem as if Elshtain is enunciating the very homophobic and stigmatiz-

---

[16] In this respect, Elshtain's position is closer to both Miller's (1997) and Kahan's (1999) than it is to Etzioni's (2001). She wants the boundary of shame to protect and express only those shared norms and values that are common to a liberal-democratic society. This shared background consensus of common values is considerably thinner than the thick communitarian consensus that Etzioni (2001) wants to support. Again, Miller and Kahan think that shame or shaming penalties should only be used to *express* a society's abhorrence of things like "rape, child abuse, torture, genocide, predatory murder and maiming" (Miller 1997, 36). However, *contra* Miller and Kahan, I agree with Nussbaum (2004) that expressivist theories of norms and laws always tend to assume that these norms are more rigid and uncontestable than is truly the case in most societies.

[17] Cultural critics like Lasch (1995) and Twitchell (1997) similarly emphasize the need to protect the public sphere from a parade of shameless perversions and degraded appetites. In other words, they also want a strict boundary between the public and private, where entry into the public is prefaced by overcoming our private perversions (Lasch, 198). Here shame is not so much the vehicle for expressing a society's values as it is the emotion that determines what gets repressed in order to enter the public sphere.

[18] Elshtain (1995), 55.

ing politics of shame that Warner is adamant to combat. She seems determined to silence or eliminate all shameless perverts who parade their sexuality in public from any access to this realm and its resources. But her position treats "arguing for a position, winning approval, or inviting dissent as a citizen" as a supposedly sexless and pure form of engagement that overlooks the many ways in which these practices instantiate a particular norm of heterosexuality.[19] The public realm is not free from expressions of sexuality, it is just that a rigid norm of heterosexuality and especially masculine, active heterosexuality is normalized such that any other expressions appear as shameless intrusions of sexuality into a nonsexual public sphere.[20] Masculine heterosexuality has "flaunted" and "made a public thing of itself" for a much longer time and in a much more successful way than any proponents of the "politics of displacement," and it has always decided which parts of the self ought to be concealed in order to display and reveal these valorized male selves. The political always was personal, it just disavowed or displaced these personal and sexual markers onto those who sought to challenge this masculine norm.[21] If militant liberationists and queer activists seek official, mandated approval of their private identities and behaviors this is only because what has passed as rational discourse has always implicitly protected and approved a certain masculine, heterosexual identity and behavior.[22]

In these ways, Elshtain *seems* to be guilty of misrecognizing the terrain of the political as one of either shame or shamelessness and of slotting her crossdressing and sadomasochistic opponents too easily into this latter category. Unfortunately, too often the debate ends here, with both parties paradoxically throwing shame at the other side for their inability to understand one another's position on shame and shamelessness. Instead, I want to move beyond this impasse, first, by arguing that Elshtain's early characterization of the boundary of shame actually fails to do justice to the complexities of the posi-

---

[19] Cf. Rosenfeld (1983), and Locke (1999).

[20] Cf. Nussbaum (2004), 173–74 and 217–19.

[21] Cf. Rosenfeld (1983), and Locke (1999).

[22] Interestingly enough, the Gay Shame conference, which I mentioned in n.10 above, was actually beset with its own controversies centering around whether or not the notion of gay shame, put forth by a number of white male academics, privileged a certain experience of white male shame that overlooked the many different ways in which racial and ethnic minorities and women experienced shame and used it as a basis for transformative experiences. As Halberstam (2005, 226) argues, the notion of gay shame put forth by some of the white male academics centered around a binary between shame and pride where shame was the experience felt by those white males who had simply failed to lay claim to the historically mandated privilege of masculinity. If this was indeed the case, then it would seem that such a notion of gay shame still works within the problematic binary between shame and shamelessness, which I diagnose in this chapter, as well as within the problematic binary between positive and negative emotions that I diagnose in the next chapter.

tion that she articulates later in the work. And second, by arguing that the complexities of this latter position actually reveal certain striking similarities between Elshtain and Warner regarding the potentially salutary role of shame in contemporary democratic politics.

ELSHTAIN AND WARNER: FINDING A COMMON GROUND

As I mentioned above, at times Elshtain articulates a kind of *rigid* boundary between the public and the private that requires veiling our bodily characteristics in order to make possible a space of commonality that transcends these characteristics. But her remarks later in the work, regarding the "Mothers of the Disappeared" in Argentina, suggest a more fluid articulation of these boundaries and the need to transgress these boundaries. According to Elshtain, what the Mothers did by protesting in the public square was to construct a common political identity, an "us" or "we," against the government by deprivatizing their grief regarding their particular sons and daughters: "By fusing a language of grief with a language of human rights, they not only kept alive the particular realities and identities of individuals, their sons and daughters, tormented and lost to state terror, but issued a call to nonviolent arms to their fellow Argentines and to the wider world: Protect mothers and families, but embrace and protect a democratic constitution as well."[23] In contrast, Elshtain argues, authoritarian systems work by dissolving the horizontal voices of citizens that are necessary for any form of democratic governance or resistance. Instead, these potential publics are isolated and privatized into tiny segments of depoliticized "I"s.

And her fear is that the contemporary politics of displacement and identity does exactly the same thing by demanding full recognition of these personal "I"s. The trajectory of such a politics is an infinite and incommensurable cacophony of voices that cannot produce any form of consensus. Instead, she argues, "We most hold in fruitful tension the 'I' of the self, the 'us' and 'ours' of the family, and the 'we' of citizens of the wider democratic civic world."[24] This in the end and on the deepest level is what she hopes the boundary of shame will do. Later, utilizing the work of Vaclev Havel, she articulates her deepest fear that a mass, consumerist democracy, which relentlessly publicizes every personal ascription or grievance, will ultimately dehumanize the individual. The individual in such a society, like the depoliticized individual in a totalitarian society, loses his reason and conscience: "He or she lives within a lie as the self is given over to the 'social auto-totality'."[25] Instead, she hopes

[23] Elshtain (1995), 130.
[24] Elshtain (1995), 129.
[25] Elshtain (1995), 134.

that the boundary of shame will prevent this total collapse of the "I" into the "We" or "social auto-totality."

But these are precisely the sorts of things that Warner himself is concerned about in his book. He argues that a politics of shame works by isolating, privatizing, and denying public access to any voices that deviate from the official norms of sexuality.[26] And when he attacks the gay pride movement from the perspective of a queer politics, his criticisms of their tactics sound very similar to Elshtain's criticisms of the politics of displacement. He is worried that the desire on the part of many gay people to become "normal" through the fight for gay marriage, etc., constitutes a similar example of giving oneself over to the "social auto-totality": "People who are defined by a variant set of norms commit a kind of social suicide when they begin to measure the worth of their relations and their way of life by the yardstick of normalcy."[27] Instead of finding sources of stigmatization in shame, he argues, we must try to find a kind of dignity in shame that will draw humanity together in a recognition of our common indignities and contingencies.[28]

Here, Warner's descriptions of the ways in which a queer politics can unite rather than separate people and can work horizontally rather than vertically sound strikingly similar to Elshtain's descriptions of the acts of the Mothers of the Disappeared. Both of them oppose a politics of shame which stigmatizes certain individuals on the basis of their personal characteristics, and then uses these stigmata to strip them of dignity and deny them political standing and recognition. Second, and most importantly, both of them oppose any form of identity politics that tries to combat hierarchical, stigmatizing regimes utilizing the very tactics of their oppressors. Instead, both Warner and Elshtain argue that we need to emphasize acts over characters, who we are over what we are, and the primacy of the deed over the fixed identity.[29]

THE CONCEPTUAL CONFUSIONS SURROUNDING SHAME

The problem is that even these commonalities still lead Warner and Elshtain to rather ambiguous articulations about shame and what we should do with our shame. Do we need some shame in one realm of our lives (the private) in order to be shameless in public? Do we need shame at all? Or should we

[26] Warner (1999), 7.

[27] Warner (1999), 59.

[28] Warner (1999), 36.

[29] *Contra* Halberstam (2005, 224), who criticizes Warner's work on shame for staying too much in the tradition of identity politics by trying to universalize a particular experience of the subject, and by focusing on rebuilding the self rather than trying to "take apart the social processes that project shame onto queer subjects in the first place." I think Warner does want to dismantle the social processes that lead to the construction of a "normal" subject in the first place, and he is

wage an all-out war on shame? Alternatively, do we need to wage war on shamelessness and reinstitute civility in order to save democracy? These ambiguities surrounding the politics of shame and civility illustrate the fact that the simple distinction between shame and shamelessness is not sufficient for articulating, let alone solving the problem regarding the place of shame in democratic politics. In fact, I have intentionally not provided a definition of what I mean by shame in the previous paragraphs because I wanted to illustrate the many different (and perhaps inexhaustible?) ways in which we use "shame" in English and in contemporary debates about this emotion.[30]

I think that our contemporary conceptual confusions surrounding shame arise from at least four sources. The first one is the different ways in which shame words can work in the English language. The second one is the different types and manifestations of shame that occur in the human psyche and in politics. The third one is the different criteria that can be used to classify shame as salutary or pernicious for democratic politics. The fourth one is the particular theoretical perspective or conceptual framework that one is using to define and analyze shame. To clarify and redress some of the confusions it is important to get clear about (1) what we mean by shame and the interrelationships between these meanings (the sense of shame); (2) which particular context or contexts we are focusing on with regard to shame (the reference of shame); (3) what criteria we are using to distinguish between different types and manifestations of shame; (4) what criteria we are using to criticize or praise shame; and (5) what conceptual frameworks or terminologies we are using to define, analyze, and criticize or praise shame.[31]

---

well aware that this would have a salutarily disorienting, perplexing, and deconstructive effect on whatever self we currently inhabit.

[30] For a similar rhetorical strategy, see Williams (1993), 75–88.

[31] Massaro (1997) does a good job of showing how cultural critics and champions of shame like Christopher Lasch and James Twitchell are confused about some of the different senses of shame (number 1 above). She (1997, 660) argues that the shame they seem to want to reinstitute is what she calls "shame the noun" or the sense of shame that is "an undeniably useful response in humans because it helps to curb appetites that may *need* to be curbed." However, she argues that this is something quite different from acts of shaming that are much more shattering to the self. Thus, she argues that by overlooking the differences between these two senses of shame, people like Lasch and Twitchell risk doing much more damage than good to our societies by advocating the elusive and dangerous tactic of shaming others to create a proper sense of shame in our society. Yet she herself tends to conflate some of the different senses and contexts of shame. First, she never makes a clear distinction between the feeling or occurrent experience of shame and the disposition or sense of shame. Secondly, she seems to conflate the shaming penalties that stigmatize and humiliate individuals by making them wear signs that advertise their crimes to any and every passerby, with the acts of shaming by parents, friends, and fellow citizens that need not have the same stigmatizing and self-shattering effects. For this reason she claims that shaming is always an unpredictable and very destructive practice for reinforcing norms. Kahan (1996) and Miller (1997) also tend to conflate these two very different contexts and types of shaming, but conversely they then argue that shaming penalties might play the same kind of role of clarifying

In what follows I want to utilize and continue to elaborate the Platonic conceptual framework that I have developed in the previous four chapters and then show (1) how this is similar to what shame means for us and (2) how it redresses some of the confusions I have identified in Warner and Elshtain's positions. Finally, I will argue that a Platonic respectful politics of shame includes elements of discomfort and pleasure, perplexity and composure, struggle and consensus, and is not flattering, stigmatizing, humiliating, authoritarian, normalizing, communitarian, or rigidly hierarchical.

Solving the Conceptual Confusions

The first confusion I want to address is the one that relates to the sense and reference of shame, and arises out of the complex way in which shame words work in the English language. When someone asks, "Have you no shame?" and another person replies, "We don't need any more shame!" they *might* but need not be referring to the same type of shame or the same psychic or political instance of shame. Instead, the first person might be referring to the disposition or sense of shame, while the second person might be referring to instances of feeling shame or to acts of shaming.[32] Or the first person might be referring to the fact that there is a certain dignity in a particular type of shame and the second person might be referring to the fact that there is a certain stigmatization that arises out of a very different type of shame. Before they can even know whether they really agree or disagree about shame they need to clarify the distinctions between the occurrent experience of shame (and the moment of recognition within this experience), acts of shaming, and the disposition or sense of shame.[33]

By the *occurrent experience of shame* I mean the moment in which a person or group experiences the discomforting and perplexing cognitive-affective recognition of the gaze of an other that reveals a certain inadequacy in the self. It is important to note here that the occurrent experience of shame does not necessarily lead one to react to it in *any* determinate way. There are a number

---

and contesting norms that is done by political acts of shaming. Braithwaite (1989 and 2000) is more careful about examining the different contexts in which shaming occurs. He argues that we should design our criminal institutions and procedures so that the shaming that occurs is not stigmatizing and expressive of contempt for the offender (as is the case with shaming penalties), but rather that shaming occurs within a community of others who both respect and care for the shamed individual, thus producing a kind of shame that treats the person as a good person who has done a bad thing and not as a bad person.

[32] Cf. Massaro (1997).

[33] Morrison (1996, 8) argues that Freud himself "was quite ambiguous in his treatment of shame, sometimes referring to it as a defense against sexuality and the drives, and at other times as a feeling and an affective experience."

of *possible* reactions to the occurrent experience of shame. The specific reaction is determined by such things as (1) the actual attitude of the other; (2) the way in which the self perceives the attitude of the other; (3) the content of the other that is doing the shaming; (4) the character and intensity of the affective awareness; (5) the self's individual, familial, social and political experience of previous shamings; (6) the individual, familial, social, and political context of the current shaming; (7) the way in which third parties tell the self that he/she/they should react to this particular shaming.[34] As I argued in my Introduction and chapter 2, this means that any particular attempt to shame a person will always involve a degree of uncertainty about just what it is that the person will be ashamed of, and how she will react to the shaming.[35] This, however, does not mean that shaming is an "extremely variable and elusive"[36] tactic that ought to be avoided in our political practices, but rather that we should be attentive to ways in which shame takes on both virtuous and vicious forms, and should try to ensure that our institutions and actions embody more of the former and less of the latter types of shame.

By the *disposition or sense of shame* I mean a person or group's temperament, habitual inclinations, or intra-psychic others developed in reaction to past occurrent experiences of shame. By *acts of shaming* I mean the actions by which an individual or collective agent attempts to produce the occurrent experience of shame within an individual or collective body (the self). I also want to use all of these terms in a political sense. In other words, I do want to anthropomorphize the polity and say that a given polity can have a "sense of shame," can engage in "acts of shaming," and that these are instantiated in the particular laws and institutions of that polity.[37] All of these manifestations of shame are not closed off from one another but rather are related both intra-psychically and inter-psychically.[38] It is precisely the inter-psychic character of shame that makes it socially and politically relevant. It is also necessary to note how significant previous experiences are in shaping the way a person or collectivity conceives of and reacts to shame, i.e., the way I (or we) shame a person and the sense of shame I (or we) have will depend in part upon the ways I (or we) have experienced shame or been shamed in the past.[39]

---

[34] I am indebted to Morrison (1996), Lu (2008), and an anonymous reviewer of an earlier version of this chapter for helping me clarify this point. See Lu (2008) for an account of the ways in political leaders play an important part in determining the kinds of reaction a polity (or collective self) will have to specific acts of shaming by other polities.

[35] Cf. Lu (2008).

[36] Massaro (1997), 655.

[37] Cf. Berlant (2008), 81.

[38] I borrow the terminology of the inter-psychic and intra-psychic character of the emotions from Morrison (1996), 9.

[39] This points to the inevitably intersubjective character of shame, which is overlooked by accounts that see shame solely as some kind of response to our finitude. For a critique of Giorgio Agamben's overly subjective understanding of shame, see Guenther (2008).

As I have shown in previous chapters, both Socrates and Plato felt there was something salutary for moral and political reflection and deliberation *within* the occurrent experience of shame. This is precisely why they tried to shame others. Notice, too, that in the case of Socrates this politically salutary use of shame was a "weapon of the weak" within the context of democratic Athens. Part of what shocked his interlocutors (and infuriated Nietzsche), was the fact that such an ugly, old, poor and hence "shameful"[40] person could inspire such awe, shame, and perplexity in his aristocratic interlocutors.[41] This use of shame as a weapon of the weak also holds true for the Mothers of the Disappeared that Elshtain talks about in her work, and for the queers who oppose the "normalizing" regimes that Warner talks about in his work. In fact, in a recent Human Rights Watch report, Executive Director Kenneth Roth argues that it is precisely because international human rights organizations often do not have the resources or institutional influence to actually shape policies in distant governments that the core of their methodology must be focused on their "ability to investigate, expose and shame."[42] Of course, this recourse to shame and exposure is no less necessary in domestic politics when the very people who do control the resources necessary to reconstruct a city devastated by a natural disaster actually fail to take the necessary actions required by common human decency, and thus disrespect the less privileged members of their own polity.

To recall my argument in chapter 2, the moment of recognition is vividly illustrated by Socrates' ability to shame each of his interlocutors into contradicting one of their deeply held beliefs. Gorgias initially declares that the rhetoric he teaches is morally neutral and has no effect on whether his students make a just or unjust use of it (*Gorg.* 456c–457c). Yet Socrates is able to momentarily shame him into admitting that no student of his will ever make an unjust use of rhetoric (460c). Gorgias is then followed by his student Polus who explicitly espouses the life of tyranny and who argues that suffering injustice is worse than doing it (469b, 474c); and yet Socrates momentarily shames him into agreeing that it is actually better to suffer injustice than to do it (475c–d). Finally, Callicles enters the discussion, espousing the life of tyranny and argues that this includes *pleonexia* (taking more than one's share) and indiscriminate hedonism (the pursuit of any and all pleasures) (491e–492c), and, once again, Socrates is momentarily able to shame him into admitting instead that some pleasures are better than others, and that some pleasures need to be restrained (499b–d).

---

[40] As I pointed out in chapter 4, more traditional and aristocratic notions of the noble (*kalon*) and shameful (*aischron*) characterized a poor, ugly, and defenseless person such as Socrates as "shameful."

[41] In the *Symposium*, Alcibiades admits that Socrates was the only person who ever made him feel shame (*Symp.* 216b).

[42] Roth (2003), 3.

That the occurrent experience of shame is discomforting and perplexing is, I think, obvious to anyone who has ever experienced it. But what is not so obvious is just what the character of this discomfort and perplexity is. The discomfort and perplexity can have a physiological, behavioral, and cognitive component, but what distinguishes shame from other emotions such as humiliation, *in a politically salient way*, is the specific cognitive component of the experience. Shame and humiliation can both be accompanied by the physiological signs of blushing or flushing red, and the behavioral signs of squirming or lowering one's head.[43] Morrison argues that shame, embarrassment, and humiliation are closely related but can be differentiated along a scale of intensity, where humiliation is the more intense and embarrassment the less intense version of what he calls "interpersonal shame."[44] But I think shame, humiliation, and embarrassment are only definitively differentiated by certain *cognitive* criteria, even if it is the case that the differences in these criteria tend to make the experience of humiliation the most searing of the three emotions. As I argued in chapter 3, *contra* Jon Elster, I think it is humiliation that is prompted by an other that displays an attitude of contempt or disgust for the self, and not shame.[45] Embarrassment and shame do not involve such a harsh condemnation of the self by the other, and in the case of embarrassment, one need not even think that any significant flaw has been revealed.[46] Here I agree with Williams that we can feel shame before an other that displays many different and considerably less negative attitudes.[47] I think these can range from admiration to respect to disappointment to disapproval; but disgust and contempt on the part of the other tend to prompt humiliation and not shame. I think the conflation of humiliation and shame is actually at the root of certain psychoanalytic or psychological accounts that mistakenly view shame as always totally devastating to the self,[48] or as involving a global assessment of one's self.[49] If one agrees with the other that one is contemptuous, disgusting, or inhuman then this kind of judgment is likely to be self-shattering and to involve a global assessment of the self as completely unworthy, but for me, this is the kind of cognitive-affective recognition that is central to humiliation and not to shame.

[43] But see Paul Ekman (2008, 93) for the argument that people who are ashamed actually don't blush.

[44] Morrison (1996), 40–41.

[45] See Elster (1999), 149. Both Elster (1999, 149) and Massaro (1997, 688) tend to conflate acts of humiliation with acts of shaming, whereas I think these are distinct forms of action.

[46] Cf. Sabini, Garvey, and Hall (2001).

[47] Williams (1993), 221–22.

[48] See for example Massaro (1997), 660–61.

[49] See for example Lynd (1958), 64; Lewis (1971), 35–37; and Tangney and Dearing ([2002], 2004), 24.

Instead, I agree with Plato, Aristotle, Williams, and Morrison that the specific *cognitive* discomfort and perplexity involved in shame arise out of the recognition of ourselves as inadequate in some specific way. Morrison describes this cognition of inadequacy as one where "we are convinced that there is something about ourselves that is wrong, inferior, flawed, weak or dirty."[50] It is important to note here that the occurrent experience of shame can arise (both for the Greeks and for ourselves) in relation to both voluntary and involuntary actions and character traits. This is true even if modern psychologists and political theorists often try to firmly differentiate guilt from shame by the fact that guilt is only related to voluntary and morally culpable actions, whereas shame is only related to involuntary character traits.[51] In the *Gorgias*, Socrates' interlocutors are predominantly made to feel shame when they recognize that their specific actions or their desires to act in specific ways are inappropriate or morally blameworthy.[52] As I pointed out earlier, this does not mean that it is easy to change these desires and reform one's actions because they arise out of what are now relatively settled character traits; but like any virtues or vices, these traits or dispositions are alterable with an investment of time and effort. What is so interesting and politically salient about shame is the fact that it can arise for voluntary actions, character traits and dispositions, or for those aspects of ourselves that we cannot change, like our vulnerability and mortality.

I would also add that, for Plato and Socrates, this latter fact about shame is true even when the other is pointing out *common* vulnerabilities that are actually shared between the shamer (other) and the shamee (self). As will be seen subsequently, it is this particular aspect of the moment of recognition that can often be important for understanding the different possible reactions to it. This discomfort and perplexity also includes the painful recognition of an impediment to some object of our interest or enjoyment, even while it "*carries the hope that the impeded good scene may return and, with it, the positive affect associated with it* [my italics]."[53] In other words, the discomforting and per-

---

[50] Morrison (1996), 13.

[51] See for example Lewis (1971), 81; Taylor (1985), chapter 4; Elster (1999), 152; Tangney and Dearing ([2002], 2004), 24; Massaro (1997), 670; and Nussbaum (2004), 207. For more on these problematic distinctions between guilt and shame, see chapter 6. Here I agree with Konstan (2006, 102) that "the borderline between modern guilt and shame seems fuzzier than one might imagine." As Konstan (2006, 102) notes, one would surely feel guilt at causing the death of another person, even if their death is the result of an unavoidable accident for which one is not morally culpable.

[52] Sokolon (2006, 113) and Konstan (2006, 104) both stress that, for Aristotle, voluntary and vicious actions are actually more shameful than involuntary actions or character traits.

[53] Nathanson (1997), 124. Nathanson is here elaborating Silvan Tomkin's notion that shame is a negative affect that works within a positive-affect complex. It includes the desire to reunite with the other whose admiration or love is temporarily sundered by the shaming experience. Cf. Berlant (2008) for the influence of Tomkin's notion of the "broken circuit" on contemporary cultural notions of shame and shaming.

plexing recognition in the occurrent experience of shame *can* motivate us to try and recapture the pleasure or positive affect associated with the good scene that the experience has impeded. Callicles' repeated attempts to squirm out of the conversation with Socrates vividly illustrate his desire to end the conversation because of its relentless attacks on the confused others of his erotic longings: imperialistic Athens and the fantasy of the tyrant.[54] It is simply more pleasant for Callicles to be in tune with or to merge with these others and thus to return to the good scene that they provide for his particular erotic longings. But what Socrates and Plato also want to show us is that the good scene *might* be the *new* scene that is occurring between the "therapist" and the "patient" or between Socrates and his interlocutors.[55]

Thus, what is potentially salutary about the moment of recognition is that it can reveal a common truth between the self and the other about the fact of our common human vulnerabilities.[56] (These include bodily and intellectual vulnerabilities. I address the first in my discussion of omnipotence and the second in my discussion of Socrates' knowledge of his ignorance.) In other words, the other who effects the shaming can be the repository of a realistic and yet still wholly new and admirable way of life. Furthermore, the person shamed and the person doing the shaming can both come to recognize this in the shame situation. Thus, discomfort and perplexity don't necessarily lead the person who is shamed to hide or withdraw from a debate or discussion. Instead, they may lead the person to transform themselves in accordance with new or old others or to contest these new or old others, or both.

The refutation of Callicles illustrates the potentially salutary moment of recognition, even though his reaction to this experience is one of hiding, squirming, and attempting to conceal the truth that he has momentarily recognized. When Callicles momentarily retracts his indiscriminate hedonism thesis, he does so because he realizes that Socrates' example of the happy cowards and fools entailed by this thesis is at odds with his (Callicles') own deeper attachment to courageous and intelligent warriors. And his assertion attests to the momentary consensus achieved between him and Socrates on the issue of good and bad pleasures: "As if you thought that I or any other human being

---

[54] As Berlant (2008, 85) puts it, "People often thrash around like monsters in that situation, not having skills for maintaining composure amidst the deflation of their fantasy about how their world is organized."

[55] For an example of this kind of positive transference, see Morrison (1996), 169.

[56] Although, in chapters 2 and 3, I emphasized the way that Socrates' shaming elenchus revealed the gaps between Callicles' actions and his (Callicles') admired but tyrannical other, it is important to note that when Callicles comes to realize that some pleasures are better than others and that some pleasures need to be restrained, he is recognizing something that is true both for himself and for Socrates. As Nussbaum (2004, 245) puts it, "Antinarcissistic shaming of a sort that reinforces common human vulnerability is much to be desired in an American all too hooked on myths of invulnerability."

did not consider some pleasures better and others worse!" (499b) Callicles momentarily recognizes a truth about himself (and the falsity of indiscriminate hedonism) that consists in the fact that for vulnerable and mortal human beings the pleasant and the good unfortunately do not completely coincide.[57]

In fact, this is precisely what Socrates hopes to do in his elenchic encounters with others. For Socrates, putting someone to shame is the very activity that first creates a potentially salutary discomfort and perplexity in the patient (i.e., the intra-psychic division between the self and the other) that is necessary for self-consciousness, self-reflection, self-criticism, and moral and political deliberation.[58] What Socrates attempts to do in his refutation of Callicles is to get him to recognize the difference between himself and the tyrant (and between himself and the tyrannical tendencies of Athenian imperial democracy) by instilling a salutary disunity within his soul in the form of the moment of recognition. As he tells Callicles, he hopes that Callicles will not agree with his thesis that the pleasant and the good are the same, "when he himself looks on himself correctly" (495e). Thus Socrates quite literally practices a politics of shame in his relentless questioning of his fellow Athenians in an attempt to make them more reflective about themselves and their collective others.

It is also precisely *this* potential in the moment of recognition that addresses the sorts of things that Elshtain and Warner are both worried about. Elshtain is worried that individuals in a democracy who practice the politics of displacement ensure their own enslavement to the totalistic gaze of publicity by coming to see themselves as simply the "cross-dressers" or "sadomasochists" that they parade about in public. This is very similar to the mistaken recognition of himself that Callicles is guilty of in his first speech when he takes himself to *be* the tyrant he shamelessly and publicly praises (483a–d). Similarly, Warner is worried that the queers who seek acceptance through gay marriage are identifying with an image of the "normal" citizen that is simply a fantastical other created by the experts and doctors in our modern disciplinary regime.

Again, if shame in its occurrent manifestation involves the recognition that we do not live up to an other that we admire, then it might have a role to play in preventing precisely this sort of complete assimilation to a "normal" but fantastical other. In the *Gorgias* Socrates is able to get his interlocutors to be momentarily ashamed by some of the acts that would be entailed by the ty-

---

[57] They may well coincide for a god and they may *almost* coincide in the philosopher's pursuit of the truth or the tyrants pursuit of money, power, praise, and sexual conquests, but they never fully coincide for any human being. This fact about the philosopher relates to the human and erotic character of his knowledge: it is knowledge of what he does and does not know, but most feels the *need* to know. As pleasant as his thinking is, it is always accompanied by the painful awareness of his *lack* of complete knowledge. The tyrannical individual, on the other hand, falsely tries to convince himself that the pleasant and the good can coincide in human life and his attempts to bring this about end up depriving him of any true freedom or friendship (*Rep.* 9.576a).

[58] For a more extensive treatment of this theme, see chapter 2.

rant's indiscriminate hedonism. Callicles doesn't recognize who he *is* when he finally admits that, like all other human beings he distinguishes between good and bad pleasures, but he does recognize that he *is not* identical to his image of the tyrant. And this kind of recognition at least momentarily prevents a complete assimilation to this other that may well be discomforting and perplexing for Callicles, but is nonetheless potentially salutary. In the occurrent experience of shame we are faced with the recognition that we are not who we thought we were, but this is a good thing if who we are can't be captured by a *fantastical* other.

And this perplexing recognition constitutes at least part of what Socrates means by knowledge of one's ignorance. Knowing *that* you are not identical to a tyrant is not the same thing as knowing *who* you are, but it might still be a necessary aspect of moral reflection, political deliberation, and the negotiation and ongoing construction of one's identity. In pursuing this kind of self-knowledge, the philosopher or lover of wisdom is performing the very negotiation of the "I," the "us," and the "we" that Elshtain speaks of in her book. Or, as Warner would put it, Socrates never gives his interlocutors any clear view of the "we" that is supposed to be different from the tyrant or the just person they are investigating, he just gets his interlocutors to see that their acts don't fully correspond to these supposedly seamless identities. And this very insight can be liberating for those engulfed by the social auto-totality of a totalitarian or normalizing regime. Following Socrates, these two thinkers want to find a radically democratic potential in the discomforting and perplexing moment of recognition within the occurrent experience of shame.

Socratic Respectful vs. Flattering Shame

By a Socratic respectful politics of shame, then, I mean a political situation in which this kind of recognition within the occurrent experience of shame is the goal of the acts of shaming or the sense of shame for all parties engaged in democratic deliberations, and/or of the structures that enable these deliberations. And I now want to clarify why this politics of shame is different from one that involves flattery, stigmatization, or humiliation. As I pointed out earlier, Socrates' refutation of Callicles momentarily sunders his identification with a particular other, the tyrant. However, there are at least five different ways in which Callicles himself might attempt to fill the gap that has now been created. He might (1) hide or withdraw from any further debate or discussion; (2) try to transform himself in accordance with a new other: either a less tyrannical democrat or Socratic philosophy; (3) try to transform himself in accordance with the old other, the tyrant or the imperial Athenian democrat; (4) try to transform the world to make it fit better with either the new or old other; (5)

try to contest the standard provided by either the new or the old others.[59] And these are not mutually exclusive alternatives. One of the interesting things about an intersubjective emotion like shame is that it evades the distinction between desires which have a world-to-mind fit and perceptions or beliefs which have a mind-to-world fit.[60] In the moment when one feels the gap that opens up between one's self and the other in the occurrent experience of shame, there is no logical or psychological necessity that this gap be filled by making oneself over in the image of the other or by making the other and the world conform to the self. Although the tyrant is characterized by his overwhelming desire to force the world and others to conform to his narcissistic self, the experience of shame does not foreclose the other possibilities mentioned above.[61] Notice, too, that the person doing the shaming might have any one or more than one of these motives when performing the shaming, and that these motives are not always transparent to the person who is experiencing the shaming. In other words, there might be consensus, disagreement, or misunderstanding about the content and/or the motives of the other that is performing the shaming.

A mature person can react to one instance of shaming and not really have it affect his own sense of shame, but over the course of a life we develop a sense of shame in response to the repeated instances of various acts of shaming by others. (Indeed, the infant or immature person first develops self-awareness and thus a sense of self in the inaugural moment of recognition at about fourteen to eighteen months.)[62] Moreover, there are various familial, political,

---

[59] I think Williams (1993) emphasizes the reactions of either hiding or transforming oneself, but not of changing the world or of simply contesting the other, yet these latter possibilities point to other political and deliberative potentials in the experience of shame. Braithwaite's (1989 and 2000) distinctions between stigmatizing and reintegrative shaming overlook these latter two possibilities as well. However, in Braithwaite's case this arises primarily because he examines shame as part of the criminal justice system where the applicability and value of the criminal law is not really in question.

[60] The notion of direction of fit is taken from G.E.M. Anscombe's 1957 book *Intention*. Robert Solomon does a nice job of articulating this two-directional or bipolar character of our emotional life. As he (2003, 37) puts it, "Virtually every emotion consists of both objective intentions and subjective intentions, intentions to change the world and transformation of one's (view of) his world."

[61] As Blitz (2005) and Tarcov (2005) argue, the tyrant's desire for eminence and power over, as well as praise from, absolutely everyone leads them to associate only with flatterers and to kill the eminent and wise in their midst, so that they never have to be shown their shortcomings by anyone. Although I agree with Strong (2005, 104) that, for Nietzsche, the tyrannical impulse lies in coming "to believe that the image that one has created is in fact the way the world is," I do not think that this is what the philosopher does. The philosophic person is the one person who is most successful at fighting off this tyrannical impulse that lingers in himself, just as it does, to some degree, in everyone.

[62] See Morrison (1996, 58–63) for a much fuller elaboration of this point from a psychoanalytic perspective and in the context of important childhood experiences.

and social structures that influence how we respond to any act of shaming. All of these will influence the sense of shame that any person develops in ways that are absolutely unique to this person, but that will also contain elements shared with any or all of the others previously encountered. I now redefine the sense of shame as that particular and absolutely unique other that resides in the soul of all of us (and in the "soul" or structures of a particular polity) and that allows us to avoid what we consider *shameful*, i.e., harmful (bad) or painful or both, and to pursue what we consider *honorable*, i.e., beneficial (good) or pleasurable or both.[63] And I want to use these criteria of the shameful and honorable to clarify and refine some of my distinctions between flattering shame and Socratic respectful shame, both in terms of the sense of shame and the politics of shame.

As I argued in chapter 1, in order to criticize Polus' and Callicles' (and imperialistic, democratic Athens') notion of flattery, Socrates distinguishes between doctors who administer painful or bitter medicines to their patients, and cooks who aim solely at the pleasures of the children who consume their pastries (464d–465a). The problem with flattery is that both parties to the relationship equate the pleasures of eating with the good of the body. Similarly, what Socrates criticizes the Athenians for, and what he would criticize in our contemporary democratic practice of flattery, is the tendency on the part of both the speaker and the audience to fixate *solely* on the pleasures of mutual recognition.[64] A false consensus then forms wherein "debate" becomes a reciprocal exchange of pleasantries, such that neither party ever has to endure the pain of having one's identity or ideals criticized by an other. Each party is thus oriented to *avoiding* the discomforting and perplexing recognition that is so characteristic of the moment of recognition.

But the problem with flattery arises because it overlooks the fact that the moment of recognition is not necessarily a pernicious experience, rather it constitutes our all-too-human openness to socialization that allows us to acquire new norms, ideals, and exemplars of different ways of living. The moment of recognition points to the *potential* divergence of the pleasant and the

---

[63] I derive this definition from lines 474d–475b of the *Gorgias*. Here Socrates explicitly defines the shameful as pain or badness or both (*Gorg*. 475a–b). See chapter 2, section 2.2, for a full elaboration of this definition of the shameful in the *Gorgias*. I believe that this potentially disjunctive definition of the shameful is the key to Plato's understanding of the phenomenon of shame, because it points to the fact that in flattering shame the painful and the harmful are conflated and the pleasant and the good are likewise conflated. In both Socratic and Platonic respectful shame, the painful is not conflated with the harmful or bad, so that what is painful (or perplexing or discomforting) may be part of a salutary recognition on the part of the person experiencing shame.

[64] This does not mean that the pleasures of mutual recognition are in themselves pernicious to democratic deliberation. I only want to argue that there is a problem when this becomes the *only* goal of our deliberations.

good in human life because it points to the possibility that what is discomforting and perplexing for us to see about ourselves might still be the most important thing for us to learn about ourselves. This is what I take to be one of the most important insights in Plato's *Gorgias*. In the moment of recognition we find ourselves falling away from an other that we had previously held dear, and losing this other has an element of discomfort and perplexity. The discomfort and perplexity that is inherent to this moment is, I think, an important source of the Greeks' (and our own) ambivalence toward shame in democratic theory and practice.[65] Perplexity is an instance where we can simultaneously feel pleasure and pain: we can feel pleasure that we are no longer living under the illusion of a false other, but we can also feel pain or discomfort precisely because we *love* this other and hold it dear.[66]

But, in the flattering reaction to the moment of recognition, one fixates on and equates the cognitive discomfort or perplexity that is inherent to this moment with its *harmfulness* or *perniciousness*. And it is this discomfort and perplexity that becomes the "harmful" situation that one's sense of shame disposes one to avoid in the future. Callicles' responses to Socrates' questions vividly illustrate how discomforting and perplexing he finds it to be shown that he doesn't live up to the standards of indiscriminate hedonism he sets for himself: "I don't know what you are saying Socrates, so ask someone else . . . How violent you are, Socrates. But if you're persuaded by me, you'll bid this argument farewell, or else you'll converse with someone else . . . (505c–d)." Callicles wants to avoid discomfort and perplexity so badly that he begs to be released from the discussion.[67]

What one considers "harmful" about the moment of recognition is the fact that the self is seen by the other as different from what one thought one was, and alternately, what one considers "beneficial" is to be recognized by the other as simply what one already takes oneself to be. But this notion of the beneficial corresponds to what both Elshtain and Warner see as the misplaced political ontology of identity politics.[68] It reflects the desire for the lost unity of an undifferentiated community standard where there could be complete transparency between individuals and thus a kind of freedom from the moment of recognition within the occurrent experience of shame. In the flattering sense

---

[65] For a different treatment of ambivalence as it relates particularly to the emotion of shame, see Williams (1993), 97, and Locke (2004), 1–4, 24.

[66] Thus, in the case of Plato and Socrates there is a certain pleasure in experiencing, reacting to, or producing perplexity in others. This is the pleasure of having one's false opinions refuted (458a).

[67] Gorgias on the other hand *is* someone who seems perplexed by and yet interested in what Socrates has to say (506a–b). For a fuller elaboration of the differences between these two interlocutors, see chapter 2.

[68] For an excellent but different critique of the mistaken ontology of the politics of identity and recognition, see Markell (2003).

of shame or politics of shame, one thus hopes to avoid the unpleasant experience of having one's identifications punctured by one's audience. But avoiding these unpleasant recognitions might well amount to avoiding the recognition of our common human vulnerabilities. It *is* discomforting and perplexing to be shown that we are human and not omnipotent, omniscient, sexless, bodiless gods. In other words, the false consensus between the self and the other that underlies this type of shame is the belief that we *ought* to be omniscient, omnipotent, and invulnerable beings who avoid all discomfort and perplexity, and who never have to learn anything new about ourselves. Accordingly, this flattering sense of shame or politics of shame motivates us to conceal our vulnerabilities and to reestablish the invulnerable, inhuman, fantastical, omnipotent other: the tyrant.

The democratic citizen motivated by this flattering sense of shame is like the child whose love and identification with his own infantile omnipotence is sundered by the moment of recognition, and who wants nothing more than to reunite with this infantile omnipotence and to eliminate the new other that threatens this reunion. But because this is impossible for self-conscious beings, such a citizen attempts to establish an omnipotent, fantastical other in his soul and in politics. And, as a secondary defense mechanism, he avoids feeling shame by displacing it onto others in the political realm or, as in the case of the tyrannical democrat in Book 8 of Plato's *Republic*, by renaming and thus misrecognizing shamelessness as "courage" and shame as "simplicity" (*Rep.* 8.560c–561a). As the tyrannical democrat, Callicles, tells Socrates, "It is fine to partake of philosophy to the extent that it is for the sake of education, and it is not shameful to philosophize when one is a lad. But when a human being who is already older still philosophizes, the thing becomes ridiculous" (485a). It is Callicles' fantasy that a person could learn everything as a child so that he would never again have to endure the pain of separation from his imperialistic community or his own infantile, omnipotent self. I follow Plato in assuming that no good democratic citizen would want to be the parent, friend, or political partner of such a person.

Here, I think it becomes possible to see why Socrates thinks that flattering shame not only unduly fixates on the pleasant (as a sufficient criterion of the good), but also why it calls in "false" witnesses of good repute (471e–472b), and why Socrates in the *Gorgias* might be the only "true" witness of bad repute.[69] The person who engages in flattery is oriented to preserving either a unitary, static, rigid, omnipotent, or fantastical other (or some combination of all of these), and is oriented to producing this kind of other either in his polity or in the psyche of his audience via his acts of shaming. And (as a secondary defense mechanism) he is also oriented to projecting his own devi-

---

[69] For a fuller treatment of the issue of "true" and "false" witnesses, see chapters 2 and 3.

ances from the other onto actual or imaginary "deviant" or "perverted" others. So this stance can be "false" in many different ways. It may involve, on the part of the speaker and/or the audience (which can be an individual, group, or political structure) (1) conscious insincerity, (2) a mistaken understanding of who one is or ought to be, or (3) a fantastical and therefore exaggerated understanding of who one is or ought to be.

And these are precisely the kinds of things that Warner is worried about when he criticizes the standard of the "normal" and when he suggests that both queers and straights may not want to assimilate themselves to this rigid and fantastical standard. The Greeks' notion of the tyrant ultimately converges with the modern notion of the "normal" citizen because both result from projecting the desire for omnipotence onto a fantastical other that no mature human being can fully live up to. Callicles' image of the tyrant and our image of the "normal" citizen is an image of shamelessness and infantile omnipotence that may have been experienced by all of us in the womb, but that is certainly never experienced when we are thrown into relations of intersubjectivity. It is the objectified image of the desire to escape all forms of restraint, intra-psychic division, or "punishment" of the self.[70] All other forms of life, according to Socrates, are not shameless because they always include some kind of prioritizing of the desires in accordance with what is beneficial in human life, and it is this prioritizing that shame enables us to do.[71] Callicles at his most shocking is still only flattering his beloved but corrupt *dēmos* and its mistaken equation of freedom with shamelessness; and we do the same thing when we equate our own democratic notion of freedom with becoming shameless.[72]

If this is in fact the case, then morality might well consist not in a blind assimilation to the norm, but in understanding the ways in which we are both like and unlike the norms of our society in specific contexts and situations. And accepting the other form of morality grounded in flattering

[70] Socrates defines punishment as "keeping [the soul] away from the things it desires" at 505b. Based on *this* Socratic definition, escaping "punishment" would include indulging all forms of desire indiscriminately. And beneficial "punishment" can include any kind of necessary and salutary restraint of one's desires: e.g., the act of respectful shaming exemplified by the Socratic elenchus.

[71] Accordingly, shamelessness should never be the goal or involved in the process of psychoanalytic therapy or democratic politics. Cf. Morrison (1996), 106. Morrison (1996, 148) states that "reformulation of ideals serving as mandates for the shape of the self is what constitutes the psychotherapy of shame." Similarly, I believe that reformulating pernicious others in our deliberations constitutes the Socratic respectful politics of shame. Only fantastical tyrants or fictional characters are completely shameless.

[72] As Tarcov (2005, 127) argues, Plato's ultimate criticism of the tyrannical democracy at the end of *Republic* 8 is that its "insatiable desire for freedom (as that which democracy defines as good) destroys democracy and leads to tyranny. Democratic citizens end up 'paying no attention to the laws, written or unwritten, in order that they may avoid having any master at all' . . . Thus the failure to moderate the democratic desire for freedom leads to its opposite for the *demos*."

shame, with its ontology of fixed identities, may well condemn us to failure and may end up producing the kind of stigmatizing politics of shame that Warner and Elshtain both criticize. Thus, a politics of shame that aims at what I mean by "flattery" endangers democracy in five ways. First, it aims only at the pleasures of mutual recognition and thus tries to avoid any discomfort or perplexity caused by misrecognition. Second, it introduces a rigid, unitary, and static other into our political structures and deliberations. Third, it introduces a fantastical or "normal" other: the ideal of a wholly active, omnipotent citizen who is never to experience discomfort, perplexity, or suffering at the hands of an other. Fourth, it tends to foreclose two of the salutary reactions to the occurrent experience of shame, i.e., contestation of new and old others, and transformation in accordance with new others. Finally, it tends to produce "normal" citizens who retain this "normality" only by projecting their own contingencies or "failures" onto others in a politics of stigmatization and humiliation. The normalizing and totalizing tendencies of flattering shame led the Athenians to pursue an imperialistic politics that stigmatized others as "barbarians," but that also led to Athens' ultimate demise. Contemporary democratic citizens and world leaders might well learn a lesson from this fact and try to avoid treating others in the domestic or international realm accordingly.[73]

Instead, I believe that Socrates' own sense of shame offers us a model of respect or, as Warner would put it, a "dignity in shame" that consists of an openness to the discomfort and perplexity that is so characteristic of the moment of recognition. In other words, producing discomfort and perplexity can be one of the goals of our political actions of respectful shaming, and one of the others that we respect in our psyche and/or establish in our deliberative structures. Such a respectful politics of shame keeps open the possibility that who we are cannot be captured by the specific others we currently possess.

This kind of politics of shame thus keeps open the other two possibilities that I mentioned earlier when speaking about how a person (or a polity) might react to the moment of recognition, i.e., we might collectively contest the others by which we are shamed or we might learn to admire and assimilate to new, more salutary and realistic others. I also hope to have shown that we need to be wary of certain false kinds of reciprocity, equality, and consensus that can exist in the relationships characteristic of a flattering politics of shame, i.e., the fixation solely on the pleasures of mutual recognition. I think that Socratic respectful shame addresses this problem as well because Socrates remains open to the possibility that his audience may show him something new and perplexing about himself that he hadn't recognized before. This kind of

---

[73] The horrific and humiliating prison abuses at Abu Ghraib perpetrated against Iraqi prisoners in the course of the Iraq war in 2003 and 2004 serve as one of the worst contemporary examples of the underside of the politics of flattery, i.e., the politics of stigmatization and humiliation.

mutual or reciprocal engagement between the speaker and the audience avoids the kind of false consensus, reciprocity, and recognition that exist in the relationship of flattery. Instead, Socratic respectful shame registers and preserves the place of uncertainty between the speaker and his audience by preserving the reciprocal possibility of being shown that one's actions do not conform to one's current set of others. A true democratic politics, for Socrates, is one that preserves the openness to this kind of discomforting and perplexing experience so central to the experience of being shamed out of one's conformity and complacent moralism. Socrates' agonistic point then is not simply that being a democratic citizen might actually require *dissolving or contesting* our political and moral projects of ordering subjects and institutions, but also that this kind of citizenship includes passivity (or suffering), discomfort, perplexity, and a salutary form of disorientation or misrecognition.

Platonic Respectful Shame and the Search for Consensus

This might still sound like we should simply replace a politics of feeling good with a politics of feeling bad and then go around relentlessly shaming and perplexing everyone we meet.[74] But as I argued in chapter 4, the *Gorgias* ultimately offers a second model of a respectful politics of shame that reflects Plato's own attempts to redress the limitations that arise from the *overly* agonistic character of the Socratic shaming elenchus. Plato's revisions to Socratic respectful shaming reflect four additional considerations. The first one is the need to emphasize the fact that not all pleasures are bad, and, indeed, certain pleasures might well be beneficial as part of the more curative aspects of a respectful rhetoric. Second, the motives behind a particular shaming are not always transparent to the one who is being shamed. Third, although respectful shame does involve the realization that we have fallen away from our ideals, it also involves an element of consensus between the self and the other. Finally, this element of consensus actually "makes Socratic negativity effective and possible."[75] In contrast to a Socratic respectful politics of shame, a Platonic respectful politics of shame does not entail that people are *constantly* feeling the painful occurrent experience of shame in public deliberations or debates. Rather it requires that people remain *open* to being shamed by an other and it does not preclude our deliberations from being filled with many pleasurable insights and with a great deal of laughter as well as tears.[76]

---

[74] For an excellent account of the "shame-induced weariness" that this kind of politics of shame produces, see Locke (2007). I also thank Reuel Rogers for bringing this point to my attention. My account of the differences between Socratic and Platonic respectful shame in this section is meant to show how a politics of *Platonic* respectful shame can avoid this specific problem.

[75] I am indebted to Peter Euben for formulating this point in this manner.

[76] I treat this theme more extensively in Tarnopolsky (2005).

For Plato, Socrates' sense of shame was so attuned to the search for truth that it often prevented him from uttering any pleasantries, or anything at all from within the background consensus or collective self that he shared with his interlocutors. Socrates himself experienced a certain amount of delight and pleasure from being perplexed and having his false opinions refuted (even while he simultaneously experienced the painful desire to overcome these limitations in his own self-knowledge), and his life exemplified an openness to this ambivalence (i.e., the simultaneous presence of pleasure and pain) within perplexity. Thus Socrates was motivated by and open to respectful shame even though his interlocutors and readers of the dialogues never see him squirm or blush. But in the early Socratic dialogues this radical devotion to searching for the truth underlies the famous Socratic strangeness and irony that his interlocutors are always complaining about. As Callicles puts it, Socrates' ideas literally turn his worldview upside down (481c). In a sense, Socrates' ironic comportment to others made him a radical other such that no lasting understanding or consensus could be achieved between him and Athens.[77]

But as Plato realized, shame can quickly spiral into anger and rage when the person who is ashamed does not fully grasp the standards by which he is being shamed. In other words, Socrates' motives may not have been fully transparent to all of his interlocutors. Thus, for Plato respectful shame requires acknowledging the place of the audience in terms of both the experiences they have suffered in the past and the others they now use to interpret these experiences. If an act of shaming is meant to introduce a new other, this requires a principle of charity, i.e., of acknowledging the shared others against which any meaningful disagreement can even be perceived.[78] For Plato then, in order to be truly radical, one cannot be simply a radical other.

Accordingly, in the *Gorgias*, Plato's Socrates doesn't just engage in a ruthless critique of every definition of a virtue and then through up his hands and walk away (as he does in many earlier dialogues.) Instead, he shows his interlocutors that although or even because they fail to live by the standards of the tyrants they profess to admire, they do actually agree with him about certain Athenian democratic others that are worthy of respect: e.g., that it is worse to do injustice than to suffer it and that some pleasures are better than others. Thus Platonic respectful shame registers the fact that a certain amount of admirable consensus is instrumental to any form of disagreement (or Socratic negativity) and that this disagreement only partially transcends its own context of meaningfulness.

This is not to say that Platonic respectful shame amounts to a blanket affirmation of the authoritative background of democratic Athens *or* the utopian idealized other of the *Republic*'s best regime. Plato himself felt that Socrates'

---

[77] For a full elaboration of this theme, see chapter 4.
[78] I borrow the terminology of charity from Davidson (1984), 183–98.

own style of justice, i.e., of speaking to each person individually and respectfully rather than calling in the many "false" witnesses of good repute (471e–472c), was vastly superior to certain *corrupt* Athenian practices and beliefs, e.g., the beliefs in indiscriminate hedonism and *pleonexia* exemplified in the practices of flattering rhetoric and Athenian imperialism. Again, as I argued in the last chapter, the moment when Callicles actually recognizes just how admirable it might be to follow Socrates' path and thus to avoid flattering and imitating the "false witnesses" of imperialistic Athens is one of the most interesting parts of the dialogue:

> CAL. In some way, I don't know what, what you say seems good to me, Socrates; but I suffer the experience of the many—I am not altogether persuaded by you.
>
> SOC. Yes, for love of the people, Callicles, which is present in your soul, opposes me. But if we investigate these same things often and better, perhaps you will be persuaded. (513c–d)

The consensus that could be achieved between them would arise out of and point back to certain salutary others of democratic Athens: that it is better to suffer injustice than to do it and that some pleasures are better than others. But, as the above quote makes clear, it would also arise out of and point forward to two new others: Socratic and Platonic philosophizing as exemplified in the conversation that takes place in the *Gorgias*. In this sense, Platonic respectful shame has the potential to simultaneously contest and transform, conserve, and conceal our collective others. In the case of the momentary consensus between Socrates and Callicles, it (1) contests and momentarily conceals aspects of the tyrannical and imperialistic democratic other; (2) contests, conserves, and transforms aspects of the Athenian democratic other; (3) contests, conserves, and transforms aspects of the Socratic other; and (4) introduces the new Platonic other into the Athenian democratic imaginary. In the *Gorgias*, the Platonic Socrates now begins to play the role of the immanent *and* transcendent critic by recalling his corrupt Athens (and its spokesperson, Callicles) back to its own best self while introducing a perplexing and awe-inspiring new conception of the philosophic way of life into this collective self.

I am aware that my notion of Platonic respectful shame brings in a whole new set of issues about the kind of authority that is being claimed by and or attributed to the Socratic and Platonic other.[79] But I follow Sharon Krause in arguing that even our modern notions of respect and distinction can refer to a salutary *hierarchical but reciprocal* relationship between a self and an other.[80] And I follow Josiah Ober in arguing that the Greek notions of honor and

---

[79] I am indebted to Sharon Krause, Fonna Forman-Barzilai, and Nancy Luxon for pointing this out to me.

[80] For an example of distinction in the case of Martin Luther King Jr., see Krause (2002), 171.

shame can refer to a salutary *egalitarian* relationship between a self and an other in ways that are similar to our modern notions of dignity.[81] The other may be one that an individual or collective self agrees with, respects, or *both*, and this is why Platonic respectful shame can be articulated within a structure of respect or dignity. Flattering shame occurs when a person mistakenly or insincerely respects or dignifies an other who is not worthy of respect or dignity. Respectful shame occurs when a person (e.g., Plato or myself) respects and dignifies, contests, and transforms an other (e.g., Socrates or Elshtain and Warner) who is worthy of respect and dignity.

Moreover, one of the salutary differences between our contemporary situation and the Athenian politics of shame is that our more democratic, liberal, and pluralistic polity makes possible a multiplicity of others within the psyche and the political context that we can respect and dignify. I think this has direct consequences for the egalitarian, reciprocal, and pluralistic structure of our own respectful politics of shame. In such a political setting, any particular act of respectful shaming can be less intense and nonreciprocally hierarchical than was the case in democratic Athens, and thus less likely to lead to the Calliclean reaction of hiding and withdrawing from the debate. There are now many more different but equally worthy notions of the best life or other that we might respect. And because of this, any particular act of shaming can be confined to a particular other within the individual's psyche, but there will be a multiplicity of alternative others that one will simultaneously respect, and that can open up different avenues of acceptance and self-acceptance.[82]

I thus want to end this chapter in a provocative but respectful way by suggesting that respectful shame *is* involved in disagreeing with a person's position in a discursive setting. I have calmly but passionately tried to respectfully shame Elshtain and Warner by showing them that their disagreements actually occur against a surprisingly similar, albeit weak, background consensus. Here I hope I *have* shocked the reader by suggesting that Warner and Elshtain actually make pretty good, though misrecognized, bedmates on the topic of queer politics. As I pointed out above, Elshtain criticizes the "cross-dressing, sadomasochist" queer proponents of this type of politics for shamelessly flaunting their sexuality in the supposedly sexless public sphere. Yet, as I also tried to show, the position that she ultimately articulates and her criticisms of a certain kind of "politicized ontology" end up being very similar to the position of one of these "perverted" opponents, i.e., Michael Warner. As they alternately point out, the sadomasochist queers who parade their sexuality and the Mothers of the Disappeared who parade around the public square are both challenging their respective regimes in ways that emphasize acts over characters and that

---

[81] Ober (1996), 101–3.
[82] I am indebted to Morrison (1996) and David Leitch for this point.

challenge the gaze of the "social auto-totality."[83] This is not to say that the two groups share a comprehensive moral background culture: both groups would probably be horrified by this suggestion. They are, however, weakly linked together by their similar mode of opposition to the unitary and totalizing image of the "normal" citizen. Similarly, Warner and Elshtain are weakly linked together in their mutual opposition to any form of identity politics that requires a static and essentialized view of the group that is contesting the public image or unitary standard of the citizen. But discovering this consensus required respectfully shaming these thinkers in the very act of refusing to flatter or stigmatize them as a "prude," "pervert," or "tyrant."

[83] Elshtain (1995), 134.

Chapter Six

WHAT'S SO NEGATIVE ABOUT THE

"NEGATIVE" EMOTIONS?

IN THE LAST CHAPTER I argued that a Platonic notion of respectful shame can offer us a model of civility that incorporates the kind of painful recognitions that are necessarily involved in trying to come to an agreement with others who may be quite different from ourselves. I also argued that this kind of agreement does not require the thick consensus or unitary background of shared values that are often presumed to be necessary for civility and that so often lead to a pernicious stigmatization of the other. In this chapter, I want to look at some of the other criteria that have been used to characterize shame, and the emotions more generally, as "negative" or pernicious for contemporary democratic societies. In other words, I want to expand my treatment beyond the particular debates about shame and civility in order to see how the notion of Platonic respectful shame I have derived from Plato's *Gorgias* might shed light on some of the broader debates about reason and the emotions more generally.[1]

DEFINING THE "NEGATIVE" EMOTIONS

Discussions of the emotions and their place in democratic politics too often take one of four forms:[2] (1) they articulate the differences between reason and the emotions and then argue for the benefits of reason (usually in terms of its impartiality, neutrality, or objectivity) and against the corresponding dangers of the emotions;[3] (2) they divide the category of emotions into "interests"

---

[1] As I argued in the last chapter, Plato's notion of respectful shame does not reject the salutary production of perplexity so central to Socratic respectful shame, but rather preserves this even as it transcends it by focusing on the salutary forms of consensus and pleasure that can also be involved in coming to a new understanding of ourselves in and through the experience of shame. Thus, in this chapter, whenever I speak about Platonic respectful shame, I mean to include within it those elements of Socratic respectful shame that involve the salutary but painful production of perplexity in one's fellow citizens.

[2] For a discussion of the role of emotions in politics that evade all of these problematic tendencies, see Koziak (2000); Hall (2005); Sokolon (2006); Krause (2008); and Kingston and Ferry (2008).

[3] For a discussion of this problematic tendency, see Hall (2002), 732; Hall (2005), 22–24; Nussbaum (2004), 24; Sokolon (2006), 3; Krause (2008), 1; and Kingston and Ferry (2008), 3.

and "passions" and argue for the salutary character of interests while carefully excluding the dangerous, irrational, and warlike passions;[4] (3) they simply overlook the emotions in their models of political deliberation and norm-justification (even if they allow a place for them in motivating political action and disposing people to adhere to the norms that reason has justified);[5] or (4) they try to find a place for the more "positive" emotions, such as love, compassion, and guilt as elements within democratic deliberations, while carefully excluding the "negative" emotions of shame, humiliation, and disgust.[6]

Moreover, these perceptions of the problematic character of the emotions have a long history in Western political thought. As Martha Nussbaum argues, the first strategy was perfected by the Greek and Roman Stoic philosophers who saw emotions as linked to those "external goods" that were beyond human control and thus disruptive of the self-sufficiency, autonomy, and invulnerability that the philosopher strove to achieve.[7] Medieval philosophers combined this with a Christian (and primarily Augustinian) view of the emotions as linked to our dangerous sexuality and therefore in need of repression.[8] Then, in the early modern period, classical liberals revised the first strategy and developed the second one in the "wake of the violence of the religious wars."[9] Classical liberals marginalized the emotions by specifically focusing on their problematic character and then proscribing them from politics, but now in order to deal with their tendency to produce instability and war.[10] In the case of the second strategy, early moderns like Adam Smith and John Locke chose to use greed and avarice to counter the passions for honor and vainglory that were allegedly at the heart of political and religious wars.[11] In a second move, the former passions (greed and avarice), condemned by the ancients as some of the lowest forms of human motivation and by the medievals as cardinal sins,

---

[4] For a discussion of this problematic tendency, see Koziak (2000), 6–8; Walzer (2002), 617–18; Hall (2002), 733; Hall (2005), 25–26; and Brennan and Pettit (2004), 7–8.

[5] For a discussion of this problematic tendency, see Hall (2002), 734; Hall (2005), 26–67; and Krause (2008), 2–3.

[6] I discuss this problematic tendency below. For a discussion of how Aristotle's view of the emotions counters this problematic tendency, see Sokolon (2006), 179–82.

[7] Nussbaum (2004), 6–7.

[8] Koziak (2000), 8; Jacobs (2008), 72; and Berlant (2008), 81.

[9] Kingston and Ferry (2008), 1.

[10] Hall (2002), 732–34; and Hall (2005), 21–27. Cf. Koziak (2000), 6–8; Walzer (2002), 625; and Brennan and Pettit (2004), 7–8. All of these authors cite Albert Hirschman's 1977 book, *The Passions and the Interests: Political Arguments for Capitalism before its Triumph*, as the first one to outline the classical liberal strategy of distinguishing between passions and interests (strategy 2). Hall cites Stephen Holmes' 1995 book, *Passions and Constraints: On the Theory of Liberal Democracy*, for the liberal strategy of designing institutions to keep the passions out of politics and to safeguard reason from the passions (strategy 1).

[11] For a full account of this strategy, see Hirschman (1977); Holmes (1995); and Hall (2003) and (2005).

were reclassified as "interests."[12] Finally, these theorists accorded "interests" the status of rationality by arguing that they, unlike the "hot-blooded" passions, were calm, calculable, and communicable to others.[13] Linked with this was a tendency to see people still moved by passions, rather than reason or interests, as "ignorant," "primitive," and part of the "lower orders."[14]

The fact that many contemporary liberals and deliberative democrats now marginalize the passions by simply overlooking them rather than by explicitly targeting them (strategy 3) is due, in part, to the fact that the classical liberals did such a good job of proscribing them from politics.[15] Finally, I would argue that the fourth strategy of distinguishing between "positive" and "negative" emotions, which now seems to be prevalent in certain contemporary discussions of emotions, actually constitutes a (perhaps misrecognized) revival of strategy 2, but now within a very different political context. Three or four centuries after thinkers like Locke and Smith extolled the virtues of greed and avarice, few political theorists remain convinced that such emotions lead to a *decline* in aggressive warfare or to an overall *increase* in the wealth of nations. However, theorists have still adopted a number of elements of this early liberal strategy, including the distinction between "positive" and "negative" emotions, the distrust of certain "primitive" emotions, and the belief that such emotions must be carefully excluded from the public sphere.[16] While the criteria now used may not be exactly the same as those used by the early liberal theorists, some contemporary theorists still target certain emotions as characteristic of more primitive stages of human development, and, as I show below, shame is often among those targeted for exclusion for this very reason.

The criteria that have been put forth by various psychological, philosophical, anthropological, psychoanalytic, moral, political, legal, phenomenological, sociological, or neuroscientific perspectives to distinguish between "negative" and "positive" emotions include, but are not limited to: pain/pleasure, hierarchical/egalitarian, moral/nonmoral, political/apolitical, advanced/primitive, active/passive, masculine/feminine, rational/irrational, cognitive/affective, calm/agitated, relational/non-relational, competitive/cooperative, egoistic/altruistic, autonomous/heteronomous, arising from primitive parts of brain

[12] Hirschman (1977), 33; Holmes (1995), 4; Koziak (2000), 8; Hall (2003), 733 and (2005), 25–26.

[13] Hirschman (1977), 33, 50, 58; Hall (2002), 733; and Hall (2005), 26.

[14] Walzer (2002), 619–22.

[15] Hall (2003), 732–34; and Hall (2005), 21–27.

[16] Hall (2005, 17) argues that another way of distinguishing between "negative" and "positive" emotions is to distinguish between passions and sentiments, where the latter are positive because they are calm, mild, reasonable, and moderate. I do not deal with this problematic distinction, but for excellent treatments of why *both* passions and sentiments are important components of political deliberations, see Hall (2005) and Krause (2008).

responsible for fight and flight responses/arising from higher centers of the brain, related to actions/related to characters or natures, related to external or actual others/related to internalized or imaginary others, involved in zero-sum games/involved in non-zero sum games, indicative of our common humanity/ indicative of a belief and desire for godlike omnipotence. Many of these criteria have also been used to distinguish between reason and the emotions more generally. These include the criteria of rational/irrational, cognitive/affective, calm/agitated, political/apolitical, moral/nonmoral, masculine/feminine, arising from higher centers of the brain/arising from primitive parts of the brain responsible for fight and flight responses, active/passive, autonomous/ heteronomous, and advanced/primitive.

When we think of an emotion like shame it is possible to see why it might be construed as a "negative" emotion. This is because it is often interpreted as including one or more of the following characteristics: painful, hierarchical, nonmoral, apolitical, aggressive, primitive, feminine, passive, irrational, affective, searing, competitive, egoistic, heteronomous, related to external or actual others, involved in zero-sum games, and/or indicative of a desire and belief in a godlike omnipotence. Freud focused on guilt rather than shame in his psychoanalytic theories because he construed shame as primitive, passive, and feminine.[17] As his focus shifted from the study of narcissism to the study of dynamic structural conflict, Freud came to see guilt as the active and moralizing, masculine, and mature voice of the superego.[18] As Andrew Morrison points out, "this psychoanalytic viewpoint influenced the anthropologists' differentiation between shame and guilt cultures, with guilt judged to be the more advanced and evolved emotion."[19] According to Bernard Williams, Kant favored guilt over shame because he considered shame to be nonmoral, primitive, egoistic, and heteronomous, and Williams' chapter on shame in his book *Shame and Necessity* is partially devoted to criticizing Kant's oversimplistic views of shame.[20] More recently, Martha Nussbaum has criticized shame, or to be more precise, a certain form of shame that she calls "primitive" shame, for being primitive, aggressive, irrational, narcissistic, egoistic, and indicative of a desire and belief in a godlike omnipotence.[21] And she argues that guilt

[17] Morrison (1989), 3,12–13; and Morrison (1996), 9.

[18] Morrison (1989), 8–15. (This does not mean that Freud felt that all forms of guilt were salutary for human life, and *Civilization and Its Discontents* obviously focuses on the less salutary and more destructive aspects of this moralizing emotion.)

[19] Morrison (1996), 9. For an account of the distinction between shame and guilt cultures in Ruth Benedict's *The Chrysanthemum and the Sword: Patterns of Japanese Culture*, see Ivy (2008), 64–68.

[20] Williams (1993), 75–102.

[21] Nussbaum (2004), 172–221. As I will show in section 6.3, she thinks this kind of "primitive" shame continues to lurk behind the more constructive forms of shame, thus making all forms of shame problematic for political life.

is less aggressive, more mature, more potentially creative and connected to "reparation, forgiveness, and the acceptance of limits to aggression."[22]

But I think that there are actually four problems with these criteria that have been used to mark shame as a "negative" emotion for democratic politics. The first one arises out of the binary and exclusive nature of the criteria themselves, and this is, I think, a remnant of the early modern dualisms between mind and body, and reason and passion, which have plagued the study of emotions and rationality for centuries.[23] As Cheryl Hall points out, Merriam-Webster's Dictionary still explicitly defines "passion" as an "intense, driving or overmastering feeling or conviction," and the plural form, "passions," as "the emotions *as distinguished* from reason."[24] Moreover, as Sharon Krause points out, the neo-Kantian view that practical reason alone can motivate our ethical decisions has cast a long shadow over many contemporary theories of deliberation and judgment, and thus has allowed many contemporary theories to overlook the role played by emotions, passions, and sentiments in practical reasoning and judgment.[25] However, as I have argued throughout this book, an emotion like shame is active *and* passive, cognitive *and* affective, and this is no less true for the other emotions like compassion and pity. In fact, as I will argue below, understanding shame allows us to understand why exclusive categories like altruism/egoism, autonomy/heteronomy, cognitive/affective, and active/passive simply fail to capture the essence of our emotional, rational, moral, and political life.

The second problem is that some of these criteria are simply not sufficient to classify shame, or any other emotion for that matter, as "negative" or "positive." As I argued in the last chapter, it is wrong to equate the physiological and mental discomfort and perplexity of shame with its perniciousness to democratic politics. The same is true of the criteria of hierarchy, passivity, and relation to actual or external others. Third, some of the criteria have been wrongly applied to shame. These include the criteria of nonmoral, apolitical, heteronomous, and egoistic. Finally, some of the criteria only apply to the particular form of shame that I have been calling flattering shame and do not apply to the notion of respectful shame that I derive from Plato. These include the criteria of being involved in a zero-sum game, and being indicative of a belief and desire for a godlike omnipotence.

---

[22] Nussbaum (2004), 208.

[23] As Hall (2005, 136 n.6) notes, it is difficult to convey a sense of passion or emotion and reason as deeply intertwined "while using the words with which they have long been distinguished."

[24] Hall (2002), 729. See also *Merriam-Webster Online Dictionary*: http://www.merriam–webster .com/dictionary/passion.

[25] Krause (2008), 9. In contrast to this view, Krause and I both believe that recent neuroscientific evidence (which I discuss later in this chapter) actually gives us very good reason to doubt that reason alone can motivate any practical decisions. Interestingly enough, the neo-Kantian view that reason alone motivates practical action is often imported back into interpretations of Plato,

In order to address the first problem, that is, the problematic binaries that have been used to distinguish the emotions from reason or rationality, I want to turn to Antonio R. Damasio's neuroscientific work on the emotions, *Descartes' Error: Emotion, Reason and the Human Brain*.[26] Here, I will show that Plato's argument about the cognitive value of Platonic respectful shame for democratic deliberations is actually supported by this recent neuroscientific research on the place of the emotions in human reasoning. I will also argue that both Plato and Damasio give us good reasons for discarding the problematic binaries that we have inherited from the early modern tradition when thinking about the place of emotions in our contemporary liberal-democratic practices. Finally, they also give us good reasons for discarding the neo-Kantian view that reason alone can motivate our practical and ethical judgments.[27]

In the second part of the chapter, I will turn to one of the most prominent defenders of the cognitive theory of the emotions, Martha Nussbaum, and examine her recent attempt to distinguish between certain positive and negative emotions based on a new version of the liberal harm-principle. Here I will address her argument that certain emotions like anger, compassion, and guilt are much more likely to be connected to a constructive contestation of legal and political norms and to realistic conceptions of our humanity, whereas emotions like disgust and shame are more likely to be linked to attempts to

---

even though Plato explicitly includes *erōs*, *aidōs/aischunē*, and *thumos* in his descriptions of practical reasoning and judgment, especially in his middle and later works.

[26] Damasio's work has been supplemented by other neuroscientists such as Joseph LeDoux (e.g., *The Emotional Brain: The Mysterious Underpinnings of Emotional Life*), and both of them have been adapted by George Marcus in his 2002 book, *The Sentimental Citizen*, in order to understand the role of emotions in politics from a neuroscientific perspective. However, I primarily examine Damasio's work in this chapter because he remains focused on what he calls the "higher emotions" that are conscious and complex, and that do include many learned behavioral patterns and norms. In contrast, LeDoux ends up focusing more on the emotional processes that go on solely at an unconscious level. (This indeed may be why the subtitle of his book is "The *Mysterious Underpinnings* of our Emotional Life" [my italics]). For his part, Marcus (2002) tends to focus more on these unconscious emotional processes and their role in either *initiating or enabling* political deliberations (75–78). Both LeDoux (1997) and Marcus (2002) designate as "emotions" the kinds of automatic and unconscious processes that underlie our ability to catch a cup that is rolling off a table or that underlie our "gut feelings" that something bad is about to happen. Although these unconscious processes and judgments may play a role in human ethical and political life, I do not include them in my notion of emotions, and I do not think that they correspond to the kinds of emotions that Plato and Aristotle examined in their accounts of human ethical and political decision making. I think Gross (2006) is correct to argue that these kinds of neuroscientific accounts leave out the socially or politically constructed character of our emotions; however, I think this criticism is only true of the kinds of unconscious "emotions" that people like LeDoux (1997) and Marcus (2002) focus on. Thus, although I agree with Krause (2008, 55–56) that the use of neuroscience in Marcus' work fails to account for the role of emotions *within* rational deliberation and instead sees them only as supplements to rational decision making, I do not think that this is true of Damasio's account of "higher emotions" that I analyze in this chapter.

[27] Cf. Krause (2008) and n.25 above.

hide from this humanity. In contrast to this, I will argue that no emotion can simply be classified as "positive" or "negative" for democratic politics or legal judgments (the primary focus of Nussbaum's book) but rather that every emotion, just like every form of reasoning, can partake of a kind of irrationality and infelicity for democratic deliberations and legal judgments when they manifest themselves in certain forms or contain certain problematic contents and attitudes toward the self or others.[28] In the final section of the chapter, I will offer some concluding remarks on the positive character of the seemingly negative criterion of pain in an emotion like shame.

RATIONALITY AND THE EMOTIONS

In his book *Descartes' Error: Emotion, Reason and the Human Brain*, Antonio Damasio argues that those parts of the brain concerned with processing our emotions—the limbic system, the prefrontal cortices, the somatosensory cortices, the amygdala, and the hypothalamus—are integral to the structure of rationality necessary to make decisions about our future courses of action and plan our lives in ways that are meaningful and felicitous both for the individual himself and for those around him.[29] He also shows that individuals who sustain injuries to these parts of the brain are unable to make decisions even when they can enumerate all of the possible courses of action with clarity, can access the social knowledge and norms of behavior that ought to constrain these actions, and can understand the consequences that would issue from any particular course of action.[30] Their defect, as he puts it, comes in "at the late stages of reasoning, close to or at the point at which choice making or response selection must occur."[31] The cold-blooded or emotionless person has a flat decision-making landscape such that she cannot assign different values to different options, and a flat mental landscape that is "too shifty and unsustained for the time required to make response selections."[32] It is important to point out here that, for Damasio, the neural arrangement that underlies our rational

---

[28] Cf. Elster (1999) who articulates the many different ways in which emotions can be considered rational or irrational in and of themselves, and can be supportive or disruptive of rationality and political deliberations in their relationship to reasons, interests, and other emotions/passions. Cf. Sokolon (2006), especially 179–182. See Damasio (1994), Hall (2003), and Solomon (2003) for accounts of just how pathological purely instrumental rationality can be in certain instances. Both Koziak (2000, 23) and Krause (2008, 3) argue that one of the problems with certain contemporary theories of emotions in politics is that they fail to articulate any normative criteria for distinguishing between good or bad uses of the emotions in politics, and both Koziak and Krause go on to redress this oversight in their own works.

[29] Damasio (1994).

[30] Damasio (1994), 46–49. Cf. Marcus (2002), 32; and Krause (2008), 53–54.

[31] Damasio (1994), 50.

[32] Damasio (1994), 51. Cf. Blackburn (1998), 126.

decision making and our mature emotional responses is not confined to the "high and new" brain structures of the neocortices, but rather it consists of the combination, and requires the simultaneous activity of both the "low and old" brain structures, such as the hypothalamus and limbic system, and the "high and new" brain structures of the neocortices.[33]

Damasio's fascinating discoveries have two important implications for the understanding of our mature, higher-order or "secondary" emotions and our rational decision-making processes. The first one is that we cannot simply separate the primary emotions or affect programs that constitute flight or fight responses (and that can produce physiological changes in an organism without the involvement of consciousness or the mind), from the higher-order emotions and decision-making processes.[34] As Damasio's clinical evidence shows, when the primitive system (the limbic or the hypothalamus) is disrupted, the higher-order decision-making process and emotions collapse as well. As Simon Blackburn puts it, "The whole point is that there is no dualism, in which one floats free of the other."[35] All of the mechanisms of behavior beyond drives and instincts use "both the upstairs and the downstairs" and "rationality results from their concerted activity."[36] The second important implication of Damasio's theory arises from the fact that what provides the bridge between the upstairs and downstairs, the cortical and subcortical, or the rational and nonrational processes are emotions and feelings.[37] In other words, we cannot change people's preferences and their practical decision-making abilities without engaging their emotions and emotional dispositions. As I have argued throughout this book, this was one of the primary contentions of Plato's middle dialogues, and one of the reasons he began to examine the emotions and emotional dispositions in a much deeper way than had his teacher, Socrates.

How do emotions and feelings work as a bridge between the rational and nonrational processes of the brain? Feelings for Damasio are the positive or negative perception of changes in our body states by which we monitor and regulate our biological states in order to survive.[38] Pain and pleasure arise out of certain chemical changes in the body in response to its external or internal environment, but these do not fully constitute what we mean by positive or negative human feelings. Instead, feelings arise when certain neurotransmitters, working simultaneously and in response to the chemical and hormonal

---

[33] Damasio (1994), 128. Similarly LeDoux (1996, 165) argues that our mature or higher emotions involve "parallel transmission to the amygdala from the sensory thalamus and sensory cortex. The subcortical pathways provide a crude image of the external world, whereas more detailed and accurate representations come from the cortex."

[34] Cf. LeDoux (1996), 165.

[35] Blackburn (1998), 129.

[36] Damasio (1994), 128.

[37] Damasio (1994), 128.

[38] Damasio (1994), 143–47.

changes that produce pain or pleasure, change the speed with which images of the body are formed, discarded, attended, or evoked, and they also change the style of reasoning operating on those images.[39] The feeling of elation is accompanied by rapid generation of multiple images and a rapid associational process, whereas the feeling of sadness is accompanied by "slowness of image evocation and production, poor association in response to fewer clues," and "overconcentration on the same images."[40] (The extreme form of elation is mania and the extreme form of sadness is depression.[41]) And "by dint of juxta-position, body images give to other images a *quality* of goodness or badness, of pain or pleasure."[42] It is this process that makes it painful and negative to perceive the loss of a person one might love. These are the feelings that are involved in the emotions, and they involve both the cognition of bodily changes and of events or things in the world. Feelings are what allow us to begin forming systematic connections between categories of objects and situations in the world and the primary emotions and instincts that more closely regulate our bodily functions. And the combination of these two things is what constitutes a secondary, or higher-order, emotion.

An emotion then "is the combination of a *mental evaluative process*, simple or complex, *with dispositional responses to that process*, mostly *toward the body proper*, resulting in an emotional body state, but also *toward the brain itself* (neurotransmitter nuclei in the brain stem), resulting in additional mental changes."[43] When we see a bear charging at us, our heart will race, our face may flush red, and many other innate and instinctive responses will occur, but the feeling of these primitive emotional states allows us to intervene in the instinctual responses in a more flexible way using our acquired secondary emotional dispositions: those based on one's particular experience and knowl-edge of bears, and one's strategies for dealing with charging bears. If it is a grizzly then I had better run up a tree, if it is a black bear then I had better play dead. All of these dispositional responses, then, are included in the mature person's fear of bears. Emotions cue you to the fact that there is danger in the world by juxtaposing an image of your body state with an image of the charg-ing bear. Their negative or positive valence will speed up or slow down the cognitive process by which you process all of the images that are coming into play, and the dispositional repertoire they activate will allow you to quickly access a strategy of behavior to deal with the problem. In the case of the charg-ing bear, the response needs to be so quick that no real deliberation of alterna-tives is possible.

[39] Damasio (1994), 163.

[40] Damasio (1994), 163–64.

[41] Damasio (1994), 164. Cf. Elster (1999), 298. I return to this topic in the final section of this chapter.

[42] Damasio (1994), 159.

[43] Damasio (1994), 139.

But emotions perform a similar function even when we have the time to deliberate about our future courses of action without bears charging at us. For Damasio, the secondary emotions provide the negative or positive somatic markers that operate as biasing devices to highlight certain future favorable or dangerous outcomes based on our dispositional knowledge of predicted future outcomes to certain scenarios. "When a negative somatic marker is juxtaposed to a particular future outcome the combination functions as an alarm bell. When a positive somatic marker is juxtaposed instead, it becomes a beacon of incentive."[44] Emotions work to quickly focus our decision-making faculty on a number of salient options in a world where the number of logically possible options are too vast to be held by the limited capacity of our attention span and working memory. In other words, emotions work to make the decision-making process more efficient and even practically possible because they put us in touch with strategies for coping and with predictions about future outcomes, both of which are stored as emotional dispositions. And they work as motivators, that is, as alarm bells or beacons of incentive pushing us in one direction, preventing us from moving toward another. As Simon Blackburn puts it, "We can see our cognitive relations with the world, our capacity to represent it as being one way or another, as tied in partnership with the mechanisms of emotion and of affect that turn the input into output. Our emotional dispositions and our representations act together to issue in action, with neither apparently able to achieve its results without the other."[45] In other words, a proper understanding of our emotions allows us to see that the binaries traditionally used to distinguish between the emotions as passive, affective, and agitated, and reason as active, cognitive, and calm, fail to capture the full character of human emotions and practical decision making. In fact, Damasio's cool and calm patients, who sustained damage to the emotional centers of the brain, were *incapable* of actively choosing any course of action or deciding on any future plans for their life.[46]

Thus, instead of seeing emotions as disruptive of our rationality, Damasio and Blackburn are committed to a view of the emotions that sees them as constitutive of and integral to human rationality. Emotions are the very psychic mechanisms by which we move into a world of rationality and thus acquire our ability to reflect and deliberate on our selves in relation to a social and external world that is beyond our control and that constrains us in very specific ways. Moreover, Damasio's somatic-marker hypothesis illustrates another im-

[44] Damasio (1994), 174.

[45] Blackburn (1998), 131.

[46] Though see Elster (1999, 297) for the argument that Damasio's evidence proves only a correlation between emotions and practical decision making and not causality. Although this might be true, it seems to be the best evidence we can muster given that proving causality definitively would probably violate all ethical rules for dealing with human subjects.

portant way in which emotions work to connect the mind and the body, so that our perceptions of the external world, and our cognition of the moral and political norms governing our social world come to be inscribed in the body in the form of dispositional knowledge. Emotions do not simply register and express our cognition of certain bodily states, but rather they serve as a bridge between our dispositional representations of these bodily states and our dispositional representations of the external and social world. They allow us to connect certain bodily responses and processes with our cognition of the world outside this body that threatens it in various ways. Thus it is only by understanding the emotions that we can understand how power and power relationships come to be inscribed in the body in the form of settled dispositions which act as "alarm bells" or a "beacons of incentive" for our daily actions.

All of our higher emotions have this cognitive-affective structure such that certain affectual programs and chemical processes, registered as pain or pleasure, come to be associated with an intensional object in the world, whose content intricately determines the character and structure of the emotion itself. Flushing red or a rapid heartbeat can be characteristic of the emotions of anger, fear, embarrassment, shame, and humiliation. But what distinguishes each of these things as separate emotions is the cognition of what it is that we are angry about, or ashamed or afraid of. And the content of these beliefs will be comprised not just of facts about the world, but also of evaluative standards about the ways in which people ought to behave or interact. I might have a red face and a racing heartbeat, and I might also believe that a certain fact is true about the world, e.g., my beloved new Mercedes is now damaged beyond repair. But my red face will indicate anger only if I believe in addition that, for example, a person has just smashed into my car intentionally, and that this is an unjust thing to do. Conversely, my red face might indicate shame if I myself have just smashed my car into the wall while driving under the influence of alcohol. The evaluative content of the emotion points to the fact that emotions don't simply register the fact that such and such is the case in the world, but rather they also register certain norms and rules that have been developed for dealing with the world and with others, and with the sorts of harm and suffering that can befall human beings in these interactions.

The other important implication of this view of the emotions is that the structure and prevalence of an emotion depends in part on the particular structures and norms of any given society. The very structure of shame or compassion will be different in a society that is more egalitarian than others. In fact, as Rousseau argued in his *Second Discourse* and Tocqueville in his *Democracy in America*, certain hierarchical social structures will produce people who don't actually feel much compassion for a poor beggar on the street (Rousseau) or a person who is being drawn and quartered (Tocqueville). Notice too that such an aristocratic person won't even feel ashamed to be shown that they have not helped such a person. In contrast, in our more egalitarian societies, the gay pride movement can fight for the right for gay people to feel pride and engage in same-sex marriages and it can reciprocally shame governments that refuse to give them the rights and resources they require to flourish in their societies, but it can do so without thereby asserting the kind of pride that a baron would have felt in relation to his feudal serfs. In other words, their pride in contemporary democracies will take the form of a desire for the respect and dignity that is owed to all citizens, without thereby taking this respect and dignity away from the other citizens. Pride and shame can work in a non-zero-sum game in those regimes where respect and dignity are considered basic goods to which all citizens are entitled.[47]

All of Damasio's findings, then, support the claims that I have been making about the salutary potential for a respectful politics of shame within our own contemporary democratic polities. Like Damasio, Plato felt that the emotions were not simply involved in *motivating* individuals to contest or transform themselves in accordance with the norms of their society, but rather that they were intricately involved in *registering, justifying, and transforming* the very substantive content of these norms themselves. As I have argued in my previous chapters, our recognition of just what it is that we are in fact ashamed of shows us what we human beings deem worthy of respect and dignity in our ongoing interactions with the world and with other people.

Of course, one might respond to this whole line of argument by saying that while the emotions do serve a place in our rational, deliberative processes, it is not altogether clear that *all* of the emotions ought to be allowed to serve this purpose. Here the argument might be that certain emotions have no salutary role to play in registering and justifying the content of our normative ideals. The argument might even be more subtle than this: i.e., that while they do play a salutary role in some instances, their tendency for harm outweighs their tendency for good, and their tendency for good can be secured by other less "negative" and more advanced emotions. This is the strategy for dealing with shame that Martha Nussbaum outlines in her recent work, *Hiding from Humanity: Shame, Disgust and the Law*, and I know want to look at the specifics of this argument and its treatment of shame.

PRIMITIVE VS. ADVANCED EMOTIONS

Martha Nussbaum's strategy is to differentiate the emotions that entail a denial of our vulnerability and humanity (e.g., disgust and shame) from those that

---

[47] Shame, pride, honor, and esteem did originally arise out of Greek aristocratic competitions in wartime and in the public sphere. However, Ober (1996, 101) shows that even in the fifth and fourth centuries BC the Athenians developed ways of talking about a more demotic (and less aristocratic) form of honor (*timē*) that is somewhat closer to our modern notions of dignity and respect. The positive content of this form of honor (*timē*) was defined by the intersection of individual freedom (*eleutheria*), political equality (*isotēs*), and security (*bebaiotēs, asphaleia*).

serve as "valuable reminders of our common humanity."[48] According to Nussbaum, these latter emotions can help us to enact reasonable laws that will respond to the types of damages and harms that might befall vulnerable human beings who live in a "world of significant events that [they] do not fully control."[49] Here she lists anger, fear, grief, compassion (and later guilt) as emotions that are inextricably linked to our normative conceptions of what a "reasonable" person should do in response to such circumstances as these come to light against a background of what matters to vulnerable human beings.[50] It is reasonable to feel anger against a person who has just murdered one's child, reasonable to fear such a person might murder again, reasonable to feel a considerable amount of grief for the loss of a child, reasonable to feel a certain amount of compassion for someone who has lost their child, and finally it is reasonable to feel guilt if one's drunken driving has led to the loss of one's child. Again, as Nussbaum, Damasio, and I have all argued it is actually a sign of a faulty kind of reasoning and a pathological personality not to have the requisite emotions in response to the sorts of calamities, accidents, and losses that human life necessarily subjects us all to. This does not mean that for Nussbaum all forms of anger, grief, fear, compassion, and guilt are rational and ought to be recognized in our legal systems of punishment. As she points out, anger or fear, like all emotions, might be "irrational" because they are based on false beliefs or false values: "They may be based on false information, as when someone gets angry at X in the belief that X has assaulted her child, but no such crime has occurred (or someone else did it). They may also be irrational because they are based upon false values, as would be the case if someone reacted with overwhelming anger to a minor insult."[51]

According to Nussbaum, however, certain emotions are more likely than others to be linked to faulty values about our humanity; more specifically, they are linked to a denial of our human, needy, vulnerable natures. The thought content of these emotions contains "impossible aspirations to purity, immortality, and non-animality, that are just not in line with human life as we know it."[52] Here she includes the emotion of disgust and what she calls "primitive" shame. The fact that Nussbaum finds "primitive" shame to be pernicious for liberal democratic institutions, which should produce and sustain a respect for both liberty and equality, and a norm of humanity as "a condition of shared incompleteness"[53] is actually quite consistent with the view of flattering shame that I have articulated in the previous chapters. Plato agrees with Nussbaum

[48] Nussbaum (2004), 7.
[49] Nussbaum (2004), 7.
[50] Nussbaum (2004), 8–12.
[51] Nussbaum (2004), 12.
[52] Nussbaum (2004), 14.
[53] Nussbaum (2004), 16.

that a certain type of shame is oriented to instituting and preserving a fantastical norm of omnipotence in democratic deliberations and practices. It is for
precisely this reason that I have consistently argued that flattering shame
should not have a place in contemporary democratic practices and deliberations. And she even suggests that a more mature or "constructive" shame may
have a positive role to play in human development and social and political life
when it is connected to valuable ideals and aspirations.[54] Here, she argues, as
I have with regard to Platonic respectful shame, that shame can occur against
a background of mutual respect and dignity, where both parties acknowledge
their mutual neediness and incompleteness.[55] The problem, according to Nussbaum, is that primitive shame is not always transcended by all human beings,
and even those who have transcended it in some ways are very likely to carry
a good deal of primitive shame around with them. Thus shame is "likely to be
normatively unreliable in public life, despite its potential for good."[56]

Nussbaum and I actually agree to rather a rather striking degree on many
of these issues. The kind of Platonic respectful shame that I advocate in this
book consists of a rejection of any kind of rigid, static norms or idealized
others in our political deliberations (especially when these take the form of an
omnipotent and wholly autonomous other). Insofar as laws are necessarily
rigid and static there is a sense in which respectful shame can't ever be fully
and finally articulated by such a brute instrument. But it seems to me that this
would apply equally well to her notions of reasonable anger, grief, compassion,
or fear and their role in the law. As she herself points out, "If a man in ancient
Athens believed that women are inferior, we may judge his view to be mistaken
but reasonable, or at least not unreasonable, while such a belief in today's
America would be both mistaken and unreasonable."[57] Because, as both Nussbaum and I argue, if our norms and thus the contents of our emotional judgments change in a reciprocal fashion over time, then the conception of what
it is reasonable to be angry at or ashamed of will change as our norms and
laws incorporate different conceptions of what it means to be a democratic
citizen and a reasonable human being. The role of a competent judge is to
interpret the laws in a flexible way so that they can reflect and incorporate the
changing norms and situations that any society will face over time. Just as our
compassion and anger must be linked to a reasonable conception of the person
and what matters to such a person, so must our shame be linked to such a
reasonable conception, and judges as well as members of protest movements
must be ready to contest any laws which currently fall below these standards
of reasonableness. Indeed, as I argued in the last chapter, the ongoing contesta-

[54] Nussbaum (2004), 15, 211–16.
[55] Nussbaum (2004), 213.
[56] Nussbaum (2004), 15.
[57] Nussbaum (2004), 34.

tion of our collective others is one of the most important goals of a Platonic respectful politics of shame.

However, our difference arises from the fact that she argues that certain emotions can be seen as more reasonable, and more attuned with a realistic notion of humanity, than other emotions. To put it more precisely, for her some emotions are more likely to attune us to the real vulnerabilities that befall human beings, while others attune us to a notion of the reasonable as the "normal," where the "normal" consists of a fantastical, omnipotent being which all human beings fall below in some ways.[58] But this view seems to be in tension with her own theory of the emotions more generally, which states that *all* emotions are responses to "areas of vulnerability [to harm and damage], responses in which we register the damage we have suffered, might suffer, or luckily have failed to suffer."[59] Shame and disgust, like grief, fear, anger, guilt, and compassion, can all alert us to important problems in our physical, social, and political environment. Without feeling ashamed of myself as a drunken driver, it is unlikely that I will take the necessary steps to stop this pernicious behavior and thus *more* likely that I will end up harming either myself or others.[60] Even more problematically, her argument that shame is one of the emotions that inclines us to conform to the problematic standard of the "normal" seems to be in tension with her view of shame as the painful emotion that responds to our discovery that we are in some ways abnormal: "Because we all have weaknesses that, if known, would mark us off as in some ways 'abnormal,' shame is a permanent possibility in our lives, our daily companion."[61] Shame, then, would seem to be a very valuable emotion precisely because it shows us that we have fallen below the standards of the "normal" that our society sets for us. Indeed, this is precisely what I have argued with respect to the painful moment of recognition within the occurrent experience of shame. In this moment the person recognizes that they are in some sense inadequate or weak in relation to an ideal they hold dear, and it can then serve as a valuable reminder to us that we are not the omnipotent, autonomous beings that tend to be valorized in our notions of the "normal" citizen. Indeed, Nussbaum herself later admits that this type of recognition can underlie the more positive and constructive shame that humans acquire as they become mature adults: "A good development, we have suggested, will allow the gradual relaxation of omnipotence and transcendence in favor of trust, as the infant learns not to be ashamed of neediness and to take a positive delight in the playful and creative 'subtle interplay' of two imperfect beings."[62]

---

[58] For a full discussion of the concept of the "normal," see chapter 5, n.8.

[59] Nussbaum (2004), 6. Cf. Nussbaum (2001), 27–33.

[60] Cf. Elster (1999), 154.

[61] Nussbaum (2004), 173.

[62] Nussbaum (2004), 191.

The problem then, for Nussbaum, is not that a constructive and mature form of shame might actually serve as an important source of motivation for human beings. This would occur, she argues, if shame were felt in connection with morally good norms "that are very basic to the shared political conception of the United States, and shared by people who otherwise differ politically about goals and ends" and that actually reinforce "a sense of common human vulnerability."[63] The real problem for her arises out of the fact that this is much too optimistic. As she puts it, "The idea that reciprocity is the stable human norm and that most people come to accept their incompleteness, lack of control, and mortality is much too optimistic. After all, it is just bad not to be able to have what one wants and thinks one ought to have, especially immortality; much of human life is caught in this painful state of affairs."[64] But if we pair this with her view of the emotions more generally, then it would seem that human life is caught in a rather difficult dialectic in which our emotions both register our vulnerability in an uncertain world, and seek to hide our vulnerability from ourselves in order for us to get through a life "in which we are soon bound for death, and in which the most essential matters are in fact beyond our control."[65] It is this necessity for self-deception that underlies the "unreasonable" emotions like shame and disgust. These emotions, according to Nussbaum, hide our vulnerabilities from us and "make the struggle to achieve appropriate emotions something of an uphill battle in all human beings."[66] For her, even mature, constructive, or what I would call respectful shame, never fully overcomes the "primitive" shame that points backwards in time to an ever-present but deceptive longing for the infantile omnipotence of the womb, and also inwards in space to a concern with the narcissistic self. Shame makes us want to hide from our humanity, because, according to Nussbaum "its reflex is to hide from the eyes of those who will see one's deficiency, to cover it."[67] In contrast, emotions like compassion, guilt, anger, or grief point outwards to a world of distinct others with whom we share a world, and they also point forward to a mature acceptance of our incompleteness, vulnerability, and relatedness to others who have their own desires, plans, and life projects.

There are, however, a number of problems with this position. First, is it so clear that the emotions of guilt, compassion, and anger are so easily separated from an emotion like shame, or is it not the case that these emotions are much more interconnected in our lives? If I steal a stereo from my best friend, I will feel guilty that I have done this to my friend and I may want to repair the situation by buying that friend a new and better one. But I will also feel

[63] Nussbaum (2004), 213.
[64] Nussbaum (2004), 188–89.
[65] Nussbaum (2004), 17.
[66] Nussbaum (2004), 36.
[67] Nussbaum (2004), 183.

ashamed that I am a thief, and I will hope that the new stereo will make this person accept me again as a trustworthy friend rather than as a potential thief. In other words, shame and guilt often work together to motivate us to change ourselves in response to actions that we deem unworthy of our ideals or exemplars for action that are encapsulated in our various others. In fact, as Jon Elster points out, "Because avoidance of shame cannot take the easy option of self-deception, it has to use the hard option of behavior modification."[68] Thus, I would argue that it was only because enough members of the collective self that is America actually felt truly ashamed of America's actions in Abu Ghraib or New Orleans or on Wall Street that members of this collective self felt the need to change it by voting in a new kind of administration. Although Nussbaum follows Kant in arguing that guilt is a more salutary emotion because it is connected with reparation and forgiveness, with agency rather than with thoughts about the whole self, and with treating other people as "separate beings with rights, who ought not to be harmed,"[69] I think that this strict separation of shame and guilt actually falls apart when we think about the ways in which these emotions motivate us in our ethical and political lives.

This is not to say that guilt and shame are identical, and I follow Bernard Williams in thinking that the important distinction is not between guilt that targets only our actions and shame that targets our entire self, but rather in the direction of concern of these emotions in response to any action. As he

---

[68] Elster (1999), 154. Similarly, Braithwaite (1989 and 2000) argues that shame is actually more likely than guilt to get a person to change his behavioral patterns precisely because shame is felt before those admired others whose opinion and judgment actually matter to the criminal.

[69] Nussbaum (2004), 209. Cf. Locke (2007, 149) who treats shame as involving a "negative global self-assessment." Nussbaum is also following the predominant trend in psychological and psychoanalytic literature, which distinguishes between shame as an emotion that targets the entire self, and guilt as an emotion that focuses only on specific actions. See for example Lynd (1958); Lewis (1971); Taylor (1985); and Tangney and Dearing ([2002], 2004). However, as I argued in chapter 5, this distinction depends on conflating all instances of shame with humiliation and I think this conflation becomes clear in Nussbaum's own work when she defines humiliation accordingly (203–4): "Humiliation I understand to be the active, public face of shame. To humiliate someone is to expose them to shame; and to shame someone is, in most cases, to humiliate them (at least if the shaming is severe enough) . . . Humiliation typically makes the statement that the person is low, not on par with others in terms of human dignity." This conflation of humiliation with all acts of shaming also characterizes Massaro's (1997) work on shaming penalties. I think that this conflation occurs, in the case of Nussbaum (2004) and Massaro (1997), because they are thinking primarily of the shaming penalties that were introduced into various legal systems in recent years, and which really were about publicly humiliating criminals. I think the conflation occurs in much of the psychoanalytic literature because they are drawing conclusions based on clinical experiences (where their patients probably are feeling humiliated) rather than from the ways in which we talk about and engage in shaming in our political and everyday practices. The person motivated by flattering shame might well be more apt to humiliate other people, but there is no need for all forms of shame to devolve into a stigmatization of individuals or groups who are seen as "not on par with others in terms of human dignity."

puts it, any action "stands between the inner world of disposition, feeling and decision and an outer world of harm and wrong. *What I have done* points in one direction toward what has happened to others, in another direction to what I am. Guilt looks primarily in the first direction and it need not be guilt about the voluntary . . . Shame looks to what I am . . . [and it can help us] to understand how a certain action or thought stands to ourselves, to what we are and to what realistically we can want ourselves to be."[70] In the occurrent feeling of shame the direction of concern is toward the self that has now been revealed to be inadequate in some way, but this self is also simultaneously revealed to be changeable and not static, especially when we feel shame for an action we have just done.[71] It is always possible to transform the very self that some psychologists worry can only be shattered or silenced by the experience of shame. In other words, both guilt and shame are always intertwined in our ongoing construction and negotiation of our identities in relation to others, and shame is rarely reflective of a static and unchangeable self and its relation to static internal or external others. Identities don't always change easily, or as the result of one action (although they can in some cases), but they do change over time as a result of the kind of actions we undertake in life in relation to others. And guilt and shame register the ongoing reciprocal connection between actions and the self, and between our agency and the structures within which we express this agency. It is for this reason that a proper understanding of the role of guilt and shame in human life actually undermines the strict dichotomies between moral/nonmoral, autonomy/heteronomy, altruism/egoism that have traditionally been used to differentiate guilt from shame. Both of these emotions register the ways in which human life is lived between the ever-elusive poles of a complete immersion in the self and an immersion or merger with others. And it is just as pathological to be immersed in the

---

[70] Williams (1993), 92–93.

[71] It is certainly true that we can feel shame for things that we cannot do much about. For example, I might feel shame about my big nose, even if, barring cosmetic surgery, there is not much I can do about it. Konstan (2006), Sokolon (2006), and Williams (1993) all stress that shame is neutral on the distinction between "moral" and "nonmoral" qualities. As Williams (1993, 92) puts it, "We, like the Greeks, can be as mortified or disgraced by a failure in prowess or cunning as by a failure of generosity or loyalty." This however does not render the shame we feel at either or both of these things ethically or politically irrelevant or necessarily pernicious. As I have argued throughout this book, respectful shame about our vulnerability or mortality both discloses this fact to us and offers us the possibility of constructing norms that are more attuned to this fact about human existence. Finally, it is simply not the case that guilt tracks only moral qualities. A person would probably feel both shame and guilt about one's lack of cunning or prowess if this fact about oneself led one to be unable to defend one's family or country from attack. Again, I follow Williams (1993, 92) and Konstan (2006, 102) in thinking that the line between modern shame and guilt is much fuzzier than many psychologists and moralists want us to believe, and it is certainly not true that we can differentiate them according to the criterion of nonmoral (shame) and moral (guilt) emotions.

narcissistic self as it is to be overcome and ruled by the guilt that one feels for an other. As Nussbaum herself puts it, "Guilt can, of course, be excessive and oppressive, and there can be a corresponding excessive focus on reparation, one that is unhealthily self-tormenting."[72]

These kinds of interconnections also occur in the case of the other emotions. The person whose sense of shame does attune them to a desire for the infantile omnipotence of the womb is the same person who will feel angry and lash out at those people who show them that they are vulnerable. Such a person will also fear this exposure in any of their social engagements and will feel compassion only for those who share their desire for omnipotence. In other words, their fear, guilt, anger, and compassion will be no less "irrational," "unreasonable," or attuned to the infantile desire for omnipotence and the need to hide from their humanity as would be the case with the person who is experiencing primitive shame. On a more positive note, the new doctrine of humanitarian intervention, which is allegedly tied to a globalized compassion for the victims of tyrannical and unjust regimes, is as much an outgrowth of our universal shame at the Holocaust as it is an outgrowth of an ever-expanding compassionate concern for others.[73] In other words, the contents of one's emotional beliefs in anger, compassion, grief, and shame will *all* be attuned to the same notion of what it is to be a democratic citizen or a humanitarian nation, whether this consists of a fantastical notion of omnipotence, the "normal" citizen, and a wholly autonomous and unilateral nation, or in the much more realistic notion of a vulnerable and needy human being and nation that is mutually and reciprocally implicated in the New World Order. Thus, if the normative content of our ideals are mistaken, fantastical or unrealistic, then it is this *content* which will make our emotions "negative" regardless of whether they are painful, pleasurable, hierarchical, egalitarian, directed toward the self, or directed toward internalized or actual others.

Second, Nussbaum's view of shame assumes that our reaction to the moment of recognition—the moment when we realize that we are "abnormal" or have fallen below a standard or other which we hold dear—is always one of hiding.[74] Here Nussbaum is criticizing not so much the cognitive content of our occurrent experience of shame, but the ways in which one will react to the painful and perplexing recognition of our inadequacy as this is revealed in the occurrent experience of shame. But as I argued in the last chapter, the

---

[72] Nussbaum (1980), 208.

[73] Ignatieff (1998). In a different vein, for an excellent account of the positive role that hatred of tyranny and even of one's own self can play in motivating positive political transformations, see Panagia (2004) and (2006), chapter 4. For an excellent account of the positive role of jealousy in preventing encroachments on state and individual freedoms by federal governments, see Levy (2007).

[74] Nussbaum (2004), 183. Cf. Massaro (1999), 89; and Elster (1999), 153.

reaction of hiding is only one of the possible ways in which a person might react to the occurrent experience of shame. The other ways include either trying to contest or transform the very standard or other by which one has been ashamed, or trying to transform oneself or one's world in accordance with the new other and new insights for action that come to light in the shaming situation. In fact, it is impossible to understand how anybody could ever move from the primitive and narcissistic shame that is supposedly characteristic of childhood to the more mature and constructive shame that Nussbaum describes, unless one learns how to transform oneself in accordance with the new knowledge and the new situations which we encounter as we move into adulthood. Of course, the way in which any person will react to a particular act of shaming will depend in part upon the way this person has been shamed in the past, the content of the other or ideals by which one is being shamed, and the attitude of the person now performing the shaming. It is hard not to try to hide from our humanity, if the person who is shaming us (and whom we admire), upholds a perfectionist and omnipotent standard of what it means to be a human being. Even if the person does not uphold such standards, it will be hard to react positively to the experience of shame if the shamer does not give us some view of the new self that we might become if we transform ourselves in accordance with their shaming criticisms.

As I argued in chapters 4 and 5, this is in fact Plato's primary criticism of the negativity of Socrates' shaming elenchus. Without giving his interlocutors any view of the new way of life that might become possible for them, or any view of the shared background consensus against which their disagreement was taking place, Socrates' acts of shaming came across as perplexing and infuriating because they seemed to turn their worlds upside down, and they seemed to require a kind of godlike indifference to the bodily concerns of his interlocutors. But as Plato and Andrew Morrison both argue, the point then is not to get rid of shame altogether, but to try to make the ideals or others involved in shaming more flexible, less omnipotent, and more cognizant of our common humanity and of the standards which we share.[75] The project of Plato's middle dialogues is to dramatize a Socrates who is more attuned to the cares and concerns that he shares with his interlocutors so that their reaction to his shaming elenchus is more positive and transformative. It was precisely this kind of therapeutic shaming that Plato felt was not being practiced either by his teacher Socrates or by the flattering rhetoricians in imperialistic Athens. As Andrew Morrison has argued, the positive task of a proper psychotherapy of shame is for both the patient and therapist alike to acknowledge their shame sensitivity and to replace the rigid ideals of perfectionist parents or societies with the more flexible ideals that are discovered within the therapy situation itself.[76]

---

[75] Morrison (1989); and Morrison (1996).
[76] Morrison (1996).

Moreover, both of these projects are, I think, compatible with the kind of politics that Nussbaum envisions. Nussbaum actually argues that modern democratic societies are now beginning to possess and ought to continue to move toward norms that don't instantiate perfectionist ideals of autonomy and invulnerability. But if this is indeed the case, then our societies will make the reaction of hiding from our vulnerability less likely. The success of movements and organizations like ACT UP or Human Rights Watch in fighting for resources for people with AIDS depends upon their ability to respectfully shame governments into recognizing that certain acts rather than certain sinful natures make all human beings vulnerable to the disease. Such movements have been successful only because the governments, which were the target of their shame, were able to alter their policies and transform their conceptions of human agency in the more realistic direction offered by these movements. Their success is difficult to understand unless we understand respectful shame as a valuable weapon of the weak, who do not have the political clout or financial resources to directly influence policy.

In contrast, Nussbaum's point against shame depends upon her belief that there is something inherent in the structure of human life itself that makes us try to hide from our vulnerabilities and our mortality. Nussbaum actually argues that it is precisely for this reason that primitive shame is likely to be an ongoing danger, at least to some extent, in all of us.[77] But there is a potential for this to become a far more elitist conception than I think she would want to adopt. The implication is that the average person does not overcome primitive shame and that only truly exceptional people can do so. In fact, her position begins to sound like the canonical view of Plato (to which this book is opposed), which asserts that only a truly exceptional individual like a philosopher can come to accept his mortality without trying to hide from it or becoming angry at those who expose this to him.

Moreover, she admits that compassion, anger, and fear can often be just as childlike or primitive as shame and that a reasonable compassion is a difficult achievement: "Even though compassion has the potential to connect us to a larger group of humans, it will not do so without a moral achievement that is at least coeval to it, in which we focus on the suffering person or people as among our significant goals and ends, as part of our circle of concern."[78] As she later argues, "Compassion has many potential roles in public life. It can provide crucial underpinnings for social welfare programs, for foreign aid and other efforts toward global justice, and for many forms of social change that address the oppression and inequality of vulnerable groups."[79] This might well be true, but is it easier to feel a mature and productive compassion for a person in Iraq than it is to feel productive or respectful shame? In fact, I would argue

---

[77] Nussbaum (2004), 192.
[78] Nussbaum (2004), 51.
[79] Nussbaum (2004), 55.

that the shame which Americans felt at the photographs coming out of Abu Ghraib did more to get this country's administration to move toward international cooperation in the fight against terrorism than any photographs that depicted the innocent victims of either U.S. or Iraqi aggression as a means for eliciting compassion.

Indeed, if we follow Damasio then it becomes clear that all emotions have the potential to be exhibited in primitive forms precisely because there is a meaningful link between the simpler goals and drives of the instincts and the more fully developed, cognitively rich, higher-order emotions that guide us in social life. In other words, there is a permanent possibility in human life for the emotions of shame, compassion, grief, anger, and guilt to take on primitive forms, because we were all once children in the safe and secure womb, we all share remnants of our animalistic past, and we will all have to come face to face with our mortality at various points throughout our lives. Finally, we might all, like Leontius in Plato's *Republic*, curse our eyes for showing us our mortality when we gaze upon corpses. However, our anger, compassion, grief, shame, and guilt might instead spur us on to deal with this fact about human life in a realistic and reasonable manner. All of the emotions serve the necessary function of warning us about our mortality and vulnerability, but what makes them "irrational" or "primitive" depends on whether we try to cover this insight up with pleasant but false myths about our omnipotence and autonomy or whether we try to come to terms with our vulnerabilities in our mutual engagements with others. It is simply a fact about human history that the animals and peoples who have reacted by denying their vulnerability come to suffer death or defeat in an uncertain and dangerous world far faster than those who accept it.[80] In other words, if primitive shame really lingered in all of us to the extent that Nussbaum fears, it would be hard to understand how we could ever have moved toward more democratic and egalitarian institutions in which we all necessarily share in ruling and being ruled, shaming and being shamed, in order to survive in an uncertain world. If our respectful shame doesn't open us up to our vulnerabilities in an uncertain world and jolt us out of our false desires for omnipotence, then surely our anger, fear, grief, and compassion won't do much to assuage the situation either.

THE POSITIVITY OF NEGATIVITY

But I want to end this book on a more positive note and suggest why and how Platonic respectful shame might actually surpass emotions like love and compassion in its ability to promote rather than discourage democratic deliberations and a real concern for others. One of the most prevalent criteria that

[80] As Blitz (2005), Tarcov (2005), and Beiner (2005) all point out, Plato and Aristotle both supplemented their normative arguments against tyranny with the empirical evidence that tyrants

have been used to distinguish between the "negative" and "positive" emotions has been the criterion of pain. Joy, pride, honor, and love are certainly more pleasant than disgust, shame, envy, or anger, and I am sure that we all wish our lives were filled with more of the former emotions and less of the latter emotions. Indeed, there is a tendency to equate the pleasantness of an emotion with its beneficial character, and the painfulness of an emotion with its harmful character. However, one of the most important arguments of Plato's *Gorgias* is the argument that the pleasant and the beneficial do not correspond in human life, and that equating the painfulness of shame with its perniciousness for democratic deliberations is an oversimplistic strategy for dealing with this emotion. And Damasio's work on the role of the "negative" and "positive" emotions actually supports this Platonic thesis in a way that has direct relevance to our contemporary situation.

As I argued in the previous chapter, Platonic respectful shame is directed at producing the salutary, but painful, perplexing, and discomforting recognition of a certain discrepancy between the self and the others by which we measure this self. It produces a certain painful feeling of inadequacy in relation to an actual or imaginary other because it shows us how we have fallen below a standard or exemplar of action which we hold dear or value. As I also argued, this can happen even when, as in the case of Socrates and Plato, this other is attempting to point out our common human vulnerabilities. In imperialistic Athens, most of the citizens were actually experiencing the pleasant and seamless merger with the objectified image of their tyrannical regime and its mistaken equation of freedom as freedom from all forms of pain and restraint. The other that they admired and held dear was the objectified image of shamelessness and indiscriminate hedonism, i.e., the pursuit of any and all forms of pleasure. Their sense of shame was thus attuned to and motivated them toward seamlessly merging with their tyrannical and imperialistic regime that, like the grandiose child, attempted to subject and dominate every other around its self in its pursuit of indiscriminate pleasure.

In a sense, then, this regime was experiencing the pathological but pleasurable mania that both Damasio and Morrison describe in different ways. As Morrison describes it, in mania the "real, the fantasized ideal and the self-image are experienced as the same."[81] As Damasio argues, elation and its pathological form, mania "permits the rapid generation of multiple images such that the associative process is richer and associations are made to a larger variety of cues available in the images under scrutiny. The images are not attended for long. The ensuing wealth promotes ease of inference, which may become overinclusive. This cognitive mode is accompanied by an enhance-

---

don't actually preserve their rule for very long. Fortunately, this also seems to have proven true for both the petty and the not so petty tyrants who have plagued the twentieth century.

[81] Morrison (1996), 184.

ment of motor efficiency and even disinhibition, as well as an increase in appetite and exploratory behaviors."[82] It is not too much of a stretch to say that
this kind of mania and elation captures the emotional state that characterized
America's (and its allies') initial decision to go to war with Iraq and to pay for
such a war with immoderate consumerism and a deregulation of the economy.

Of course, such elation was progressively shattered by the horrific images
coming out of Abu Ghraib, the reports of missing weapons of mass destruction, and the collapse of just about every financial bubble that was blown up
over the past eight years. In an important sense, the exposure of these facts by
the media can be seen as a self-shaming of the American regime and public,
and a salutary disruption of its easy inference between the war on terrorism
and an omnipotent unilateralism. It also puts to shame any people who believe
that deregulation and rampant consumerism can somehow amount to fiscal
responsibility. If, as Damasio argues, the painful or "negative" emotions have
the effect of slowing down our thinking processes and making us concentrate
on an image and actually attend to it for a while, then the occurrent experience
of shame ought to have this paradoxically "positive" ability of slowing down
the polity and making it more reflective about its collective self-image or
others.[83] This "negative" emotion then would have the salutary effect of self-
criticism, which, as we all know, is painful but necessary for us to act in relation
to other human beings as respectful citizens or nations rather than as tyrants.
If, as deliberative democrats argue, deliberation requires transforming or tran-
scending one's initial preferences in the very act of coming to an agreement
with others, then such a transformation is often going to involve a certain
amount of pain, *especially when achieving this agreement might well require
giving up substantial components of our pre-deliberative preferences or interests.*
The very painfulness of shame can thus indicate a salutary break or rupture
in the seamless identity that we have with our physical, social, and political
environment. From this perspective, the negativity of shame can play a positive
role in democratic deliberations because it can make us conscious of just
what our collective others are or ought to be, and of how we have now fallen
below them.

As I argued in chapter 4, Plato's respectful shame incorporated but also
transcended the negativity of Socratic respectful shame by specifically focusing
on the kinds of images and myths that can supply a memorable and lasting

---

[82] Damasio (1994), 163–64.

[83] In a slightly different vein, Elster (1999, 299–300) argues that one of the most interesting
findings to come out of psychological studies of the emotions in recent years is the fact that sad
and depressed people make far more unbiased and evenhanded appraisals of themselves, of the
world, and of others. Cf. Marcus (2002), chapter 6 for the argument and empirical evidence that
the unpleasant emotion of anxiety actually prompts more deliberation, and a conscious consideration of policy alternatives in democratic polities.

reminder of the rewards that are open to those individuals who have the courage to undergo the revelations of their injustices, and to transform themselves
in accordance with the insights gleaned from their experience of shame. In
our current worldwide perplexity about just how we should transform our
democratic polities in order to become more moderate and just toward the
citizens within these polities and the others with whom we share this new
world order, Plato's model of respectful shame suggests that we use this salutary perplexity to open up rather than foreclose discussions about the kinds
of democratic polities or selves that we might now want to become.[84]

Plato's own respectful shaming of his imperialistic democratic polity was
an attempt to prevent the kinds of pathological deliberations that were made
by the Athenians during the Peloponnesian War, and to open up a space where
transformation of the very self that led to this war was possible. One can only
hope that our current domestic and international institutions will continue
to protect the rights of all citizens and nations to shame regimes out of the
problematically pleasant elation of their own fantastical omnipotence.

---

[84] Thus my notion of Platonic respectful shame does not preclude but rather fosters the production of the kinds of "counterpublics" valorized by Warner (2005) and Locke (2007).

BIBLIOGRAPHY

Abdel-Nour, Farid. 2003. "National Responsibility." *Political Theory* 31 (5): 693–719.

Abizadeh, Arash. [2002], 2008. "The Passions of the Wise: *Phronēsis*, Rhetoric and Aristotle's Passionate Political Deliberation." In *Bringing the Passions Back In: The Emotions in Political Philosophy*, eds. Rebecca Kingston and Leonard Ferry. Vancouver: University of British Columbia Press: 60–77.

Abu-Lughod, Lila, and Catherine A. Lutz, eds. 1990. *Language and the Politics of Emotion*. Cambridge: Cambridge University Press.

Adkins, A. H. 1960. *Merit and Responsibility: A Study in Greek Values*. Oxford: Oxford University Press.

Allen, Danielle. 2000a. "Envisaging the Body of the Condemned: The Power of Platonic Symbols." *Classical Philology* 95:133–50.

———. 2000b. *The World of Prometheus: The Politics of Punishing in Democratic Athens*. Princeton and Oxford: Princeton University Press.

Annas, Julia. 1981. *An Introduction to Plato's Republic*. New York: Oxford University Press.

———. 1982a. "Plato's Myths of Judgment." *Phronesis* 27 (2): 119–43.

———. 1982b. "Plato on the Triviality of Literature." In *Plato on Beauty, Wisdom and the Arts*, eds. Julius Moravcsik and Philip Temko. Totowa, NJ: Rowman & Allanheld: 1–28.

Anscombe, G.E.M. 1957. *Intention*. Oxford: Blackwell.

Arendt, Hannah. 1958. *The Human Condition*. Chicago: University of Chicago Press.

Balot, Ryan K. 2001. *Greed and Injustice in Classical Athens*. Princeton: Princeton University Press.

———. 2008. "Socratic Courage and Athenian Democracy. " In *Ancient Philosophy* 28: 49–69.

Beck, Hans. 2003. "Freiheit und Herrschaft in der Athenischen Demokratie: Aristoteles, Nicklas Luhmann und die Archai der Polis." *Electrum* 9: 40–55.

Beiner, Ronald. 2005. "The Soul of the Tyrant, and the Souls of You and Me: Plato's Understanding of Tyranny." In *Confronting Tyranny: Ancient Lessons for Global Politics*, eds. Toivo Koivukoski and David Edward Tabachnick. Lanham: Rowman & Littlefield Publishers, Inc.: 181–96.

Benardete, Seth. 1991. *The Rhetoric of Morality and Philosophy: Plato's Gorgias and Phaedrus*. Chicago and London: The University of Chicago Press.

Benhabib, Seyla. 1986. *Critique, Norm, and Utopia: A Study of the Foundations of Critical Theory*. New York: Columbia University Press.

———. 1992. *Situating the Self: Gender, Community and Postmodernism in Contemporary Ethics*. Cambridge: Polity Press.

———, ed. 1996. *Democracy and Difference: Contesting the Boundaries of the Political*. Princeton: Princeton University Press.

Benjamin, Jessica. 1988. *The Bonds of Love: Psychoanalysis, Feminism and the Problem of Domination*. New York: Pantheon Books.

Benjamin, Jessica. 2004. "Beyond Doer and Done To: An Intersubjective View of Thirdness." *Psychoanalytic Quarterly* 73: 5–46.

Berlant, Lauren (interviewed by Sina Najafi & David Serlin). 2008. "The Broken Circuit: An Interview with Lauren Berlant." In *Cabinet: A Quarterly of Art and Culture: Special Issue on Shame*: 81–85.

Black, Edwin. 1958. "Plato's View of Rhetoric." *The Quarterly Journal of Speech* 44 (4): 361–74.

Blackburn, Simon. 1998. *Ruling Passions*. Oxford: Clarendon Press.

Blitz, Mark. 2005. "Tyranny, Ancient and Modern." In *Confronting Tyranny: Ancient Lessons for Global Politics*, eds. Toivo Koivukoski and David Edward Tabachnick. Lanham: Rowman & Littlefield Publishers, Inc.: 9–24.

Bradley, A. C. [1909], 1963. *Oxford Lectures on Poetry*. 2nd ed. London: Macmillan.

Bradshaw, Leah. 2005. "Tyranny and the Womanish Soul." In *Confronting Tyranny: Ancient Lessons for Global Politics*, eds. Toivo Koivukoski and David Edward Tabachnick. Lanham: Rowman & Littlefield Publishers, Inc.: 161–80.

Braithwaite, John. 1989. *Crime, Shame and Reintegration*. Cambridge and New York: Cambridge University Press.

———. 2000. "Survey Article: Repentance Rituals and Restorative Justice." *The Journal of Political Philosophy* 8 (1): 115–31.

Brandwood, Leonard. 1992. "Stylometry and Chronology." In *The Cambridge Companion to Plato*, ed. R. Kraut. Cambridge: Cambridge University Press: 90–120.

Brennan, Geoffrey and Philip Pettit. 2004. *The Economy of Esteem: An Essay on Civil and Political Society*. Oxford: Oxford University Press.

Brickhouse, Thomas C. and Nicholas D. Smith. 1989. *Socrates on Trial*. Princeton: Princeton University Press.

———. 2000. *The Philosophy of Socrates*. Boulder: Westview Press.

Broucek, Francis. 1991. *Shame and the Self*. New York: Guilford Press.

Butler, Judith. 1997. *The Psychic Life of Power: Theories in Subjection*. Stanford: Stanford University Press.

———. 2004. *Precarious Life: The Powers of Mourning and Violence*. London and New York: Verso.

Cairns, Douglas L. 1993. *Aidōs: The Psychology and Ethics of Honour and Shame in Ancient Greek Literature*. Oxford: Clarendon Press.

Calhoun, Cheshire. 2004. "An Apology for Moral Shame." *Journal of Political Philosophy* 12 (2): 127–46.

Calhoun, Cheshire and Robert C. Solomon, eds. 1984. *What Is an Emotion: Classic Readings in Philosophical Psychology*. New York and Oxford: Oxford University Press.

Clarke, Simon, Paul Hoggett, and Simon Thompson, eds. 2006. *Emotion, Politics and Society*. Hampshire and New York: Palgrave Macmillan.

Cooper, John M. 1999. *Reason and Emotion: Essays on Ancient Moral Psychology and Ethical Theory*. Princeton: Princeton University Press.

Damasio, Antonio R. 1994. *Descartes' Error: Emotion, Reason and the Human Brain*. New York: Harper Collins.

Davidson, Donald. 1984. "On the Very Idea of a Conceptual Schema." In *Inquiries into Truth and Interpretation*. Oxford: Clarendon Press: 183–98.

de Romilly, Jacqueline. 1992. *The Great Sophists in Periclean Athens*. Oxford: Oxford University Press.

de Sousa, Ronald. 2001. *The Rationality of Emotions*. Cambridge: Cambridge University Press.

Densham, Andrea. 2006. "Introduction: Politics as a Cause and Consequence of the AIDS Pandemic." *Perspectives on Politics* 4: 641–46.

Dodds, E. R. 1951. *The Greeks and the Irrational*. Berkeley: University of California Press.

———. 1959. *Gorgias*. Oxford: Oxford University Press.

Dover, K. J. 1978. *Greek Homosexuality*. Cambridge, MA: Harvard University Press.

———. 2002. "Classical Greek Attitudes to Sexual Behaviour." In *Sexuality and Gender in the Classical World*, ed. L. K. McClure. Oxford: Blackwell Publishing: 19–33.

Drumbl, Mark A. 2002. "Punishment, Postgenocide: From Guilt to Shame to Civis in Rwanda." *New York University Law Review* 75:1221–326.

Edmonds, Radcliffe. 2009. "Whip Scars on the Naked Soul: Myth and Elenchos in Plato's *Gorgias*." Unpublished Manuscript, forthcoming from Brill: 1–22.

Eisenstadt, Oona. 2001. "Shame in the *Apology*." In *Politics, Philosophy, Writing: Plato's Art of Caring for Souls*, ed. Z. Planinc. Columbia and London: University of Missouri Press: 45–59.

Ekman, Paul (interviewed by Christopher Turner). 2008. "Shamefaced: An Interview with Paul Ekman." *Cabinet: A Quarterly of Art and Culture: Special Issue on Shame* 31: 91–94.

Elshtain, Jean Bethke. 1995. *Democracy on Trial*. New York: Basic Books, Harper Collins.

Elster, Jon. 1999. *Alchemies of the Mind: Rationality and the Emotions*. New York, Cambridge and Melbourne: Cambridge University Press.

Etzioni, Amitai. 2001. *The Monochrome Society*. Princeton: Princeton University Press.

Euben, J. Peter. 1986. *Greek Tragedy and Political Theory*. Berkeley: University of California Press.

———. 1990. *The Tragedy of Political Theory: The Road Not Taken*. Princeton: Princeton University Press.

———. 1994. "Democracy and Political Theory: A Reading of Plato's *Gorgias*." In *Athenian Political Thought and the Reconstruction of American Democracy*, eds. J. P. Euben, J. R. Wallach, and J. Ober. Ithaca and London: Cornell University Press: 198–226.

———. 1997. *Corrupting Youth: Political Education, Democratic Culture and Political Theory*. Princeton: Princeton University Press.

———. 2003. *Platonic Noise*. Princeton: Princeton University Press.

Euben, J. Peter, John R. Wallach, and Josiah Ober, eds. 1994. *Athenian Political Thought and the Reconstruction of American Democracy*. Ithaca: Cornell University Press.

Farrar, Cynthia. 1988. *The Origins of Democratic Thinking: The Invention of Politics in Classical Athens*. Cambridge: Cambridge University Press.

Ferry, Leonard and Rebecca Kingston. 2008. "Introduction: The Emotions in the History of Political Thought." In *Bringing the Passions Back In: The Emotions in Political Philosophy*, eds. Rebecca Kingston and Leonard Ferry. Vancouver: University of British Columbia Press: 3–18

Finley, M. I. 1985. *Democracy Ancient and Modern*. Second Edition. London: Hogarth Press.

———. 1991. *The Ancient Greeks*. New York: Penguin Books.

Fisher, Paul. 2002. *The Vehement Passions*. Princeton: Princeton University Press.

Fornara, C. W. and L. J. Samons II. 1991. *Athens from Cleisthenes to Pericles*. Berkeley: University of California Press.

Fortenbaugh, W. W. [1975], 2002. *Aristotle on Emotion: A Contribution to Philosophical Psychology, Rhetoric, Poetics, Politics and Ethics*. London: Duckworth Press.

Foucault, Michel. 2001. *Fearless Speech*. Los Angeles: Semiotext(e).

Frank, Jill. 2005. *A Democracy of Distinction: Aristotle and the Work of Politics*. Chicago and London: The University of Chicago Press.

———. 2007. "Wages of War: On Judgment in Plato's *Republic*." *Political Theory* 35 (4): 443–67.

———. 2008. "Vying for Authority in Plato's *Republic*." Presented at the 2008 Annual Meeting of the American Political Science Association Meeting, August 28-31st, Boston, MA: 1–33.

Friedländer, Paul. 1964. *Plato: The Dialogues: First Period*. Translated by H. Meyerhoff. Vol. 2. New York: Pantheon Books.

Garver, Eugene. 1994. *Aristotle's Rhetoric: An Art of Character*. Chicago: University of Chicago Press.

Gebauer, Gunter and Christoph Wulf. 1995. *Mimesis: Culture—Art—Society*. Translated by Don Reneau. Berkeley: University of California Press.

Gentzler, Jyl. 1995. "The Sophistic Cross-Examination of Callicles in the *Gorgias*." *Ancient Philosophy* 15: 17–43.

Geuss, Raymond. 2001. *Public Goods, Private Goods*. Princeton and Oxford: Princeton University Press.

Gish, Dustin. 2006. "Rivals in Persuasion: Gorgianic Sophistic Versus Socratic Rhetoric." *Polis* 23 (1): 46–73.

Goffman, Erving. 1963. *Stigma: Notes on the Management of Spoiled Identity*. New York: Simon and Schuster.

Goldhill, Simon. 1986. *Reading Greek Tragedy*. Cambridge: Cambridge University Press.

Gooch, Paul W. 1988. "Red Faces in Plato." *The Classical Journal* 83 (2): 124–27.

Green, Jeffrey. 2005. "The Shame of Being a Philosopher." *Political Theory* 2 (33): 266–72.

Griswold Jr., Charles L. 1986. *Platonic Writings, Platonic Readings*. New York: Routledge Press.

Gross, Daniel M. 2006. *The Secret History of Emotion: From Aristotle's Rhetoric to Modern Brain Science*. Chicago and London: University of Chicago Press.

Guenther, Lisa. 2008. "Resisting Agamben: The Biopolitics of Shame and Humiliation." Unpublished Manuscript: 1–26.

Gulley, Norman. 1968. *The Philosophy of Socrates*. London: Macmillan and Co., Ltd.

Gurstein, Rochelle. 1996. *The Repeal of Reticence: A History of America's Cultural and Legal Struggles over Free Speech, Obscenity, Sexual Liberation, and Modern Art*. New York: Hill and Wang.

Halberstam, Judith. 2005. "Shame and White Gay Masculinity." *Social Text* 23: 219–33.

Hall, Cheryl. 2002. "Passions and Constraint: The Marginalization of Passion in Liberal Political Theory." *Philosophy and Social Criticism* 28 (6): 727–48.

———. 2005. *The Trouble with Passion: Political Theory beyond the Reign of Reason*. New York: Routledge.

Halliwell, Stephen. 2002. *The Aesthetics of Mimesis: Ancient Texts and Modern Problems*. Princeton: Princeton University Press.

Hansen, Mogens Herman. 1991. *The Athenian Democracy in the Age of Demosthenes: Structure, Principles and Ideology*. Translated by J. A. Cook. Oxford: Blackwell Press.

———. 1995. *The Trial of Sokrates—from the Athenian Point of View*. Vol. 71. Copenhagen: Munksgaard.

Havelock, Eric. 1957. *The Liberal Temper in Greek Politics*. London: Cape Publishers.

Hirschman, Albert O. 1977. *The Passions and the Interests: Political Arguments for Capitalism before Its Triumph*. Princeton: Princeton University Press.

Holmes, Stephen. 1995. *Passions and Constraints: On the Theory of Liberal Democracy*. Chicago: University of Chicago Press.

Ignatieff, Michael. 1998. *The Warrior's Honor: Ethnic War and the Modern Conscience*. New York: Henry Holt and Company.

Irwin, Terence. 1977. *Plato's Moral Theory: The Early and Middle Dialogues*. Oxford: Oxford University Press.

———. 1979. *Plato: Gorgias*. Oxford: Oxford University Press.

———. 1995. *Plato's Ethics*. Oxford: Oxford University Press.

Ivy, Marilyn. 2008. "Benedict's Shame." *Cabinet: A Quarterly of Art and Culture: Special Issue on Shame* 31: 64–68.

Jacobs, Allen. 2008. "In the Garden." *Cabinet: A Quarterly of Art and Culture: Special Issue on Shame* 31: 69–72.

Jaegar, Werner. 1943. *Paideia: The Ideals of Greek Culture*. New York: Oxford University Press.

Jones, A.H.M. [1957], 1978. *Athenian Democracy*. Oxford: Basil Blackwell.

Kahan, Dan. 1999. "The Progressive Appropriation of Disgust." In *The Passions of Law*, ed. S. A. Bandes. New York: New York University Press: 63–79.

———. 1996. "What Do Alternative Sanctions Mean?" *University of Chicago Law Review* 63: 591–653.

Kahn, Charles H. 1983. "Drama and Dialectic in Plato's *Gorgias*." In *Oxford Studies in Ancient Philosophy*, Volume I: 75–121.

———. 1996. *Plato and the Socratic Dialogue: The Philosophical Use of a Literary Form*. Cambridge: Cambridge University Press.

Kalyvas, Andreas. 2007. "The Tyranny of Dictatorship: When the Greek Tyrant Met the Roman Dictator." *Political Theory* 35 (4): 412–42.

Karp, David. 1998. "The Judicial and Judicious Use of Shame Penalties." *Crime and Delinquency* 44 (2): 277–94.

Kastely, James L. 1991. "In Defense of Plato's *Gorgias*." *Publications of the Modern Language Association of America* 106 (1): 96–109.

Kaufer, David S. 1978. "The Influence of Plato's Developing Psychology on his views of Rhetoric." *Quarterly Journal of Speech* 64 (1): 63–78.

Kennedy, George. 1964. *The Art of Persuasion in Ancient Greece*. Princeton: Princeton University Press.

Kerferd, George. 1981. *The Sophistic Movement*. Cambridge: Cambridge University Press.

Kingston, Rebecca. 2008. "The Political Relevance of the Emotions from Descartes to Smith." In *Bringing the Passions Back In: The Emotions in Political Philosophy*, eds. Rebecca Kingston and Leonard Ferry. Vancouver: University of British Columbia Press: 108–25.

Klosko, George. 1983. "The Insufficiency of Reason in Plato's *Gorgias.*" *The Western Political Quarterly* 36 (4): 579–95.

———. 1984. "The Refutation of Callicles in Plato's *Gorgias.*" *Greece and Rome* 31: 126–39.

Konstan, David. 2006. *The Emotions of the Ancient Greeks: Studies in Aristotle and Classical Literature.* Toronto: University of Toronto Press.

Koziak, Barbara. 2000. *Retrieving Political Emotion: Thumos, Aristotle and Gender.* University Park: The Pennsylvania State University Press.

Krause, Sharon. 2002. *Liberalism with Honor.* Cambridge, MA and London: Harvard University Press.

———. 2008. *Civil Passions: Moral Sentiment and Democratic Deliberation.* Princeton: Princeton University Press.

Kraut, Richard. 1983. "Comments on Gregory Vlastos' *The Socratic Elenchus.*" In *Oxford Studies in Ancient Philosophy.* Oxford: Oxford University Press: 59–70.

Lanni, Adriaan. 2005. "Relevance in Athenian Courts." In *The Cambridge Companion to Ancient Greek Law,* eds. Michael Gagarin and David Cohen. Cambridge: Cambridge University Press: 112–45.

Lasch, Christopher. 1979. *The Culture of Narcissism: American Life in an Age of Diminishing Expectations.* New York: W.W. Norton and Company.

———. 1995. *The Revolt of the Elites and the Betrayal of Democracy.* New York: W.W. Norton and Company.

Latimer, John Francis. 1926. *The Meaning of Aidōs.* Dissertation Submitted to the Faculty of the Graduate School of Arts and Literature in Candidacy for the Degree of Master of Arts in the Department of Greek Language and Literature. Chicago.

Lear, Jonathan. [1998], 1999. *Open Minded: Working Out the Logic of the Soul.* Cambridge, MA and London: Harvard University Press.

———. 2001. "Inside and Outside the Republic." In *Essays on Plato's Moral Psychology.* Lanham and Oxford: Lexington Books: 169–203.

LeDoux, Joseph. 1996. *The Emotional Brain: The Mysterious Underpinnings of Emotional Life.* New York: Simon and Schuster.

Lee, Everett Hunt. 1962. "Plato and Aristotle: Rhetoric and Rhetoricians." In *Studies in Rhetoric and Public Speaking: In Honor of James Albert Winans.* New York: Russell: 3–60.

Levy, Jacob. 2007. "Federalism, Liberalism, and the Separation of Loyalties." *American Political Science Review* 101 (3): 459–77.

Lewis, Helen Block. 1971. *Shame and Guilt in Neurosis.* New York: International Universities Press.

Lewis, Thomas J. 1986. "Refutative Rhetoric as True Rhetoric in Plato's *Gorgias.*" *Interpretation* 14: 195–210.

Liddell, H. G. and Robert Scott. 1996. *A Greek-English Lexicon.* Oxford: Oxford University Press.

Locke, Jill. 1999. "Hiding from Whom? Obscurity, Dignity and the Politics of Truth." *Theory & Event* 3 (3).

———. 2004. "Unashamed Citizenship." Paper presented at the Western Political Science Association Annual Meeting, March 2004: 1–30.

———. 2007. "Shame and the Future of Feminism." *Hypatia* 22 (4): 146–62.

Lu, Catherine. 2008. "Shame, Guilt and Reconciliation after War." *European Journal of Social Theory* 11 (3): 367–83.

Lutz, Catherine A. 1986. "Emotion, Thought and Estrangement: Emotion as a Cultural Category." *Cultural Anthropology* 1 (1): 287–309.

Lynd, Helen Merrell. 1958. *On Shame and the Search for Identity*. New York: Harcourt Press.

Mackenzie, Mary Margaret. 1981. *Plato on Punishment*. Berkeley: University of California Press.

Makari, George. 2008. "Unspeakable Subjects." *Cabinet: A Quarterly of Art and Culture: Special Issue on Shame* 31: 79–80.

Marcus, George. 2002. *The Sentimental Citizen: Emotion in Democratic Politics*. University Park: The Pennsylvania State University Press.

Markell, Patchen. 2003. *Bound by Recognition*. Princeton: Princeton University Press.

Massaro, Toni M. 1997. "The Meanings of Shame: Implications for Legal Reform." *Psychology, Public Policy, and Law* 3 (4): 645–704.

———. 1999. "Show (Some) Emotions." In *The Passions of Law*, ed. S. A. Bandes. New York: New York University Press: 80–120.

McClure, Laura K. 1999. *Spoken Like a Woman: Speech and Gender in Athenian Drama*. Princeton: Princeton University Press.

McKim, Richard. 1988. "Shame and Truth in Plato's *Gorgias*." In *Platonic Writings, Platonic Readings*, ed. C. L. Griswold, Jr. New York: Routledge Press: 34–48.

Meiggs, Russell. 1972. *The Athenian Empire*. Oxford: Oxford University Press.

Miller, William Ian. 1993. *Humiliation: And Other Essays on Honor, Social Discomfort, and Violence*. Ithaca: Cornell University Press.

———. 1997. *The Anatomy of Disgust*. Cambridge, MA: Harvard University Press.

Monoson, Sara. 2000. *Plato's Democratic Entanglements*. Princeton: Princeton University Press.

Morrison, Andrew P. 1989. *Shame: The Underside of Narcissism*. Hillsdale, NJ: The Analytic Press.

———. 1996. *The Culture of Shame*. New York: Ballantine Books.

Murray, James Stuart. 2001. "Plato on Power, Moral Responsibility and the Alleged Neutrality of Gorgias' Art of Rhetoric (*Gorgias* 456c–457b) " *Philosophy and Rhetoric* 34 (4): 355–63.

Nathanson, Donald L. 1997. "Shame and the Affect Theory of Silvan Tomkins." In *The Widening Scope of Shame*, eds. Melvin R. Lansky and. Andrew P. Morrison. Hillsdale: The Analytic Press: 107–38.

Nehamas, Alexander. 1998. *The Art of Living: Socratic Reflections from Plato to Foucault*. Berkeley: University of California Press.

———. 1999. *Virtues of Authenticity: Essays on Plato and Socrates*. Princeton: Princeton University Press.

Newell, Waller R. 2000. *Ruling Passion: The Erotics of Statecraft in Platonic Political Philosophy*. Lanham, MA: Rowman & Littlefield Publishers, Inc.

———. 2005. "Is There an Ontology of Tyranny?" In *Confronting Tyranny: Ancient Lessons for Global Politics*, eds. Toivo Koivukoski and David Edward Tabachnick. Lanham: Rowman & Littlefield Publishers, Inc.: 141–60.

Nietzsche, Friedrich. 1967. *The Birth of Tragedy and the Case of Wagner*. Translated by W. Kaufmann. New York: Vintage Books.

Nieuwenburg, Paul. 2004. "Learning to Deliberate: Aristotle on Truthfulness and Public Deliberation." *Political Theory* 32 (4): 449–67.

Nussbaum, Martha. 1980. "Shame, Separateness and Political Unity: Aristotle's Criticism of Plato." In *Essays on Aristotle's Ethics*, ed. Amélie Oksenberg Rorty. Berkeley: University of California Press: 395–435.

———. 2001. *Upheavals of Thought: The Intelligence of Emotions.* Cambridge: Cambridge University Press.

———. 2004. *Hiding from Humanity: Disgust, Shame and the Law.* Princeton: Princeton University Press.

Ober, Josiah. 1989. *Mass and Elite in Democratic Athens: Rhetoric, Ideology, and the Power of the People.* Princeton: Princeton University Press.

———. 1996. *The Athenian Revolution: Essays on Ancient Greek Democracy and Political Theory.* Princeton: Princeton University Press.

———. 1998. *Political Dissent in Democratic Athens: Intellectual Critics of Popular Rule.* Princeton: Princeton University press.

Ober, Josiah and Charles W. Hedrick. 1996. *Demokratia: A Conversation on Democracies, Ancient and Modern.* Princeton: Princeton University Press.

Olmsted, Wendy. 2006. *Rhetoric: An Historical Introduction.* Malden, MA: Blackwell Publishing, Ltd.

Panagia, Davide. 2004. "The Force of Political Argument." *Political Theory* 32 (6): 825–48.

———. 2006. *The Poetics of Political Thinking.* Durham: Duke University Press.

Penner, Terry. 1992. "Socrates and the Early Dialogues." In *The Cambridge Companion to Plato*, ed. R. Kraut. Cambridge: Cambridge University Press: 121–69.

Piers, Gerhart and Milton B. Singer. 1953. *Shame and Guilt: A Psychoanalytic and a Cultural Study.* Springfield: Thomas.

Plato. 1924. *Laches, Protagoras, Meno, Euthydemus.* Translated by W.R.M. Lamb. Cambridge, MA: Harvard University Press.

———. 1925. *Lysis, Symposium, Gorgias.* Translated by W.R.M. Lamb. Cambridge, MA: Harvard University Press.

———. 1926. *Cratylus, Parmenides, Greater Hippias, Lesser Hippias.* Translated by H. N. Fowler. Cambridge, MA: Harvard University Press.

———. 1927. *Charmides, Alcibiades I and II, Hipparchus, The Lovers, Theages, Minos, Epinomis.* Translated by W.R.M. Lamb. Cambridge, MA: Harvard University Press.

———. 1930. *The Republic, Books I-V.* Translated by P. Shorey. Cambridge, MA: Harvard University Press.

———. 1935. *The Republic, Books VI-X.* Translated by P. Shorey. Cambridge, MA: Harvard University Press.

———. 1961. *The Collected Dialogues of Plato*, eds. E. Hamilton and H. Cairns. Princeton: Princeton University Press.

———. 1968. *The Republic of Plato.* Translated by A. Bloom. Second edition. New York: Basic Books.

———. 1992. *The Republic.* Translated by G.M.A. Grube and C.D.C. Reeve. Indianapolis: Hackett Publishing Company, Inc.

———. 1998. *Plato: Gorgias.* Translated by J. H. Nichols, Jr. Ithaca: Cornell University Press.

Popper, Karl. 1945. *The Open Society and Its Enemies, Volume 1: The Spell of Plato*. London: Routledge and Sons, Ltd.

Raaflaub, Kurt A. 1994. "Democracy, Power, and Imperialism in Fifth-Century Athens." In *Athenian Political Thought and the Reconstruction of American Democracy*, eds. J. Peter Euben, John R. Wallach and Josiah Ober. Ithaca, N.Y.: Cornell University Press: 103–46.

Rawls, John. 1971. *A Theory of Justice*. Cambridge, MA: Harvard University Press.

Redding, Paul. 1999. *The Logic of Affect*. Ithaca: Cornell University Press.

Reddy, William M. 1997. "Against Constructionism: The Historical Ethnography of Emotions." *Current Anthropology* 8 (3): 327–51.

Rhodes, P. J. 2006. *A History of the Classical Greek World: 478–323 BC*. Malden, MA: Blackwell Publishing.

Riedinger, J.C. 1980. "Les deux *aidōs* chez Homère." *Revue de Philologie* 54: 62–79.

Riezler, Kurt. 1943. "Comment on the Social Psychology of Shame." *American Journal of Sociology* 48 (4): 457–65.

Roberts, Jennifer Tolbert. 1994. *Athens on Trial: The Antidemocratic Tradition in Western Thought*. Princeton: Princeton University Press.

Rocco, Christopher. 1996. "Liberating Discourse: The Politics of Truth in Plato's *Gorgias*." *Interpretation* 23 (3): 361–85.

———. 1997. *Tragedy and Enlightenment: Athenian Political Thought and the Dilemmas of Modernity*. Berkeley: University of California Press.

Rorty, Amélie Oksenberg. 1980. "Introduction." In *Explaining Emotions*, ed. Amélie Oksenberg Rorty. Berkeley: University of California Press: 1–9.

Rosen, Stanley. 1993. *The Quarrel between Poetry and Philosophy: Studies in Ancient Thought*. New York: Routledge Press.

Rosenfeld, Richard. 1983. "Gay Liberation and Social Feminism: A Comment on Elshtain's 'Homosexual Politics.' " *Salmagundi* 61: 138–42.

Rosenstock, Bruce. 1983. "Rereading the *Republic*." *Arethusa* 16: 219–46.

Roth, Kenneth. 2003. "International Human Rights Organizations and Economic, Social, and Cultural Rights: A Practical Defense." Newsletter for Human Rights Watch.

Rowe, Christopher. 1976. *An Introduction to Greek Ethics*. London: Hutchison & Co., Ltd.

Rubinstein, Lene. 2005. "Differentiated Rhetorical Strategies in the Athenian Courts." In *The Cambridge Companion to Ancient Greek Law*, eds. Michael Gagarin and David Cohen. New York and Cambridge: Cambridge University Press: 129–45.

Rudebusch, George. 1999. *Socrates, Pleasure and Value*. New York: Oxford University Press.

Sabini, John, Brian Garvey, and Amanda L. Hall. 2001. "Shame and Embarrassment Revisited." *Personality and Social Psychology Bulletin* 27 (1): 104–17.

Samons II, Loren J., ed. 1998. *Athenian Democracy and Imperialism*. Boston: Houghton Mifflin.

———. 2004. *What's Wrong with Democracy? From Athenian Practice to American Worship*. Berkeley: University of California Press.

Santas, Gerasimos. 1979. *Socrates' Philosophy in Plato's Early Dialogues*. London: Routledge and Kegan Paul.

Saxonhouse, Arlene. 1983. "An Unspoken Theme in Plato's *Gorgias*: War." *Interpretation* 11: 139–69.

Saxonhouse, Arlene. 1996. "Plato and the Problematical Gentleness of Democracy." In *Athenian Democracy: Modern Mythmakers and Ancient Theorists.* Notre Dame, IN.: University of Notre Dame Press: 87–114.

———. 1998. "Democracy, Equality and *Eidē*: A Radical View from Book 8 of Plato's *Republic.*" *American Political Science Review* 92 (2): 273–84.

———. 2006. *Free Speech and Democracy in Ancient Athens.* Cambridge: Cambridge University Press.

Schacter, Stanley. 1962. "The Interaction of Cognitive and Physiological Determinants of Emotional State." *Psychology Review* 69: 372–99.

Scheff, Thomas. 1987. "The Shame-Rage Spiral: A Case Study of an Interminable Quarrel." In *The Role of Shame in Symptom Formation,* ed. Helen Block Lewis. Hillsdale, NJ: Erlbaum: 109–49.

———. 1997. "Shame in Social Theory." In *The Widening Scope of Shame,* eds. M. R. Lansky and A. P. Morrison. Hillsdale: The Analytic Press: 205–30.

Seery, John Evan. 1988. "Politics as Ironic Community: On the Themes of Descent and Return in Plato's *Republic.*" *Political Theory* 16: 229–56.

Segal, Charles. 1970. "Shame and Purity in Euripides' *Hippolytus.*" *Hermes* 98: 288–299.

———. 1988. "The Myth Was Saved: Reflections on Homer and the Mythology of Plato's *Republic.*" *Hermes* 106: 315–56.

Sharp, Hasana. 2005. "Why Spinoza Today? Or, 'A Strategy of Anti-Fear'." *Rethinking Marxism* 17 (4): 591–608.

Shorris, Earl. 2004. "Ignoble Liars: Leo Strauss, George Bush and the Philosophy of Mass Deception." *Harper's Magazine,* June 2004: 65–71.

Sokolon, Marlene. 2006. *Political Emotions: Aristotle and the Symphony of Reason and Emotion.* DeKalb: Northern Illinois University Press.

Solomon, Robert. 1980. "Emotions and Choice." In *Explaining Emotions,* ed. Amélie Oksenberg Rorty. Berkeley: University of California Press: 251–81.

———. [1998], 2008. "The Politics of Emotion." In *Bringing the Passions Back In: The Emotions in Political Philosophy,* eds. Rebecca Kingston and Leonard Ferry. Vancouver: University of British Columbia Press: 189–208.

———. 2003. *Not Passion's Slave: Emotions and Choice.* Oxford and New York: Oxford University Press.

Stauffer, Devin. 2002. "Socrates and Callicles: A Reading of Plato's *Gorgias.*" *The Review of Politics* 64 (4): 627–57.

———. 2006. *The Unity of Plato's Gorgias: Rhetoric, Justice, and the Philosophic Life.* New York: Cambridge University Press.

Ste. Croix, G.E.M. de. 1972. *The Origins of the Peloponnesian War.* London: Duckworth Press.

Straus, Erwin. 1979. "Shame as a Historiological Problem." *Phenomenological Psychology* 25: 122–40.

Strauss, Barry. 2005. "In the Shadow of the Fortress." In *Confronting Tyranny: Ancient Lessons for Global Politics,* eds. Toivo Koivukoski and David Edward Tabachnick. Lanham: Rowman & Littlefield Publishers, Inc.: 233–41.

Strong, Tracy B. 2005. "Tyranny and Tragedy in Nietzsche: From the Ancient to the Modern." In *Confronting Tyranny: Ancient Lessons for Global Politics,* eds. Toivo Koivukoski and David Edward Tabachnick. Lanham: Rowman & Littlefield Publishers, Inc.: 103–21.

Tangney, June Price and Ronda L. Dearing. [2002], 2004. *Shame and Guilt.* New York and London: The Guilford Press.

Tarcov, Nathan. 1996. "The Meanings of Democracy." In *Democracy, Education, and the Schools*, ed. R. Soder. San Francisco: Jossey-Bass Publishers: 1–36.

———. 2005. "Tyranny from Plato to Locke." In *Confronting Tyranny: Ancient Lessons for Global Politics*, eds. Toivo Koivukoski and David Edward Tabachnick. Lanham: Rowman & Littlefield Publishers, Inc.: 123–40.

Tarnopolsky, Christina. 2003. "Shame and Guilt in the Psyche and in Politics." Paper presented to the American Political Science Association Annual Meeting.

———. 2004. "Prudes, Perverts and Tyrants: Plato and the Contemporary Politics of Shame and Civility." *Political Theory* 32 (4): 468–94.

———. 2005. "Reply to Green." *Political Theory* 33 (2): 273–79.

———. 2007a. "The Bipolar Longings of *Thumos*: A Feminist Rereading of Plato's *Republic*." *Symposium: The Canadian Journal of Continental Philosophy* 11 (2): 291–314.

———. 2007b. "Platonic Reflections on the Aesthetic Dimensions of Deliberative Democracy." *Political Theory* 35 (3): 288–312.

———. 2008a. "Plato on Shame and Frank Speech." In *Bringing the Passions Back In: The Emotions in Political Philosophy*, eds. Rebecca Kingston and Leonard Ferry. Vancouver: University of British Columbia Press.

———. 2008b. "The Pedagogies of Shame." *Cabinet: A Quarterly of Art and Culture: Special Issue on Shame* 31: 99–103.

Taylor, C.C.W. 1997. "Plato's Totalitarianism." In *Plato's Republic: Critical Essays*, ed. R. Kraut. New York: Rowan and Littlefield: 31–48.

Taylor, Gabrielle. 1985. *Pride, Shame and Guilt: Emotions of Self-Assessment.* Oxford and New York: Oxford University Press.

Thür, Gerhard. 2005. "The Role of the Witness in Athenian Law." In *The Cambridge Companion to Ancient Greek Law*, eds. Michael Gagarin and David Cohen. Cambridge: Cambridge University Press: 146–69.

Todd, Stephen. 1990. "The Purpose of Evidence in Athenian Courts." In *Nomos: Essays in Athenian Law, Politics and Society*, eds. Paul Cartledge, Paul Millett, and Stephen Todd. Cambridge: Cambridge University Press: 19–40.

Tormey, Simon. 2005. "What Is 'Tyranny'?: Considering the Contested Discourse of Domination in the Twenty-first Century." In *Confronting Tyranny: Ancient Lessons for Global Politics*, eds. Toivo Koivukoski and David Edward Tabachnick. Lanham: Rowman & Littlefield Publishers: 67–79.

Twitchell, James B. 1997. *For Shame: The Loss of Common Decency in American Culture.* New York: St. Martin's Press.

Vernant, Jean-Pierre. 1988. *Myth and Society in Ancient Greece.* Translated by J. Lloyd. New York: Zone Books.

Vernant, Jean-Pierre and Pierre Vidal-Naquet. 1990. *Myth and Tragedy in Ancient Greece.* Translated by J. Lloyd. New York: Zone Books.

Vickers, Brian. 1988. *In Defense of Rhetoric.* Oxford: Clarendon Press.

Vidal-Naquet, Pierre. 1955. *Politics Ancient and Modern*. Translated by J. Lloyd. Cambridge: Polity Press.

Villa, Dana. 2001. *Socratic Citizenship*. Princeton: Princeton University Press.

Vlastos, Gregory. 1983a. "The Socratic Elenchus." In *Oxford Studies in Ancient Philosophy, Volume I*. Oxford: Clarendon Press: 27–58.

———. 1983b. "Afterthoughts on the Socratic Elenchus." In *Oxford Studies in Ancient Philosophy, Volume I*. Oxford: Clarendon Press: 71–73.

———. 1983c. "The Historical Socrates and Athenian Democracy." *Political Theory* 11 (4): 495–516.

———. 1991. *Socrates, Ironist and Moral Philosopher*. Ithaca: Cornell University Press.

———. 1994a. "The Socratic Elenchus: Method Is All." In *Socratic Studies*, ed. M. Burnyeat. Cambridge: Cambridge University Press: 1–33.

———. 1994b. "Postcript to 'The Socratic Elenchus'." In *Socratic Studies*, ed. M. Burnyeat. Cambridge: Cambridge University Press: 33–37.

———. 1995. "Was Polus Refuted?" In *Studies in Greek Philosophy*, ed. D. Graham. Princeton: Princeton University Press: 60–4.

Wagner, Aleksandra. 2008. "The Woman Who Knew Too Much." *Cabinet: A Quarterly of Art and Culture: Special Issue on Shame* 31: 61–63.

Wallach, John R. 1997. "Plato's Socratic Problem and Ours." *History of Political Thought* 18: 377–91.

———. 2001. *The Platonic Political Art: A Study of Critical Reason and Democracy*. University Park, PA: Pennsylvania State University Press.

Walzer, Michael. 1987. *Interpretation and Social Criticism*. Cambridge, MA: Harvard University Press.

———. 2002. "Passions and Politics." *Philosophy and Social Criticism* 28 (6): 617–33.

———. 2004. *Politics and Passion: Toward a More Egalitarian Liberalism*. New Haven: Yale University Press.

Wardy, Robert. 1996. *The Birth of Rhetoric: Gorgias, Plato and Their Successors*, ed. M. Schofield. London and New York: Routledge.

Warner, Michael. 1999. *The Trouble with Normal: Sex, Politics and the Ethics of Queer Life*. Cambridge, MA: Harvard University Press.

———. 2005. *Publics and Counterpublics*. New York: Zone Books.

Weiss, Roslyn. 2003. "Oh, Brother! The Fraternity of Rhetoric and Philosophy in Plato's *Gorgias*." *Interpretation* 30: 195–206.

Williams, Bernard. 1993. *Shame and Necessity*. Berkeley: University of California Press.

Wilson, J.R.S. 1972. *Emotion and Object*. Cambridge, MA: Cambridge University Press.

Winkler, John. 1990. "Laying Down the Law: The Oversight of Men's Sexual Behavior in Classical Athens." In *Before Sexuality: The Construction of Erotic Experience in the Ancient Greek World*, eds. David M. Halperin, John J. Winkler, and Froma I Zeitlin. Princeton: Princeton University Press: 171–209.

Wollheim, Richard. 1999. *On the Emotions*. New Haven: Yale University Press.

Yack, Bernard. 2006. "Rhetoric and Public Reasoning: An Aristotelian Understanding of Political Deliberation." *Political Theory* 34: 417–38.

Young, Iris Marion. 1996. "Communication and the Other: Beyond Deliberative Democracy." In *Democracy and Difference: Contesting the Boundaries of the Political*, ed. S. Benhabib. Princeton: Princeton University Press: 120–35.

Yunis, Harvey. 1996. *Taming Democracy: Models of Political Rhetoric in Classical Athens.* Ithaca and London: Cornell University Press.

Zerilli, Linda 2005. "We Feel our Freedom: Imagination and Judgment in the Thought of Hannah Arendt." *Political Theory* 33 (2): 158–88.

Zumbrunnen, John. 2004. "Elite Domination and the Clever Citizen: Aristophanes' *Archainians* and *Knights.*" *American Political Science Review* 32 (5): 656–57.

INDEX